Toward a Culture *of* Freedom

Toward a Culture *of* Freedom

Reflections on the Ten Commandments Today

Thorwald Lorenzen

CASCADE Books • Eugene, Oregon

TOWARD A CULTURE OF FREEDOM
Reflections on the Ten Commandments Today

Copyright © 2008 Thorwald Lorenzen. All rights reserved. Except for brief quotations in critical publications or reviews, no part of this book may be reproduced in any manner without prior written permission from the publisher. Write: Permissions, Wipf & Stock, 199 W. 8th Ave., Suite 3, Eugene, OR 97401.

Cascade Books
A Division of Wipf and Stock Publishers
199 W. 8th Ave., Suite 3
Eugene, OR 97401

www.wipfandstock.com

ISBN 13: 978-1-55635-296-6

New Revised Standard Version Bible, copyright 1989, Division of Christian Education of the National Council of the Churches of Christ in the United States of America. Used by permission. All rights reserved.

Cataloging-in-Publication data

Lorenzen, Thorwald.

> Toward a culture of freedom : reflections on the ten commandments today / Thorwald Lorenzen.
>
> viii + 254 p.; 23 cm.
>
> Eugene, Ore.: Cascade Books
> Includes bibliographical references and indexes.
>
> ISBN 13: 978-1-55635-296-6 (alk. paper)
>
> 1. Ten commandments I. Title.

BV4655 L67 2008

Manufactured in the U.S.A.

In memory of

Jürgen Meissner

A good friend who died too early

Contents

Introduction / 1

1. When God Speaks, God Says "Yes" (Exod 19:16–18, 20:1, and Deut 5:1–5): Overture to the "Ten Words" / 11

2. When God Acts, God Liberates (Exod 20:2 and Deut 5:6): Continuing the Overture to the "Ten Words" / 24

3. Who or What Is Our God? (Exod 20:3 and Deut 5:7): The First Word / 34

4. Idol or Icon (Exod 20:4–6 and Deut 5:8–10): The Second Word / 43

5. A Name Is More Than a Word (Exod 20:7 and Deut 5:11): The Third Word / 58

6. Celebrating Freedom (Exod 20:8–11 and Deut 5:12–15): The Fourth Word / 68

7. Generational Responsibility (Exod 20:12 and Deut 5:16): The Fifth Word / 81

8. Becoming Servants of Life (Exod 20:13 and Deut 5:17): The Sixth Word / 95

9. Love and Its Protection (Exod 20:14 and Deut 5:18): The Seventh Word / 111

10. The Right to Be Free (Exod 20:15 and Deut 5:19): The Eighth Word / 131

11. Speaking Truth in Public (Exod 20:16 and Deut 5:20): The Ninth Word / 152

12. Who or What Occupies Our Conscience? (Exod 20:17 and Deut 5:21): The Tenth Word / 165

Contents

Conclusion / 179

Appendix 1: *Understanding and Interpreting the Decalogue* / 189

Appendix 2: *Making Ethical Decisions from a Christian Perspective* / 209

Bibliography / 227

Author and Subject Index / 237

Scripture Index / 245

Introduction

WE ARE BORN INTO life. It is not our decision. We may even say that we are thrown into the sea of life without being able to swim. At first life is fragile. For a few years we remain dependent on our parents, especially on our mothers. Gradually we develop self-awareness. We enjoy being touched and being held tight. We begin to smile because people smile at us. We begin to talk because people talk to us. We take our first steps. Slowly but surely, we become members of the immediate family, the nation, and the human family.

As we become increasingly independent of our parents, we develop the freedom, the courage and, with these, the responsibility to act. There is much in life over which we have no control. We do not choose our parents and we have no say about the family, the country and the culture into which we are born. We are born with genetic dispositions. My wife, for instance, belongs to the 12% of people with a Celtic background who carry too much iron in their blood. Some are born as millionaires, others into abject poverty. The relationships that we experience in early days with our immediate family, especially our mothers and fathers, will determine to a significant extent whether in life we have a basic trust, whether we accept authority, and whether our attitude to life is compassionate or punitive. The class or caste of our parents determines our social status. The nature and quality of our education are significant for the professional choices that we can make. Much in life is given. We are invited to accept it and make the best of it.

But, with all that givenness we are not fated. Not everything is determined. There is no invisible force that determines everything we think and do. Although Western economists and politicians talk in personal terms about the "market" which they seem to trust for arranging everything, and Calvinist Christians expect God to plan and enact every detail in life, in fact we human beings are responsible for planning and living our own life. Within the limits of what has been given and what we cannot change, we have freedom of will, freedom of choice, and freedom to act. The challenge is to use our freedom towards a successful, meaningful, and fulfilled life. That is our interest in this book, the celebration of life. We turn to an ancient and ever modern text, a "classic," a text that has stood the test of time, with the question whether and in what way it can help us to make the best of life.

I have called this book *Toward a Culture of Freedom*. I have done so with the hope that the Ten Commandments may help us to see a culture of freedom as the best context for a meaningful and successful life. Freedom, like thinking and acting, is part of being human. It is an illusion, however, to think that freedom is doing what we feel like doing at any particular moment. It is not freedom, for instance, when intentional athletes follow their momentary desire to eat fatty sausages or take drugs. Their freedom includes discipline, patience, hard work, and good coaching towards becoming who they want to be. Martha Graham (1894–1991), the great dancer and pioneer of modern dance, once said, "Freedom to a dancer means discipline. That is what technique is for: liberation." It is not freedom when married persons follow their sexual desires to have intimate relationships with any and every person to whom they feel attracted. Their freedom includes the voluntary commitment to be faithful "for better and for worse until death do us part." Freedom needs to be lived within certain limits and conventions within a social and cultural context. Practicing freedom is the delicate challenge to find a way beyond anarchy, legalism, and control.

"Culture" describes the content, the values, the art, and the discipline of living together.[1] It provides the basic parameters for planning and living our lives. If we play football or dance flamenco, there are basic rules that must we must follow. They are given. Nevertheless, within these rules each player or dancer can freely develop and display her or his own creativity, expertise, and competence. The rules are not restrictive. They do not spoil the game or the dance—quite the opposite. They provide the context for identity, joy, and excellence. Culture includes the vision and values that provide the context for a meaningful and successful life.

Vision and values, if they are to be authentic and lasting, must include the resources that can answer basic questions in life: Why is there something and not nothing? What do I live for? How best can I live in light

---

1. The English word "culture" comes from the Latin "*colere*" which originally referred to the proper use of one's agricultural land, including the removal of weeds. In an agricultural society, it therefore described the basic parameters that guarantee a meaningful and successful life in community.

Introduction

of the certainty that one day I will have to die? What is right and what is wrong? What must I do if I want to live a meaningful and successful life? What is the place of the "other" in shaping my own identity? How can I find and occupy my place in the global family? Can we tolerate variety, can we let a thousand flowers bloom, enjoy their beauty, and still maintain our own identity?

We need to discover and name resources that can contribute toward a culture of freedom. Such a culture emphasizes that life in community carries promise and can be exciting. It can release vitality and passion. It can encourage creativity and compassion. In the long run, the cultures that will survive are those that have the spiritual and intellectual resources to live in hope rather than fear, that are committed to peace rather than war, that provide for the basic needs of their people, that will face terrorism with the resilience of people who feel good about themselves and therefore do not need to suppress others.

Such a culture of freedom is a constant challenge and is constantly threatened. Today such threats come from many different directions.

- People demand truth without ideology, and at the same time, they claim that everything is relative.
- There is an ongoing claim, indeed an ongoing experiment in many "Western" cultures to understand and live life without reference to God.
- The world has woken up to the climate crisis and its threat on the environment and on millions of people. However, contrary to political and economic rhetoric, national interest and economic profits are too often still more important than people and the environment.
- Governments and politicians operate with a politics of fear. New laws, committees of bureaucrats and statistics regulate and control our life.
- Traditional institutions such as marriage, family, universities (where intellectual enquiry rather than economic utility is the main purpose), sex (as the language of intimacy, commitment and love), and religious communities are considered old-fashioned—but no real alternatives have been put in their place.

- Individualism without restraints or commitments is encouraged by misguided self-interest and unbridled consumerism. The shopping center and the airport have become the cathedrals of modern life.

- Rationalism that leaves no room for mystery (where even love, faith, and hope are explained as the effect of hormones) and fundamentalisms that do not value the achievements of humanism and the Enlightenment sideline the resources of a creative and life-giving faith.

- Where religious needs are felt or impulses for the beyond are awakened, people often flee into a spirituality that is individualistic and comforting rather than compassionate and demanding.

- The challenge of death is suppressed or seen as an accident that should not really be there.

We must recognize these threats and remain aware of them. At the same time, we cannot afford the luxury of despair or the laziness of thoughtlessness and inactivity. A culture of freedom builds trust, hope, and responsibility and thereby strengthens the resilience of people to face the challenges that lie ahead confidently and energetically. Our meditation on the Ten Commandments aims to tease us towards a culture of freedom where liberation from coercion and oppression can pave the way for a meaningful and fulfilled life.

Such a culture of freedom entails a universal promise. The first article of the *Universal Declaration of Human Rights* says, "*All* human beings are born free and equal in dignity and rights. They are endowed with reason and conscience and should act towards one another in a spirit of brotherhood."[2] Many people question today whether there can be a universal vision of morality.

It is true, of course, that many things in life are relative. They depend on our national, cultural, and religious customs and convictions. A woman wearing a scarf (the *hijab*), tied in a certain way over her head, is demanded in Tehran, is controversial in Sydney, and is offensive in Paris. People looking each other in the eye while conversing can be a sign of openness and honesty in Berlin, and a sign of arrogance and offence in Kamasi. Building hostels for senior citizens and hospices for terminally ill people may be

---

2. The *Universal Declaration of Human Rights* can be found in United Nations, Office of Public Information, *The International Bill of Human Rights*.

Introduction

considered caring in one culture and rude or disrespectful and marginalizing in another.

While many things are relative and situational, the question is, nevertheless, whether that applies to *all* things. Is everything relative? Are all decisions situational? Is female circumcision a cultural practice that is to be respected in certain areas in the world, or is it female genital mutilation—"a way of maintaining a woman's purity by ensuring that she cannot enjoy sex while also increasing men's sexual pleasure"—that needs to be universally banned?[3] Can torture, can the rape of women as an instrument of warfare, can sexual child abuse ever be tolerated or justified? Modern human rights are universal and as such they are reminders that cultural and religious differences do not relativize or even abrogate the ethical demand—quite the contrary. Our awareness of differences raises the question as to what is right and what is wrong in different respective situations. Human existence as such includes the ethical challenge.

At the same time—and especially during this time of the Iraq war—we must realize that freedom and its values cannot be compelled. It must grow from within and it will take on different shapes in different cultures.

The affirmation that human beings "*are born* free and equal in dignity and rights" indicates that human dignity is not conferred and cannot be earned. It is given. It is not the result of empirical observations. Indeed, a look into our world reveals that many people are neither free nor equal. This assertion therefore raises the question as to where human dignity, equality, and freedom are grounded. Who says that we are "free and equal"? For people of faith, freedom and equality are the free and unconditional gift of the creator. No person, no state, and no religion can confer this dignity, nor can they take it away. Freedom needs to be recognized, guarded, and given room to flourish. As individuals and as a society, we are challenged to accept responsibility for safeguarding and filling human dignity with meaning and purpose. It is a challenge to our freedom and responsibility to determine and shape our human dignity. A cherished part of our western tradition says that human life is an end in itself and must not be used to serve other ends.[4] A culture of freedom provides the context in which human dignity can flourish.

---

3. Neustatter, "It Cuts So Deep," 2.

4. The reference is to Kant's categorical imperative: "Man and every rational being anywhere *exists as end in itself*, not merely as means for the arbitrary use by this or that will; but in all his actions . . . he must at all times be looked upon *as an end*. . . . The

As we begin our meditation on the Ten Commandments, a few introductory comments may be helpful. The first appendix contains a more comprehensive introduction to the Decalogue.

In the Bible the Ten Commandments are found in two versions, which are quite similar: Exodus 20:2–17 and Deuteronomy 5:6–21.[5] They are set in different contexts. It is only in the introduction and in the reasons given for keeping the Sabbath (the fourth word) that the substantive differences are significant. These two versions have become world famous and therefore form the basis for our reflections.

The Ten Commandments are actually never named as "laws" or "commandments." They are referred to as the ten "words" (Hebrew: *devarim*; Deut 4:13; 10:4; Exod 34:28). That is significant for our understanding of the Ten Commandments. It is the reason why they are also called the *decalogue*, from the Greek *deka* "ten" and *logoi* "words." More important to fuel the story of freedom is the indication that the "commandments" are "words." The God who "speaks" these "words" is the God who liberated Israel from bondage and slavery and at Sinai proclaimed the structures for the journey of freedom. The intention of these "words" therefore is not to replace or negate freedom, but to shape freedom in such a way that it leads to a meaningful and successful life. Freedom is grounded in love. "God is love" (1 John 4:8) summarizes the central affirmation of the Jewish and Christian faiths. As a river flows toward the sea and as a flower turns toward the sun, so our innermost human yearnings are for love. Laws cannot create love. Therefore laws cannot meet our deepest human needs. The prophets Jeremiah and Ezekiel realized this when they spoke of a new relationship with God—a relationship not grounded in law but in love. God "will forgive their iniquity, and remember their sin no more," (Jer 31:34).[6] The prophets hear God saying: "I will put my law within them, and I will write it on their hearts" (Jer 31:31–34; Ezek 36:25–28). Indeed, in Deuteronomy, where we find one of the versions of the "ten words," we are told that the

---

practical imperative will then read as follows: Act so that in your own person as well as in the person of every other you are treating mankind also *as an end, never merely as a means*" (*The Fundamental Principles of the Metaphysics of Ethics*, 46–47 [emphases mine]).

5. There are related texts like the curse ritual in Deut 27:15–26, the list of commandments in Exod 34, the prohibitions in Lev 18–20, as well as the exhortations in Ezek 18:5–18 and Ps 15.

6. Unless otherwise noted, all biblical quotations are from the New Revised Standard Version (NRSV).

Introduction

"words" are not far away—in heaven or beyond the sea—"No, the word is very near to you; it is in your mouth and in your heart for you to observe." (Deut 30:11–14) What and who one loves to talk about and what feeds the needs of one's heart is what is ultimately important—not law but love; not legalism but freedom. Jesus' affirmation of such a vision of freedom and love is among the reasons for his conflict with the religious establishment of his day. For we Christians it has therefore become central to confess that faith in Christ initiates us on a journey of freedom grounded in the love of God. Laws and regulations form the parameters for the journey of freedom. They guide us toward the central passion of life, to love God and to love our neighbor (Gal 5:1; John 8:38; Mark 12:28–31).

Nevertheless, freedom has become a word into which people read their own dreams and which people use to validate their own interests. Wars are started and fought in the name of freedom. People are tortured to further freedom's cause. Revolutions are started under the banner of freedom and soon they devour their own children. It is obvious therefore that the content of freedom needs to be spelled out and that resources are named to travel the journey and to make sure that we travel in the right direction.

We shall see that the "ten words" name their own source. It is God who calls people to the journey of freedom, and God's spirit provides wells from which to drink. At the same time, freedom needs to be measured as to whether it is true to its source, and it needs to be guided to remain on track. The measure is God's word. For Christians that word has found its fullest expression in the life, death, and resurrection of Jesus Christ. Jesus Christ is the ground and the content of faith. He mediates God who speaks freedom into our conscience—faith comes from hearing the story of Jesus (Rom 10:17)—and he provides the guidance and the resources for the journey.

Jews and Christians alike read and respect the Hebrew Bible in general and the "ten words" in particular. Jesus of Nazareth also accepted the authority of the "ten words." Indeed when Jesus, and following him the early churches, brought together Deut 6:4–5—"The LORD is our God, the LORD alone. You shall love the LORD your God with all your heart, and with all your soul, and with all your might"—with Leviticus 19:18—"you shall love your neighbor as yourself: I am the LORD"—he was summarizing the "ten words" (Mark 12:28–31; Luke 10:27; Matt 22:37–39). The difference between Jews and Christians reading the same text is that Christians interrelate all texts from both testaments with their understanding of the story of Jesus. We need to keep that in mind as we try to relate the "words" to our situation. There will be similarities and there will be differences because the final authority for the Christian is the understanding of God as it has been revealed in the story of Jesus.

We must keep in mind that the "ten words" were spoken to a nation, "all Israel" (Deut 5:1). Every culture needs a story that sustains and feeds it, a story that can be told from generation to generation, a story that transcends the business and problems of the day. Moreover, if such a story is to build a resilient culture, a culture of freedom, then it must be liberating and compassionate. For Christians the danger has often been that our faith has led to a private and personal morality. That is important, but not enough. It does not sufficiently recognize that God is the "creator of heaven and earth." Faith in the God of Moses and Jesus must be lived in the public place. It must address not only the challenges of personal morality but also of social ethics. We must therefore ask what the "ten words" mean for responsible living in the public arena.

Just as we need white lines and guard rails to keep us on the road, just as we use maps to track our journeys to their intended destinations, just as we have traffic rules and traffic signs to save us from injury, so these "words" serve as guidelines on the journey of freedom. They invite us toward a culture of freedom. Those who hear and obey the "ten words" help to create such a culture.

The "ten words" have an inherent dignity and authority that is inspiring and persuasive. Theologians, philosophers, moralists, and lawyers of past and present have viewed the "ten words" as a summary of the Judeo-Christian message and guidance to a better future.[7] Augustine, Thomas Aquinas, John Wycliffe, Martin Luther, John Calvin, Thomas Hobbes, John Locke, Jonathan Edwards, Immanuel Kant, Thomas Jefferson, Paul Lehmann and many others have emphasized the importance of the decalogue for shaping human life. When the reformer Martin Luther, to cite only one important shaper of Christian faith, went out to visit the churches in the towns and villages, he abhorred the lack of Christian knowledge, even among the clergy. In response, he wrote his *Small Catechism* (1529), which he then expanded through sermons into the *Large Catechism* (1529). Both begin with the Ten Commandments and an interpretation of them. Luther said about the importance and significance Decalogue for the journey of faith,

7. See Kuntz, *The Ten Commandments in History*; Langston, *Exodus through the Centuries*, 186–230; and Childs, *Exodus*, 431–37.

Introduction

> This much is certain: those who know the Ten Commandments perfectly know the entire Scriptures and in all affairs and circumstances are able to counsel, help, comfort, judge, and make decisions in both spiritual and temporal matters. They are qualified to be a judge over all doctrines, walks of life, spirits, legal matters and everything else in the world.[8]

I begin each chapter by citing the respective texts from Exodus 20 and Deuteronomy 5 and adding some brief theological comments. Then, in a more meditative fashion, I reflect on the message of each of the "ten words."

I must finally say a word about the designations "God" and "Lord" in our texts. The Hebrew word for "God" is *Elohim*, while the name for Israel's God is *YHWH*, which is normally pronounced today as *Yahweh* (with different vowels it has also been pronounced *Jehovah*). Since Jews are forbidden to pronounce God's name, they say *Adonai* (Hebrew for "my Lord") where the Hebrew text reads *YHWH*. The Greek translation for *Adonai* is *Kyrios*; the Latin *dominus*; and the English "Lord." However, when we render "Lord" (all capital letters), we try to capture the fact that it is the *name* for Israel's God. Consequently "*I am the Lord your God*" is the English translation for what in Hebrew reads: "*I am YHWH (Yahweh) your Elohim.*"

It remains to thank those who have inspired and helped me along the way. My family, those with whom I live (Jill, Stephan, Rachel, Cedrik, Jael and Anya) and those who are a little further away (Christina, Matthew, Ohana, Nikolai, Issha and Shanti) are important channels of life for me. I value, appreciate, and love each one of them. My special gratitude goes to my friends Matthew Anstey, Merilyn Carey, Graeme Garrett, and David Neville. They have been very generous with their time and expertise. I would also like to thank Chris Spinks of Cascade Books for his excellent editing work.

---

8. *The Large Catechism*, preface to the 1530 edition, 382. See also the modern theologian, Paul Lehmann, who writes "The thesis of this book is that the Decalogue is at once the sum of the gospel and the pathfinder toward motivations, structures, and concreteness of responsible behavior in a world being shattered and shaped, in Norbert Wiener's phrase, for 'the human use of human beings'" (*The Decalogue and a Human Future*, 19).

1

When God Speaks, God Says "Yes"

Overture to the "Ten Words"

"Then *God spoke* . . . all these *words* . . ."

Exodus 19:16–18, 20:1 and Deuteronomy 5:1–6
Related biblical texts: John 1:1–18; 2 Corinthians 1:18–20

EXODUS 19:16–18; 20:1

On the morning of the *third day* there was thunder and lightning, as well as a thick cloud on the mountain, and a blast of a trumpet so loud that all the people who were in the camp trembled. Moses brought the people out of the camp to meet God. They took their stand at the foot of the mountain. Now Mount Sinai was wrapped in smoke, because the LORD had descended upon it in fire; the smoke went up like the smoke of a kiln, while the whole mountain shook violently. . . . Then God *spoke* all these *words* . . . .

DEUTERONOMY 5:1–5

Moses convened all Israel, and said to them: Hear, O Israel, the statutes and ordinances that I am addressing to you *today*; you shall learn them and observe them diligently. The LORD our God made a covenant *with us* at Horeb. *Not with our ancestors did the LORD make this covenant, but with us, who are all of us here alive today.* The LORD spoke with you face to face at the mountain, out of the fire. (At that time I was standing between the LORD and you to declare to you the words of the LORD; for you were afraid because of the fire and did not go up the mountain.) And *he said* . . .

THEOLOGICAL COMMENTS

THE TEN COMMANDMENTS ARE found in the books of Exodus (20:2–17) and Deuteronomy (5:6–21). Both versions are very similar, but they place the Decalogue in different contexts. But in both narratives, the "ten words" are inter-related with God liberating God's people from oppression (the exodus) and then at Sinai giving instructions for their life together under God. Moses plays a major role in both stories. He is the great law-giver for the Jewish people, the father of the nation, the mediator between the people and their God—"I (Moses) was standing between the LORD and you to declare to you the words of the LORD" (Deut 5:5).

For us this means, firstly, that Moses is not only a historical person in the history of the Jewish people. He has become a symbolic figure so that even in the seventh century BCE when the Deuteronomy was written (i.e., centuries after Moses' death), people could still hear God's words spoken to them *"who are all of us here alive this day"* (Deut 5:3).

Secondly, the introduction to the Decalogue in Deuteronomy is actually a good illustration as to how every generation is invited anew to tune into the history of freedom created by the exodus event and the giving of the covenant including the "ten words." The emphasis that the covenant was made *"not with our ancestors . . . , but with us, who are all of us here alive today"* was their way of saying that the covenant must be heard and obeyed anew by each new generation. It is God's dealing with God's people and such dealings must never be frozen into the past. Similar to the *Covenant Code* in Exodus, the Decalogue in Deuteronomy is followed by the detailed laws, rules, and statutes in chapters 12–26. However, in Deuteronomy they are presented as *sermons*. They are not a legal corpus, but rather an appeal to the conscience for what it means to live responsibly under God. Again, it is important for us to remember that although the Decalogue was conceived and shaped in a certain situation, it at the same time transcends the situation and retains its moral authority for other times and circumstances. The merging of the horizons of past and present invites us to join the history of God's word, to hear it and see whether and how it can interpret and modify our lives.

Thirdly, the assertion that God "speaks" raises the whole question of how we humans can speak of God. God is different from us. God is God; we are human. God lives "in heaven"; we live on earth. Yet, as humans, we have no choice; if we want to speak of God, we can only do so with our languages. The danger is, of course, that we paint God in our image, that our thoughts and our words deprive God of God's deity, God's otherness, God's Godhood, or worse, that we use God to validate our interests and baptize our ideas.

Two thoughts may be helpful at this point. On the one hand, Christians believe that God has shared God's life with Jesus of Nazareth. The "word became flesh," we read in the prologue to the Gospel of John: "No one has ever seen God. It is God the only Son, who is close to the Father's heart, who has made him known" (John 1:14, 18). The apostle Paul comments on the same event: "when the fullness of time had come, God sent his Son, born of a woman, born under the law, in order to redeem those who were under the law, so that we might receive adoption as children" (Gal 4:4-5). This inter-locking of God with humanity through the person of Jesus of Nazareth enables and authorizes us to speak of God within the limitations of our language. At the same time, on the other hand, we need to be self-critical. We need to check our language and ask whether it coheres with the story of Jesus. It is that story which reveals and interprets God's nature. In the church it is the function and privilege of theology to recognize the story of Jesus as God's self-revelation, and it is the task of theology to measure our words and our deeds to ascertain whether they echo what the story of Jesus has revealed about God.

It is important to note that God speaks *words*, not laws, rules, commandments, or principles. We must resist the popular notion of casting God in the role of a lawgiver, or a teacher of doctrine, or as the moral principle of the universe. Our text emphasizes that God is inter-related with freedom and compassion. This constitutes a major challenge for believers today. Too many souls have been bruised, too many sincere believers have been misled, and too much faith has been distorted by a legalistic, punitive, abstract and dogmatic perception of God. Too often we have compensated our anxiety and uncertainty by creating a picture of God that is stern, authoritarian, legalistic, and punitive. The overture to the "ten words" assures us that God is the living One and that God lives for us, inviting us not into a prison of dogmatism or morality, not wanting to make us feel bad for things that we have done or not done, but calling us to a life of compassion and a journey of freedom. "If we are faithless, he (God) remains faithful—for he cannot deny himself" (2 Tim 2:13).

MESSAGE

Before we speak about the actual "words" of the Decalogue we must speak of the God in whose being these words are grounded. Theologians speak of a "theophany," God "appearing" to make God's will known, and inviting people to follow God's ways.

God "Speaks"

God is a "speaking" God. He spoke creation into being (Gen 1) and God's word will accomplish its purpose of bringing joy, peace and justice:

> . . . as the rain and the snow come down from heaven, and do not return there until they have watered the earth, making it bring forth and sprout, giving seed to the sower and bread to the eater, so shall my word be that goes out from my mouth; it shall not return to me empty, but it shall accomplish that which I purpose, and succeed in the thing for which I sent it. For you shall go out in joy, and be led back in peace; the mountains and the hills before you shall burst into song, and all the trees of the field shall clap their hands. (Isa 55:10–12)

The many words of creation in Genesis 1 reach a high point when humanity is created. One of the human organs is the ear. The human being can hear and respond. God uses the word to seek communion with humanity. When God's word has been heard and obeyed its reaches its aim: "God blessed them" (Gen 1:28).

The symbol of the "word" was taken up by the early Christians when they wanted to speak about their faith and its origin in the story of Jesus: "Long ago God spoke to our ancestors in many and various ways by the prophets, but in these last days he has spoken to us by a Son, whom he appointed heir of all things, through whom he also created the worlds" (Heb 1:1–2). In Jesus Christ "the Word became flesh." With Christ, life and joy flowered in human history. Those who hear and obey, rejoice: "we have seen his glory, the glory as of a father's only son, full of grace and truth" (John 1:14). And those "who received him, who believed in his name, he gave power to become children of God" (John 1:12). Faith comes from hearing the story of Jesus (Rom 10:17). Where grace becomes event the transformation is so powerful that new language is created. Christians in the church where the Gospel of John was written speak of new birth, of birth from above: "who were born, not of blood or of the will of the flesh or of the will of man, but of God." (John 1:13, also John 3:3) In the encounter of word and faith, the believer has already "passed from death to life" (John 5:24). God was never without the creative Word: "In the beginning was the Word, and the Word was with God, and the Word was God." (John 1:1) In light of the happiness and fulfillment that people experienced through faith in Christ, we may translate: "In the beginning was the Word, and the Word was with God, and God's Word was 'Yes.'"

God's "yes" is another way of saying that "God is love." Love takes the initiative by sharing itself. It is important to realize that before we can speak of God, God has already spoken to us! "We love because he first loved us" (1 John 4:19)! God is the ground and source of our life; God surrounds us with ever new possibilities for life's adventure. Our life, our faith, our struggles are all a response to what God has given us and what God has done for us.

God, the Mystery that Undergirds Life

One of the pictures of the British painter William Turner (1775–1851) shows a ship at sea in a snow storm. Some Turner experts have surmised that Turner had himself tied to the mast of such a ship in such a storm in order to experience the lashing of the unbridled forces of nature. A photographer with her camera could not have captured that struggle between humanity and nature. The camera would have recorded the waves and the sea and the snow and the light, but it could not have recorded what *really* went on. For that you need a poet, or a painter like Turner! A photograph captures reality as the eye sees it. Turner is able to capture reality as it affects our whole being.

Reality is more than what the eye can see or the hand can feel. Each one of us is more than we can see of each other. There are recesses of our being which we don't even know ourselves. There are parts of our life that only the Spirit of God can fathom. How impoverished we have become in our hunger for objectivity! How impoverished is a world that no longer expects God to speak, and therefore no longer listens for God's word!

This impoverishment, this shallowness, is visible at every corner. When we speak of freedom, some of us can only think of the right to have a gun or not to wear a seat belt. When we think of love, the advertising world invites us to reduce love to the sex games of stylized bodies. When we think of security, our unimaginative minds can only think of tanks and fighter planes and "star wars" to protect us from the mysterious "other." We try to reduce everything to what we are able to see.

The God who "speaks" does not live in splendid isolation. God cannot be objectified. God does not exist as other things exist. God lives in being "with us" and being "for us." "God *is* love" the Bible says in many variations. The Hebrew Bible prefers to speak of God in participles. God is in that God comes and loves and speaks. God is the mysterious, invisible, but not frightening companion on life's journey.

At the same time, we humans are defined as "hearers," as receivers of God's words. We have a conscience into which God speaks and we have the ability not only to hear but also to obey and to implement God's word.

Moses, the People, and God

Moses gets his people ready to meet God. "Prepare for the *third day*; ... On the morning of the *third day* there was thunder and lightning, as well as a thick cloud on the mountain, and a blast of a trumpet so loud that all the people who were in the camp trembled" (Exod 19:11, 15–16, emphasis mine). The "third day" is a day of promise in the history of God's people. Christians tell the story that Jesus was raised from the dead on "the third day." It is the day when God wants to do something *new* and something *good* for God's people. Let us prepare for the coming of God, Moses challenges his people. God is on his way to heal and to liberate.

And the "third day" comes. There is thunder and clouds and lightening and fire and smoke and blasts from a cosmic trumpet. The people tremble. "Moses brought the people out of the camp to meet God" (Exod 19:17). But it was too much for them. The holiness of God, God's majesty, would have consumed them. Moses and Aaron try to mediate. They want to become bridge-builders between God and God's people. And then the simple statement: *"Then God spoke all these words,"* and the "words" that he spoke we have called the "Ten Commandments," the "Decalogue" (the "ten words").

The Promise

Can the "ten words" be relevant today? Can we find meaning in them for our life and our future? Of course! They belong to the great declarations in human history. Like Jesus' *Sermon on the Mount*, the *Magna Carta Libertatum* (1215), the French *Déclaration des droits de l'homme et du citoyen* (1789), the American *Declaration of Independence* (1776), and the *Universal Declaration of Human Rights* (1948), the Decalogue has played a part in shaping our Western culture and morality. When I was a teenager we had to memorize the "ten words" and interpret them. For Christians and Jews around the world they are referred to with reverence. They are part of their worship and liturgical resources. For many they are still an unquestioned set of moral and spiritual guidelines today.

The Problem

Yet questions arise. Sometimes smaller, sometimes larger. Are not the "ten words" too old—probably over 2,500 years old!—coming to us from a completely different culture? How can they speak into our situation? How can moral rules that arose in an ancient society in the Middle East speak to a modern western technological society, a society in which the mule is replaced by the car and the airplane, in which the grazing of cattle has given way to computer-driven feeding machineries; in which the meeting of elders at the village gate is replaced by complicated legal systems and grand high court buildings? How can a narrative that was originally spoken to men in a patriarchal culture speak to men *and women* in a society that affirms their equality?

And for Christians the questions continue. Is not faith in Jesus the end of all laws and commandments and morality? We are not Israel, and our leader is not Moses! Do not the Ten Commandments presuppose God to be a law-giver, while Jesus fleshed out a merciful God, whose first words are life and love, not law and morality? Did not the apostle Paul proclaim loudly and clearly that "Christ is the end of the law" (Rom 10:4)? Is not the church already branded and often rejected as an old fashioned moral institution—with the raised finger and "the big brother is watching you" mentality? If we affirm the "ten words" are we not in danger of adding to the irrelevance of the church and of presenting God as the one who frightens people?

The Challenge

Yet, let us think again:

- At a time when many people experience emptiness and a lack of orientation, it may be good to hear of a God who can *speak* life and joy into our conscience and *liberate* us from the chains that restrain or oppress us.

- At a time when a culture of violence is rampant, when the possibility of an irresponsible use of nuclear power is in the air, when an ecology crisis threatens the survival of the human race, perhaps the commandment *"you shall not kill"* is worth pondering.
- At a time when the traditional pillars of human society are disintegrating and the family is losing its integrating power, *"you shall honor your father and your mother"* may help us to implement a postulate of the *Universal Declaration of Human Rights*: "The family is the natural and fundamental group unit of society and is entitled to protection by society and the State" (Article 16:3).
- In recent history with its colonialism, exploitation and wars, we have become painfully aware of the problems related to imperialism. We thought that we were feeding our souls by conquering the world and expanding our markets. With the resulting disillusionment, the old commandment *"you shall not covet"* may gain new meaning for us.
- The sexual revolution promised that by tearing away the fig leaves of modesty and by treating shame as psychological illusion or oppression, we could pass through the gateway to unrestrained happiness. But rising divorce rates as well as the fear of intimacy and long-term relationships suggest that *"you shall not commit adultery"* may prove to be a more reliable guide to a fulfilled life.
- At a time when the world economic structures are heavily bent in favor of the rich and powerful nations, to the detriment of those who have no voice, no friends and no power, the commandment *"you shall not steal"* may urge us toward a new understanding of life and its dignity.
- With the youth suicide rate increasing, and people searching for meaning and acceptance in the highways and by-ways of life, perhaps we need to be shocked into awareness with words from beyond: "*I am the* LORD *your God, . . . you shall have no other gods before me.*"

We shall see. Let us for the moment continue the quest for the nature and being of God in whose being those powerful words are grounded, words that we have called the "Ten Commandments" and that have influenced our history to the present day.

When God Speaks, God Says "Yes"

Again: God

"God" must be more than a word in our language. The words of the Decalogue flow from the very being of God. They assure us that God has not dismissed or abandoned God's creation; that our life is not aimlessly tossed about in the flow of history. God has not only created our world and us, God also provides structures for our lives to succeed, and for our world to have a future.

In the Bible, God's Spirit and God's words are interrelated. The Hebrew word for "spirit" is *ruach* which means "wind" or "breath." We know from our experience that when we speak, our breath is being shaped into words, which in turn interpret and modify life. Therefore, when we say that God speaks, we mean that God's Spirit aims to inter-relate God's passion with our life, making God's will known to us and empowering us to fulfill it.

But will we listen and are we willing to obey? The "ten words" are not a carefully worked out blueprint for a successful life. They do not do away with human responsibility. They are like a road map or a road sign trying to steer us in the right direction; they are like a guard rail aiming to keep us on track.

But we must be willing to listen! The God who speaks seeks for people who listen and then act upon what they hear. That has remained true from the days of Moses to our day. The early Christians heard the God of Moses speak again in the story of Jesus. He, Jesus, was for them the one word that they wanted to hear, trust and obey.

The Question of Truth

By affirming that we believe in God and that this God relates to us—that is what we mean when we say "God speaks"—we enter into the marketplace of life and raise the question of truth. Is there a truth that is worth living and therefore worth dying for? Or are we, in a different way now, like Turner's ship tossed about by the storms of life with no light to guide, no rudder to steer and no rope to pull us into a safe harbor?

With the Decalogue we affirm that God has not left this world without guidance, that there is orientation for our conscience and for our life together. We affirm that there are things that are wrong and lead to destruction, like murder and adultery and stealing and greed, and that there are things that are right and lead to life, like saving life, working for peace, enhancing justice, and caring for those who are tossed to the margin of life.

God and Conscience

At this point things become personal. Each of us has, or rather *is*, a conscience. Conscience is the centre of our personhood. It makes us who we are. It shapes our identity. It is worth understanding and caring for.

Conscience is controversial today. For some it has negative connotations. It is seen as the channel for the demands that our parents, our culture, our religion place upon us. People want to be free from such restrictions. They feel bound to the past and they want to break the chains and move into a future in which they can shape their own identity. I have met people for whom religious traditions and parental control took away the joy of life. A psychiatrist even told me that he had to murder his mother in a dream before he could be free.

Many hesitate to see conscience as a central reality in human life. It seems to be so nebulous and illusive; so easily deformed. Many religious people feel oppressed by their conscience and long for liberation. Others are so fanaticized in their conscience that they appear to have no qualms in destroying those who disagree with them. With a so-called clear conscience people have tortured, raped, and murdered. Every war, every ethnic conflict, every racial strife, every social hostility produces people on all sides who further their cause seemingly in harmony with their conscience. Aren't we all surprised at times at what people think, say and do? And their conscience seems to go along with them quite easily. When we listen to our politicians, who often claim a high moral ground for themselves, it is hardly possible to get a clear statement from them. They prefer to put a spin on things rather than speaking the truth. The human conscience seems to be very bendable and too easily made to serve all kinds of causes. One wonders at times whether a reference to "conscience" is just another way of justifying our self-interest.

But conscience is not an illusion. It is mentioned in the *Universal Declaration of Human Rights*.[1] It is real. It is a fact in human life. We all know it. Conscience is our human capacity to be aware of being woven into a network of relationship with humanity, with nature and history, and with God. In that relational network we are informed and we are responsible. If we try to deny our conscience or escape from it we not only repress its

---

1. "All human beings are born free and equal in dignity and rights. They are endowed with reason and *conscience* and should act towards one another in a spirit of brotherhood" (Article 1).

demands and promises, but we isolate ourselves from life. At the same time, we all realize that the conscience needs orientation, guidance and direction. I suggest that we can retrieve a positive and creative function of conscience if we make the following distinctions.

Firstly, conscience is the human capacity where we hear God's unconditional "yes" to us. We hear the word that can set us free to shape who we want to be. I treasure the following citation on my baptismal certificate. It comes from the prophet Isaiah:

> ... thus says the LORD, he who created you, O Jacob, he who formed you, O Israel: Do not fear, for I have redeemed you; I have called you by name, you are mine. When you pass through the waters, I will be with you; and through the rivers, they shall not overwhelm you; when you walk through fire you shall not be burned, and the flame shall not consume you. For I am the LORD your God, the Holy One of Israel, your Savior. (Isa 43:1–3)

Whatever life may bring, God, our creator, shares God's life with us, says "yes" to us, and sets us free to shape who we want to be. That divine "yes" we can only hear in our conscience.

Nevertheless, secondly, our freedom is constantly threatened by the demands of other voices that claim our allegiance. Our self-interest tempts us to use other people for our own gain. We follow the promises that much money and good sex—welcome commodities!—can bring lasting satisfaction. We get our freedom mixed up with cultural values and ambitions. It is therefore important that freedom remains grounded in God and that the content of that freedom comes from God. The human conscience is the faculty where we hear the stories of God's dealings with God's creation and relate them to our life and to our situations. For Christians the grand story by which we measure other claims upon us is the story of Jesus in which God's provision and God's passion for the world is revealed.

The challenge therefore is, thirdly, to inter-relate conscience with truth. Truth may have many colors, but it is neither arbitrary nor capricious. The "ten words" from the ancient past and human rights today have enduring significance. They stand for the fact that there are values and practices that are true and others which are false. It can, for instance, never be right and true to steal a person's freedom, to rape a woman or to murder a person. A conscience that is open to God, to other humans and to creation is open to the truth. It will negotiate truth claims, measuring them by the story that determines our ultimate allegiance and then inciting us to think and act accordingly.

When God speaks, God addresses our conscience! When we hear God's word, and when it is really God's word we hear, God frees our conscience from all kinds of garbage that binds us to the powers of hopelessness and then provides guidance to shape our freedom. God's "yes" to us is not an arbitrary declaration. It carries with it the structures for a successful and meaningful life. God frees us for a future of life and promise. The God who speaks the "ten words" into the history of Israel and thereby into the history of humanity addresses our conscience and calls us to a culture of freedom.

God and the Divine Invitation to Life

Too many people feel that God is a moral judge and that the conscience is the spoilsport of life. The word "commandment" is misleading. "Ten words"—"Decalogue"—is better. God is not a moral judge trying to tell us what to do. God wants to liberate us to affirm life and enjoy it. The "ten words" are guidelines in our quest to affirm life. That is fundamental for our understanding of the "ten words." When God speaks, God speaks words of life.

Does that not remind us of Jesus, who is also named God's word (John 1:1–14)? People experienced him as "abundant life" (John 10:10). And there are the great "I am" words with which Jesus Christ is presented as the One who dethrones all human-made gods and is confessed as the giver and fulfiller of life: "I am the door" to the mystery of life (John 10). "I am the *good* shepherd" whom you can trust for protection and guidance in life – and beware of many who want to lead you astray (John 10). "I am the bread *of life*" which can nurture you toward wholeness and meaning (John 6). "I am the *true* vine" that can fulfill your longing for life (John 15). "I am the light of the world" that can give you hope in times of darkness (John 8:12, 9:5). "I am the resurrection and the life" (11:25). "I am the way, the truth and the life" (14:6).

We may therefore say that God speaks and when God speaks, God says "yes." This "yes" is God's unconditional grace that has come to expression in the story of Jesus: In the words of the apostle Paul: "As surely as God is faithful, our word to you has not been 'Yes and No'. For the Son of God, Jesus Christ, whom we proclaimed among you, Silvanus and Timothy and

I, was not 'Yes and No'; but *in him it is always 'Yes.'* For in him every one of God's promises is a 'Yes'" (2 Cor 1:18–20, emphasis mine).

On behalf of the God of the Decalogue, Jesus invites us not into a dungeon or moral prison, but into a relationship: "Come to me, all you that are weary and are carrying heavy burdens, and I will give you rest. Take my yoke upon you, and learn from me; for I am gentle and humble in heart, and you will find rest for your souls. For my yoke is easy, and my burden is light" (Matt 11:28–30).

Perhaps we need a new understanding of life. Dethrone the gods that determine us, and put the God of Moses and of Jesus in their place. We may have to hear the invitation to life anew, that real life is life lived with God and with each other. To honor the Lord our God, to keep the Sabbath day holy, to affirm life, not to exploit others, may be some long-forgotten virtues that may help us to experience real freedom. We may have to learn again that looking after others does not restrict our freedom, but is the necessary discipline to enjoy and enhance our freedom.

God and Freedom

I therefore want to say right at the outset that the God of the "ten words" is neither a slave-owner nor a slave-driver but one who liberates his people from slavery and offers them guidance for their life together. The early Christians therefore sounded the trumpet of freedom: "For freedom Christ has set us free; stand fast therefore, and do not submit again to the yoke of slavery" (Gal 5:1, 13–14).

The Decalogue does not want to bind us with chains of morality; the "words" are not handcuffs to restrict our movements; they are not chains around our legs to hinder our freedom. They are given to name the foundation of a culture of freedom and then to structure and discipline our freedom, lest we misuse our freedom for selfish pursuits and thereby cut ourselves off from the sources of life. They are guideposts to point us in the right direction, so that we do not get lost in the jungle of life. They are guard-rails to keep us on the road of life, lest we become servants of death.

None of us will ever know God in all of God's fullness. But this ancient text reminds us that God knows us, that God is the ground of our life and that this ground is promising because it is well disposed toward us. God speaks, and when God speaks, God says "yes."

2

When God Acts, God Liberates

Continuing the Overture to the "Ten Words"

"I am the LORD your God, who brought you out of
the land of Egypt, out of the house of slavery."

Exodus 20:2 and Deuteronomy 5:6
Related biblical texts: Exodus 6:2–9; Matthew 5:1–11; Galatians 5:13–25

THEOLOGICAL COMMENTS

WE CONTINUE OUR INTRODUCTION to the "ten words." "I am the LORD your God" is found very often in the Hebrew Bible. It describes God as the ground of our freedom, as the foundation on which the history of God's people is built. At the same time this expression indicates that God takes initiatives to which people can respond, and God presents possibilities from which people can choose.

God's initiatives aim at creating space for the experience of freedom. God is the one "who brought you out of the land of Egypt, out of the house of slavery." God's being must be thought of as a presence "for us" and "with us," resulting not only in words that address the human conscience but also in deeds that liberate from situations of oppression.

Deeds of liberation call for structures of liberation. God does not liberate people so that they can fall into the hands of false gods. Freedom therefore needs discipline and structures to ensure that it remains grounded in its author. The "ten words," but also the statutes and ordinances, the cult and the prophets were all intended to preserve, protect and guide the ongoing journey of freedom.

For the believer, therefore, freedom is not freedom *from* God as suggested by the great skeptics of Western culture, from Ludwig Feuerbach and Karl Marx to Friedrich Nietzsche and Sigmund Freud, but freedom *for* God and for God's creation. Freedom needs to remain anchored in its ground, otherwise it too easily becomes an extension and intensification of our self-interest. The theological challenge is to find a way of speaking of God that is neither so abstract and removed that God does not occur in our everyday life, nor that God-talk is dissolved into morality and ethics. God's word is the necessary ground and source, as well as the content of life's journey. As such it is a *living* word, fleshed out in the life, death and resurrection of Jesus and echoed in the Holy Scriptures.

In the Judeo-Christian tradition freedom is related to community. It does not encourage individualism. The "other" is not a threat but a necessary constituent for the experience of freedom. Freedom implies communion in which the social nature of the human being—the human being created as "male *and* female" (Gen 1:27)—is realized and celebrated.

MESSAGE
An Overture to the Story of Freedom

The overture to an opera sets the tone, introduces the theme, and summarizes the message. You hear the first few sounds and you know "that is Mozart," or "that is Verdi"; "that will bring joy," or "that will deal with sadness." The overture summarizes what is then developed in the rest of the opera.

In this chapter we continue to meditate on the overture to the ten commandments. We are introduced to God's passion. It is a passion for freedom. That is the well-spring from which the "ten words" flow. These words are not primarily concerned with human rules or moral laws. They are words related to God's liberating activity in the world. When we hear the word "commandment" we tend to associate it with rules and laws and prohibitions. The immediate reaction is often that they—the commandments—and therefore God, who gives them, want to tell us what to do. They want to restrict our life. They want to limit our freedom. They want to lock us up like birds in a cage; or like wild animals in an urban zoo.

But to associate God with chains and cages is a fundamental mistake, a gross misunderstanding of the God of Moses and Jesus. God wants to open the doors of the cages we build for ourselves and for others. The Bible interprets our life as being estranged from God; as being locked into a cage, from where we dream of freedom. But at the same time the Bible insists that God wants to open the doors, God wants to break the chains, God wants to lead us into "a broad place" where we can be free. The Psalmists say it well:

> *He (the Lord) brought me out into a broad place;*
> he delivered me, because he delighted in me. (Ps 18:19)
>
> You have given me the shield of your salvation,
>   and your right hand has supported me;
> your help has made me great.
> *You gave me a wide place* for my steps under me,
>   and my feet did not slip. (Ps 18:35–36)
>
> I will exult and rejoice in your steadfast love,
>   because you have seen my affliction;
> you have taken heed of my adversities,
>   and have not delivered me into the hand of the enemy;
> *you have set my feet in a broad place.* (Ps 31:7–8)

Aberrations of Freedom

If God and freedom belong together, then we must make sure that our freedom does not get into the wrong hands and that it does not veer off the rails. Since freedom is a word that is widely used, we must be clear what freedom we are talking about.

It is not the freedom proclaimed on the posters of pro-gun rallies. "The gun assures my freedom!" Every neighbor is seen as a potential enemy from whom I need protection. The gun assures that I and my immediate family are safe and that we can do with our property what we like. This heightened individualism is indeed encouraged by the Western understanding of freedom. Its classic formulation is found in the French *Declaration of the Rights of Man and of the Citizen* (1789), in which freedom is defined as "the power of doing whatever does not injure another" (§4). This perception, while it has propelled the industrial and scientific revolutions and fuelled Western political and economic successes, it has also disadvantaged the economically powerless, and it favors seeing other persons as potential invaders of one's individual freedom.

It is not freedom when the youth magazine *Juice* has a section on "clothes *to die for*," and there presents pictures of people who have been strangled and tortured and murdered and shot; with bloody faces and bullet holes in their jackets—and then lists the prices of what they wear. This is not representative of a culture of freedom. Rather, it is the manifestation of a culture that portrays the estranging powers of death. Why would a journalist or an editor dream up something like that? And who would read it without becoming sick and disillusioned with a culture that glorifies death and violence?

Are we in the West really champions of freedom when we evaluate each other not by who we are but by what we can achieve and contribute to our society. Was that not the fate of the slaves in Egypt? Their dignity was defined by their usefulness and achievements. They were slave laborers. We may not live in material poverty, but by sidelining the disabled, the elderly and the unemployed, we are intensifying an understanding of freedom that excludes those who can not or can no longer measure up to the expectations of a culture that demands achievement and success.

Can freedom be paired with violence? The Iraq war was started in March 2003 under the American codename "Operation Iraqi Freedom." Although the immediate justification was to depose Saddam Hussein because he was (falsely) accused of harboring weapons of mass destruction and of collaborating with Al Qaeda terrorists, the long-term aim was to spread "freedom" and "democracy" to the Middle East. Returning to our text, it is a shock to find that in the immediate vicinity of the decalogue we also find the justification of war and violence. The covenant which God makes with Moses includes the driving out of "the Amorites, the Canaanites, the Hittites, the Perizzites, the Hivites, and the Jebusites. . . . You shall tear down their altars, break their pillars, and cut down their sacred poles" (Exod 34:10–16). Indeed, "when the LORD your God gives them over to you and you defeat them, then you must utterly destroy them" (Deut 7:1–6). That is not freedom. That is violence. Jesus of Nazareth turns away from such war and violence. He tunes into those elements in the Hebrew Bible that relate the messianic age to non-violence. In the Christian vision of reality freedom and violence exclude each other.

This is a good point to illustrate how a commitment to the story of Jesus can at times make us critical of biblical assertions. Jesus' relationship to God was passionate but this passion included a commitment to non-violence. When during the passion story someone in Jesus' presence resorted to violence, Jesus immediately undoes the damage and acclaims "No more of this!" (Luke 22:49–51).[1] Christian faith entails the presumption

---

1. I am aware, of course, that there are texts in the gospels that seem to portray another reality. The Jesus saying "Do not think that I have come to bring peace to the

that at the centre of reality—we may say metaphorically: "in the heart of God"—there reigns love, not hate, peace, not war, nonviolence, not violence. Jesus intentionally rejected the Zealot option of using violence in his struggle to make God manifest on earth. But his alternative was not withdrawal, passivity or quietism. Indeed, it was Jesus' praxis, his active involvement in the affairs of his society that caused opposition, rejection, torture, and finally brought about his execution. Jesus exhorted his followers not only to love their neighbors, but their enemies "so that you may be children of your Father in heaven; for he makes his sun rise on the evil and on the good, and sends rain on the righteous and on the unrighteous" (Matt 5:43–48). With his execution the way of violence seemed to have triumphed. But "God raised Jesus from the dead!"[2] With this divine initiative, God *validated* Jesus' way of non-violence and at the same time also defeated the powers of violence that led to Jesus' crucifixion. God showed that ultimately love is stronger than death. On that basis we can re-affirm, in a world of war and violence, that peacemakers are the children of God (Matt 5:9). We can confess in a world where political, economic and military power seems to dictate what is right and what is wrong, that ultimately the meek will inherit the earth (Matt 5:5).

---

earth; I have not come to bring peace, but a sword" (Matt 10:34) refers to the "division" (cf. Luke 12:51) that the new vision of God's ways brings into one's personal networks (Matt 10:34-36; Luke 12:51-53), and which are to be expected as part of letting the story of Jesus determine one's life (Matt 10:37-39). A similar metaphorical use of *"sword"* is found in Luke 22:35-38. It stands for the increasing opposition that Jesus and his friends encounter on the way to the cross. More often, the so-called *temple cleansing* is mentioned as a possible illustration that Jesus resorted to violence (Mark 11:15-17; Matt 21:12-13; Luke 19:45-46; John 2:14-17). The imagery of Jesus "making a whip of cords" (only in John), turning over tables and driving the money changers out seems to point in that direction. But those who are familiar with prophetic symbolism, and realising that the text refers to two major prophets (Isaiah and Jeremiah) who used such symbolism, makes it much more likely that Jesus used prophetic symbolism, what we may call a demonstration or street drama, to make the point that in his view the temple cult was seeking God in the wrong direction. Hays speaks for many when he concludes: "Thus, from Matthew to Revelation we find a consistent witness against violence and a calling to the community to follow the example of Jesus in *accepting* suffering rather than *inflicting* it" (*The Moral Vision of the New Testament*, 332, see 317-46).

2. This early Christian confession is still transparent in texts such as Rom 4:24; 8:11; 10:9; 1 Cor 6:14; 15:15; 2 Cor 4:14; 1 Thess 1:9-10; Gal 1:1; Col 2:12; Eph 1:20; 1 Pet 1:21; and Acts 3:15; 4:10; 5:30; 10:40, 13:30-37.

When God Acts, God Liberates

Dimensions of Freedom

Freedom grounded in God has individual, social and historical dimensions. On the individual level it assures people that their dignity is a precious gift of a God who calls people into freedom. Our inner freedom is not dependent on whether we are rich or poor, whether we have a job or not, whether we are disabled or a decathlon champion, whether we went to university or not. Our freedom is a gift that we are invited to accept and put into practice.

Such God-given freedom can give extraordinary courage to people who are prepared to swim against the stream. During the time of the "third Reich" in Germany, when the dictator Adolf Hitler demanded ultimate obedience from his subjects, the Lutheran theologian and ecumenical diplomat Dietrich Bonhoeffer helped Jewish people escape from Nazi oppression to Switzerland. He also engaged in a conspiracy to kill Hitler. He paid for his courage by being hanged in Flossenbürg concentration camp.

An Austrian peasant and devoted Roman Catholic Christian, Franz Jägerstätter, was the only person in his village, St. Radegund in upper Austria, to oppose Austria's *Anschluss* (annexation) to Hitler's Germany. Later he refused military service—against the explicit advice of his priest and bishop. He could not imagine how Hitler's racism and violence could be an expression of God's will. He was imprisoned and then beheaded. The book that tells his story, *In Solitary Witness*,[3] influenced Daniel Ellsberg decades later in the United States in his decision to oppose the Vietnam War by publishing the Pentagon Papers.

Although God's freedom conveys dignity and courage to the individual, it does not individualize people. Freedom is a community experience. We need God and other humans for our experience of freedom. Christians therefore affirm with the apostle Paul that faith "comes" to individuals, but when it arrives and is celebrated then it creates a community of equals (Gal 3:23–28).

There is also a historical dimension to freedom. The ten commandments are related to the story of Israel's liberation from oppression. The story has become an icon of hope for people and nations in their struggle for freedom. Men and women like Mahatma Gandhi, Aung San Suu Kyi, Xanana Gusmao, Nelson Mandela, and Martin Luther King, Jr.; and people groups in Burma (Myanmar), Rwanda, Burundi, Palestine, and Nagaland

---

3. Zahn, *In Solitary Witness*.

in their struggle for democracy, justice, and peace can draw courage and resilience from the story of the liberation that God provided for Israel.

The Bible and Freedom

The "ten words" must therefore be understood as an invitation to a culture of freedom. That is indeed the underlying theme of the Jewish and Christian Scriptures.

We are reminded of Moses, when God appeared to him in a flaming bush: "I am the God of your fathers, the God of Abraham, the God of Isaac, and the God of Jacob . . . . I have seen the affliction of my people who are in Egypt, and have heard their cry . . . I know their suffering, and I have come down to deliver them . . . and . . . bring them . . . to a good and broad land. . . . Come, I will send you . . ." (Exod 3:1–10). Moses is overwhelmed by the challenge. The experience of holiness, fear and uncertainty are pervasive. Who am I to face Pharaoh? What can I do? But the great "I am" speaks again: "I will be with you" (3:12). So, Moses, go and say to the people of Israel in Egypt: "I am the LORD, and I will free you from the burdens of the Egyptians and deliver you from slavery to them. I will redeem you with an outstretched arm and with mighty acts of judgments. I will take you as my people, and I will be your God!" (Exod 6:6–7).

We are also reminded of Jesus at the Lake of Galilee, looking at Simon and Andrew and James and John as they went about their daily tasks—then breaking into their lives: "Come and follow me" (Mark 1:16-20).

We are reminded of Paul who sounds the trumpet of freedom: "For freedom Christ has set us free; stand fast therefore, and do not submit again to the yoke of slavery" (Gal 5:1, 13-14).

God takes the initiative. God is waiting at the door of our life, at the gate of our conscience, not to invade us but to invite us to a journey of freedom. The great overture which must guide our understanding of the "ten words" as a whole, and of each "word" in particular, is that God comes into our lives as a liberating reality.

Liberation is a little more than freedom. Freedom can be abstract, liberation is concrete. Freedom can be discussed, liberation must be practiced and experienced. Freedom can be an idea in our mind, liberation aims to be fleshed out in our daily life. God wants to free us from the chains that bind us to the past. That is the central point, which we must not forget as we consider the decalogue. The commandments are not to restrict but to shape and discipline our freedom. They are invitations to a life of freedom. If we forget that, then everything will be distorted.

A Gracious God

The God who calls people to freedom is a *gracious* God: "I am the LORD your God . . . ." The one who speaks the commandments is not only a living and liberating God but a God who lives *for us*. God is a loving and a gracious God. That is the experience of faith. We recognize, suddenly or gradually, not only that God *is* but that God is *for us*; that God is not a deity who lives out there somewhere in splendid isolation, but that God is *our* God. "In him we live and move and have our being" (Acts 17:28).

There will be times when we fail and falter on our journey of faith. When we become tired and disillusioned. When we become comfortable and lazy. When the dream of freedom has subsided because we don't want to take risks any more. How can God surprise people who want to control and administer the kingdom of God? At times like that it is good to know that God can and does forgive, that God can and does renew, that God can and does give us another chance—because God's being includes the passion for freedom.

God Creates History

God is introduced not only as a living and liberating God, not only as a loving and gracious God, but also as a God who creates history. "I am the LORD your God, who brought you out of the land of Egypt, out of the house of slavery." What does that mean? How did God do it? God calls people into the process of liberation. God invites people like Moses and Joshua and the other countless women and men who were prepared to echo God's passion for justice and peace and salvation. God's plans become history when God's people hear the call and do something about it.

God provides the possibilities for our life. Will we centre our conscience on God or will we serve other gods? Will we use the word "god" to validate our own interests, or will we honor God's name? Will we add to a culture of violence or will we learn not to kill in thought and deed? Will we honor our promises of love or will we commit adultery? Will we make our own interest and welfare and comfort the primary ambition of our life, or will we learn not to steal and not to covet?

We can choose! But remember that with our choices we create history, we determine the future not only of our lives but of our society. We can become partners with God in creating a future of justice and peace and reconciliation. With our thoughts and our deeds we can resist a culture of death and enhance a culture of life.

The Ingredients of Liberation

Let us finally ask how we can become God's liberated people? What are the ingredients to fuel the process of liberation[4] and create a culture of freedom?

The first step is that we must *want* to be free. God's liberating grace is already at work when we experience the desire for freedom and meaning. Remember the story: God heard the cry of his people long before they wanted to be free. He sent Moses. And Moses had to speak to them of a liberating God: What shall I say to the people when they want to know who you are, God? Tell them, I am the God of their fathers and I will want to start a new journey with them: "I am the One whom they will experience as freedom if and when they get up and walk!" (paraphrase of Exod 3:14). Telling them of a liberating and gracious God aroused their desire. They got up and started to walk—and they began to create history.

This means, secondly, that there must be the realization that we *can* be free. How often do we find ourselves in hopeless situations, in the dead-end streets of life. Our marriage seems to be at an end; a friendship is broken and the future is gone; I am caught in the vicious cycle of drugs and alcohol; my employment is taken away, and I see no hope for another one. Yet, life goes on, and as long as there is life, there is hope, because God is the author of life, and God will not abandon God's world. In the fullness of time, yes, in the fullness of our time, "God sent his Son, born of a woman, born under the law, in order to redeem those who were under the law, so that we might receive adoption" as children of God (Gal 4:4–5).

We may be frustrated, we may be disheartened, we may at times want to lie down with Job in the dust of the earth and say to God: I have had enough, leave me alone (Job 7:11–21). We may be tired and say with Jesus: Father, let this cup pass away from me! (Mark 14:36) We may even hang on

---

4. I roughly follow the analysis of Gutierrez, *A Theology of Liberation* (1988) 36–37, 168–78.

one of the many crosses of life and say: My God, my God, why have you forsaken me (Mark 15:34)?

The good news is not that we shall have easy lives. The good news is not that believers shall be spared from the trials and temptations of life. The good news is not that we shall not have to walk through the valleys of shadow and death. The good news is that we shall not walk alone; that God cares; yes, God cares like a shepherd who will leave his many sheep and search for the one who is lost in the stony desert of life (Luke 15:4-7). The great "I am" is the "Lord" who is with us until the end of the age (Matt 28:18-20); and from whom nothing can separate us (Rom 8:31-39)! The first step toward a life of freedom is that we want to be free. The second step is the promise and the assurance that we can be free because God has laid the foundation for our freedom and empowers us for the journey ahead.

That brings us to the third and deepest level of liberation. A level that is already implied in the previous steps. By raising Jesus from the dead, God has liberated us from the power of death, sin and estrangement. In Jesus Christ, God has shared God's life with our human story. God's story and our story are interwoven. When Christians through the ages have spoken about forgiveness of sins, of redemption and of reconciliation, they have gratefully confessed that God has healed their broken relationship with God; that their estrangement from God has given way to a deep trust; that their quest for meaning has found its answer in Jesus Christ. And that has made them free.

Conclusion

The ten commandments are not intended to be laws and dogmas. This is why Jesus never quoted all the commandments, and at times was even critical of some of them.[5] We also recognize that we live in a different world and in a different society from the one in which these commandments were shaped. But we come to them with the question for guidance, how we can live our faith and our freedom in the world today. We expect that they will help us, not to restrict the liberation which we have experienced through our faith in Jesus Christ, but to shape our responsibility toward a culture of freedom.

---

5. See, for instance, our discussion of the "sabbath" commandment in chapter 6.

3

Who or What Is Our God?

The First Word

"You shall have no other gods but me."
or
"You won't need any other gods besides me."

Exodus 20:3 and Deuteronomy 5:7
Related texts: Isaiah 44:1–2, 6–8, 21–23; John 10:11–16

THEOLOGICAL COMMENTS

THE VERB IS NOT an indicative ("you *have*"), but an imperative ("you *shall* have"). Yet in light of the introduction to the "ten words," which emphasizes that God has liberated God's people from slavery, we may also read: because God has set his people free, therefore "you *will* have no other gods" or "you *won't need* any other gods besides me." That gives to this "word" the dimension of being "a declaration of theological emancipation."[1]

The Hebrew "but me" or "besides me" is very difficult to capture in English. Attempts include: "before me," "before my face," "over against me." The intention is clear. For the followers of Yahweh, he is the all-encompassing deity. Worshippers of Yahweh cannot divide their loyalty.

"*No other gods.*" The decalogue took shape in a world of many deities. We know the stories where other gods, like Molech (Lev 20), Dagon, the god of the Philistines (1 Sam 5:1–7), Baal, a deity of many faces (1 Kgs 18:17–40; Num 25:1–3) and Baalzebub, the god of Ekron (2 Kgs 1) were

---

1. Brueggemann, *Exodus*, 841.

confronted with the overwhelming power of Yahweh. Israel was different to the surrounding peoples in that it made an exclusive claim for its God Yahweh. Later in Israel's history this led to the universal assertion that "in the beginning" Israel's God "created the heavens and the earth" (Gen 1:1),[2] which implied the affirmation that other deities don't really exist.[3] Monotheism—faith in *one* God which entails a denial of the existence of other gods—came to be a distinguishing mark of Israelite religion.

The only adequate response to Israel's God is total allegiance. Partial commitment would question or deny that Yahweh is really God. Emphasizing Yahweh's exclusiveness and uniqueness was new in the ancient world and Israel was continually reminded of it in its life and worship: "you shall worship no other god, because the LORD, whose name is Jealous, is a jealous God" (Exod 34:14).[4]

Israel's monotheism is not merely a theoretical monotheism, intellectually affirming the existence of Yahweh and denying the existence of other deities. It is mainly a practical monotheism. It asserts that while there may be other gods being worshipped, Israel for its own life and worship recognizes only Yahweh as the one true God. The emphasis is not theological theory whether one or many gods exist, but the praxis of life as to who deserves to claim our allegiance as individuals and as a society.[5] "Hear, O Israel: The LORD is our God, the LORD alone. You shall *love* the LORD your God with all your heart, and with all your soul, and with all your might" (Deut 6:4–5, emphasis mine).

---

2. The same is affirmed in Isaiah 44:24 "I am the LORD, who made *all* things, who *alone* stretched out the heavens, who *by myself* spread out the earth" (emphases mine).

3. This is polemically asserted by the prophets Isaiah and Jeremiah: "You are my witnesses, says the LORD, and my servant whom I have chosen, so that you may know and believe me and understand that I am he. Before me no god was formed, nor shall there be any after me" (Isa 43:10). "Thus says the LORD, the King of Israel, and his Redeemer, the LORD of hosts: I am the first and I am the last; besides me there is no god" (Isa 44:6). "But the LORD is the true God; he is the living God and the everlasting King. At his wrath the earth quakes, and the nations cannot endure his indignation" (Jer 10:10).

4. See also our discussion of the second commandment which describes Yahweh as a "jealous God" (Exod 20:5 = Deut 5:9). There are many other texts in the Hebrew Bible that emphasize the exclusiveness and uniqueness of Yahweh, for instance Exod 22:20, 23:13; Deut 4:39, 6:4, 13:5; Josh 23:7; 2 Sam 7:22; 1 Kgs 8:60; 2 Kgs 5:15, 19:19; Hos 13:4; Isa 26:13; Ps 81:9.

5. Schmidt comments that *theoretical* monotheism is the *consequence* rather than the *basis* for Old Testament faith (*Die Zehn Gebote*, 51).

MESSAGE

God Talk—God-Walk[6]

A mother brings her little boy to the Rabbi for religious instruction. The Rabbi challenges the boy: "I'll give you a dollar, if you can tell me where God lives!" The boy thinks for a moment. Then he responds: "Rabbi, I'll give you two dollars if you can tell me where God does not live!"

That is in essence how most discussions about God are carried on. They are discussions *about* God. Does God exist, or doesn't God exist? Is God here, or is God there? Is God everything, or is God nothing?

The biblical message does not encourage such a procedure. In the Bible there is very little discussion *about* God. It presupposes the being of God and then asks what difference that makes in our lives. Modifying the eleventh thesis of Karl Marx's on Feuerbach (1845),[7] we may say Christian faith is not primarily interested in thinking about God, but rather in participating in God's passion to change history in the direction of what is helpful to make human life human, in the direction of life, freedom, truth and justice.

Unmasking the Gods

Martin Luther, who placed the ten commandments right at the beginning of his *Large Catechism*, names "God" as our ultimate point of reference: "A 'god' is the term for that to which we are to look for all good and in which we find refuge in all need. . . . Anything on which your heart relies and depends, I say, that is really your God."[8] Applying Luther's definition to our situation, we may ask: Where do we anchor our hearts? In what do we put our trust—ultimately? Who or what are our gods?

Is money our God? That would be nothing new. Money and the "heart," money and religion, have been bed-fellows for a long time. Jesus said: "where your treasure is, there will your heart be also" (Matt 6:21). And he interprets this: "No one can serve two masters; . . . You cannot serve

---

6. "*God-Walk*" is the title of Herzog's book on theology from a liberation perspective.

7. "The philosophers have only *interpreted* the world, in various ways; the point, however, is to change it." (Marx, *Theses on Feuerbach* [1845] 72). Moltmann applies the same principle to theology: "The theologian is not concerned merely to supply a different interpretation of the world, of history and of human nature, but to transform them in expectation of a divine transformation." (*Theology of Hope*, 84).

8. Luther, "The Ten Commandments," 386.

Who or What Is Our God?

God and money" (Matt 6:24). When a young man came to Jesus, one who thought that he had kept all the commandments, Jesus proceeded to give a diagnosis naming where this person had anchored his heart. "Jesus looking upon him loved him, and said to him, 'You lack one thing; go, sell what you have, and give to the poor, and you will have treasure in heaven; and come, follow me.'" But the young man "went away sorrowful; for he had great possessions" (Mark 10:17–22). This is the only incident in the gospels where a person rejects the call of Jesus. And it was because of money.

Is consumerism our God? The more we have the more we are! We want to have life. The aspiration to get the most out of life is a legitimate quest. But where is the source and the sustenance of *real* life? Modern shopping centers are built as cathedrals of consumerism. They are designed to appeal to our religious instincts! You drive up to them, and the spire, often made of glass, and a clock tease into your subconscious the intimation of "church" or "temple." You drive into the parking lot. You get out of the car and walk up to the great entrance with its columns, lights, trees and flowers. The glass doors open automatically and soft music greets you. Reverently you walk around, amazed by the overwhelming riches of the offerings. Finally you settle on the pair of shoes or the suit or the watch and you experience a good feeling. Satisfied, you eat a hamburger, have a coffee and drive home again.

Is activism our God? Consumerism implies activism. Activity and hard work are important. We know that. But it is not of *ultimate* importance. Listen to what the great German mystic of the Middle Ages, Meister Eckhart (1260–1328), said:

> People should not worry as much about what they do but rather about what they are. If they and their ways are good, then their deeds are radiant. If you are righteous, then what you do will also be righteous. We should not think that holiness is based on what we do but rather on what we are, for it is not our works which sanctify us but we who sanctify our works.[9]

Our activism must be grounded in something real. Otherwise it becomes an escape from the real questions in life, and the end-result is what psychologists call "burn out."

---

9. Meister Eckhart Quotes. Online: http://historymedren.about.com/od/quotes/a/quote_eckhart_2.htm. This emphasis on "being" as the foundation for "having" or "doing" is at the centre of the Christian vision of reality, but it is also found in other traditions as the wonderful book by Fromm, *To Have or To Be?* shows.

Is sexuality our God? Sexuality is part of the gracious gift of a good God. Sexuality is the language of love, and the church has made terrible mistakes in this area when it has denigrated and even demonized sexuality. But outside the circle of love and respect, sexuality can lead to violence and disrespect. The world into which the "ten words" were spoken knew many fertility cults in which sexuality played a dominant role. Religion and sexuality have often been associated in the history of humanity. Today sex tourism is a billion-dollar business. Sexually arousing pictures increase the sales of many newspapers, magazines and internet sites. Child prostitution and sex slavery constitute one of the major human rights problems in our time.[10] Do we expect from sex what only God can give?

Is the yearning for power our God? The historian Lord Acton suggested long ago that the craving for power is the most serious threat to liberty: "Power tends to corrupt, and absolute power corrupts absolutely."[11] Religion and power have often been wedded. An incident which has shaped the Christian understanding of God more than the decalogue or the Sermon on the Mount was when in the fourth century Constantine became Emperor of the Roman Empire. The decisive battle in his conquest to become emperor in Rome was fought on the Milvian bridge. Just before the battle he had had a vision of Christ, telling him that he should fight this battle under the banner of the cross. He did it—and he won! He made Christianity the state religion, and church and clergy began to enjoy privileges. His messianic ambitions led to his being baptized in the river Jordan, and he used the church to unify his empire. Ever since, the cross has all too often been aligned with political power, rather than with liberating and redemptive service and suffering. Is the church today a voice for those who have no voice, a friend for those who have few friends and a power for the powerless? Are we open to the power of love or have we succumbed to the love of power?

Is the bomb our God? A poster shows an altar in the desert and on the altar a bomb, pointing to heaven. It is declared policy of the governments of all powerful nations that "defense" has priority in all decision-making. Not the aged or the sick or the invalids in our midst. Not health and education. Not the children of the world, 30,000 of whom die every day under the

---

10. See the recent book by Batstone *NOT for Sale: The Return of the Global Slave Trade—and How We Can Fight It* (2007), and the "NOT for sale" campaign associated with it.

11. Lord Acton, "Letter to Mandell Creighton" (April 5, 1887), 364.

age of five. Half of them could be saved tomorrow with a fraction of our military budgets. Not the social security schemes. Not the unemployment problem. Not development aid. No, military defense and the associated industrial-military complex and "intelligence" industry! We accept the fact that 12 million children die each year for want of food, water and medical treatment, while we spend billions on arms. We accept the fact that our best brains and engineers are working for the military complex, even though we desperately need their brain power for planning a human future of justice for all people. There is no question of course that we need structures like government, police, military, and a legal system to organize human life together. But has not a militaristic mindset taken on religious dimensions? Do we need the arms race to defend ourselves against aggressors, or do we need it to sustain our markets, fuel our industries and protect our possessions? Do we trust God also in our public life or have we reduced him to be redeemer of our souls, while in the public arena we trust other gods?

Has our longing for security replaced God in our lives? The psychology is simple. The existential anxiety that is part of our human finitude becomes intensified with events like the terrorist attacks on September 11, 2001 in New York, Washington and Pennsylvania, the two bomb attacks in the tourist areas of Bali (2003 and 2005), as well as the horrifying attacks in Madrid (2004), London (2005), New Delhi (2005) and Amman (2005). Thousands of innocent people were killed and many more injured. The message is loud and clear: it could happen anywhere, at any time, to any one. Anxiety spreads quickly. How did politicians and governments respond? With security measures. The Australian government, for instance, within a short time issued 37 new laws, questioned the absolute authority of human rights and even withdrew from strengthening the world-wide struggle for the abolition of torture.[12] Some of these measures may be important, perhaps even necessary. But it is an illusion to think that security measures can deal with fear. It is like a child going into a dark cellar pressing its favorite doll close to the chest. It gives the feeling of security. But it is an illusion. We have to learn to have confidence in life and then simply go on living. It is an illusion to run after other gods to fill the deepest longings of our life.

Is religion our god? Even in the church we urgently need to hear the warning not to follow other gods. We confess that "*Jesus* is Lord," but then we want to defend the infallibility of the Bible, the deity of our religious

12. For details see Lorenzen, "Freedom or security," 339–51; "Freedom from fear," 193–99.

experience, and the sinlessness of the church. The Bible, our experience, and the church can be icons that reflect or allow access to the divine. They become idols, other gods, if we assign to them the status of divinity. "Where the church is soft on idols, it becomes muted on social criticism."[13]

Ultimate and Penultimate Concerns

To get a better handle on the difference between God and the gods we can take a brief look at Dietrich Bonhoeffer's *Ethics*. Bonhoeffer distinguishes between an ultimate concern and penultimate concerns.[14] They are different, but they are not disconnected. They are related. A person's relationship to God—the "justification of the sinner by grace alone"—is ultimate. It is the "origin and essence of all Christian life." But this ultimate reality seeks echoes in our daily lives. With reference to the Matthean parable of the last judgment (Matt 25:31–46), Bonhoeffer describes life in the penultimate as "being human" and "being good." Concretely that means giving bread to the hungry, shelter to the homeless, justice to the deprived, freedom to the oppressed, community to the lonely and discipline to the lazy. Failing to do that "would be blasphemy against God and our neighbor." Indeed, how can those who are hungry, deprived and oppressed hear about ultimate things of grace, faith and justification of the sinner? "The entry of grace is the ultimate," nevertheless "to bring bread to the hungry is preparing the way for the coming of grace." Even worthy causes like love for our family, our responsible citizenship (patriotism), our possessions can distort our lives if they become our ultimate concerns, if we hang our hearts on them, if they become our gods.

Here we find also the deeper reason why the Judeo-Christian heritage insists on monotheism (that there is one God) and maintains that God's ways have a universal claim. The intention is not imperialism or conquest. The intention is to underline that the God who is over against us makes a liberating claim on our whole life and on all of our life. As human beings we are woven into a global network of relationships. Only a God who is "global" and who is "one" can meet our deepest needs. A religion with many gods tends to project human needs and then create gods to meet them. There is a god for peace and for war, for life and for death, for food and for sex. Monotheism is the recognition and assertion that there is one God

---

13. Brueggemann, *Exodus*, 844.
14. Bonhoeffer, "Ultimate and Penultimate Things," 146–70.

Who or What Is Our God?

who calls us to faith and invites our obedience. The so-called projection theory claims that we deal with our needs and deficiencies by creating our own gods. We feel weak and are aware of our failures—therefore we create a strong and sinless deity. The "cargo cult" in New Guinea and Melanasia came into being when the native people observed that large aeroplanes were bringing goods to white people. So, by adopting "white man's" way of worship they thought that the heavenly messengers would bring such good also to them. The first commandment therefore has an anti-religious dimension. Not religion as such is its goal, but to point people to the one place, the one reality, where true fulfillment can be found.

God's Liberating Claim on Our Life

Against the popular projection theory of Ludwig Feuerbach and Sigmund Freud, we insist that God is not a human creation. God is not the projection of our needs and interests. God is the source of our life and the ground of our freedom. There is discernible content to God and that content is not simply a validation of human interests. Faith in God therefore has a critical edge.

In 1934, shortly after Adolf Hitler had claimed near-total allegiance of the German people, some Christian theologians met in a little town near Cologne and issued the so-called *Barmen Theological Declaration*. Its first paragraph reads:

> I am the Way and the Truth and the Life; no one comes to the Father except through me. (John 14:6)
>
> Very truly, I tell you, anyone who does not enter the sheepfold through the gate but climbs in by another way is a thief and a bandit. I am the gate. Whoever enters by me will be saved. (John 10:1, 9)
>
> Jesus Christ, as he is attested to us in Holy Scripture, is the *one* Word of God whom we have to hear, and whom we have to trust and obey in life and in death.
>
> We reject the false doctrine that the Church could and should recognize as a source of its proclamation, beyond and besides this one Word of God, yet other events, powers, historic figures and truths as God's revelation.

This does not mean that God's presence cannot be found in our lives, in history and in nature. But it does mean that for Christians, God is not arbitrary. God has defined and interpreted God's nature in the story of Jesus and it is that story which alone is the source of the church's proclamation and the measure for what is divine and what is not.

This implies an exclusiveness which opponents to faith consider as being intolerant and even arrogant. Here we need to tread carefully. The ancient world was full of gods. The Greek and Roman worldview included many deities, both male and female. They corresponded to human life and human ambitions. There was a god for life, a god for war, a god for love and a god for sex, a god for agriculture and a god for trade. As we said before, these deities were relevant for *partial* aspects of human life. It was therefore a significant advance in human development when *one* deity replaced the *many* deities. If we believe that relationship to the divine is an important dimension to human life, then only if the deity is *one* and *universal* can it provide an "over against" to human life and thus speak something *new* and *different* into our lives.

"You Shall Have No Other Gods"

At this point things become personal. We do not properly respond to God if we talk *about* God. God is portrayed as setting people free, as claiming their allegiance, as wanting to shape their life. God's claim entails the elements of unconditional love (*agape*) and at the same time the invitation (*eros*) to live a responsible and meaningful life. Those who have experienced God as a liberating and personal reality "won't need any other gods," and therefore, "you shall have no other gods but me." The conflict with the despisers of religion is not whether God is or whether God is one or many, but whether we need God at all for a fulfilled and successful human life.

Freedom entails responsibility and discipline. We recall Joshua's great sermon to the people of God (Josh 24). He first reminds them of God's great liberation from slavery in Egypt, but with it comes the personal challenge:

> put away the gods that your ancestors served beyond the River and in Egypt, and serve the LORD. . . . Choose this day whom you will serve, whether the gods your ancestors served in the region beyond the River, or the gods of the Amorites in whose land you are living; but as for me and my household, we will serve the LORD. (Josh 24:14–15)

4

Idol or Icon

The Second Word

"You shall not make for yourself a carved image of God . . . ;
you shall not bow down to them or worship them . . . ."

Exodus 20:4–6 and Deuteronomy 5:8–10

"You shall not make for yourself an *idol (image),* whether in the form of anything that is in heaven above, or that is on the earth beneath, or that is in the water under the earth. You shall not *bow down to them or worship them*; for I the LORD your God am a *jealous* God, punishing children for the iniquity of parents, to the *third and the fourth* generation of those who reject me, but showing steadfast love to the *thousandth* generation of those who love me and keep my commandments."[1]

Related texts: Deuteronomy 4:9–40; Exodus 32; Psalm 136; Jeremiah 10:1–16; Isaiah 44:9–20; John 1:1–18; Romans 1:18—2:1; Colossians 1:15–20; Hebrews 1:1–4

THEOLOGICAL COMMENTS

THIS WORD, TOGETHER WITH the sabbath commandment, is longer than the others, and it is the only one which includes a sanction. It is of special importance for Israel's identity, and the text has grown as it was applied to ever changing situations.

The Hebrew word *pesel* is better translated with "image" rather than "idol." Its focus is the prohibition of objectifying God in a representation of God, a carved image. Such representations of Yahweh, the God of Israel,

---

1. The text is the same in Exodus and Deuteronomy. *Italics* are for emphasis.

were well known (Judg 17:4, 18:17–18, also Isa 40:19, 44:10). They were carved from wood, hewn from stone or shaped from metal. The emphasis of the "second word"—whether we use "idol" or "image"—is "not the creation of a rival that detracts from Yahweh, but an attempt to locate and thereby domesticate Yahweh in a visible, controlled object."[2] This includes two emphases: objectifying God and taking the stuff for the objectification—wood, stone, metal—from creation and thereby tending to overlook the difference between creator and creation.

"Bowing down" and "worshiping" such images is idolatry, an aberration of worship. It is an inappropriate response to Yahweh. The story of the golden calf in Exodus 32 provides an instructive illustration. The Israelites gather their jewelry, cast a molten calf and call it "Yahweh": "These are your gods, O Israel, who brought you up out of the land of Egypt!" (Exod 32:4–5)

This instruction not to represent Yahweh or even to name God has been a significant dimension to Israel's faith. In contrast to the religions surrounding Israel, the Jewish temple and the Holy of Holies (the inner sanctuary) did not have a representation of Yahweh. This influence is still felt in the Christian Bible when, for instance, the "kingdom *of God*" in the Gospel of Matthew is named the "kingdom *of heaven*." There seems to be no parallels for such a prohibition in the religious world around Israel.

At the same time, we are aware that visible manifestations of the divine are very popular. They have also been helpful in the history of Christian faith. Icons, for instance, have communicated the story of Jesus to people who can't read. The elements of bread and wine, indeed the Lord's Supper as a whole, represent the presence of Christ. In fact, is it not true that most of us—with the exception perhaps of mystics—need representations, pictures, word-pictures to relate to the divine? Jesus spoke of God in word-pictures (parables). The Bible calls God "father" and "mother" and "shepherd" and "judge"—all images. We need to ask whether and why such representations may be problematic.

The following theological guidelines may help us to understand and appropriate the second commandment.

- A major threat to Israel's faith was posed by the Canaanite cults of various deities named "Baal," "Ashtarte" and other names. Many Yahweh-worshippers simply used or adapted representations of those deities when they made images of Yahweh. Applying this to our situation, it

---

2. Brueggemann, *Exodus*, 842.

Idol or Icon

would mean using cultural values—consumerism, militarism, racism, nationalism, sexuality—to shape our understanding of God.

- The deeper theological meaning is to protect the godhood, the otherness, of God. Not for its own sake, but to safeguard human freedom. The world, God's creation, is in need of salvation because humanity has broken the covenant and has rebelled against God. The great experiment of the West has been to live without God. Not God, but self, has become the major focus of humanity. The relational structure of human life has been distorted. The needed reconciliation can only come from God. It cannot come from any part of God's creation. Creation is "fallen." Healing can only come from beyond creation, from the creator. This "word" therefore emphasizes the otherness of God and God's difference from what God has created. The intention is not to make God unavailable to human longing. The intention is to demonstrate that God is not part of the problem. God can and God does provide an answer because God is the "other." In Deuteronomy 4:9–40 the warning not to make idols is rooted in the assertion that "the LORD has taken you and brought you out of the iron-smelter, out of Egypt, to become a people of his very own possession, as you are now" (Deut 4:20). Therefore the "otherness" of God is intimately inter-related with the reality of human freedom.

- Nevertheless, in the divine economy, otherness and difference do not mean separation. The earliest Christians affirmed the message of the Hebrew Bible that God, in a free and voluntary decision, has remained faithful to God's creation and has made covenant after covenant with God's people. While God's people became godless, God remained faithful to God's promises. In Jesus Christ, God's commitment has been confirmed (2 Cor 1:18–20) and at the same time God has interpreted God's nature in and through the story of Jesus (2 Cor 4:4; Col 1:15; Heb 1:3, John 1:14, 18).

- God is a dynamic personal reality. God relates himself to God's people, providing possibilities to lead people into freedom. This dynamic reality of God and faith cannot be adequately represented in a picture or a statue. Objects therefore become idols when they freeze or petrify God. They tend to remove the mystery of God (Rom 1:23).

- Objectifying God is part of the human longing to define God and then make God pliable to our schemes, desires and interests.

The *sanctions* speak of God as punishing not only the perpetrators, but also their succeeding generations. We become forcefully aware that disobedience has actual historical consequences. These consequences are related to God's passion which "warms" and encourages those who live within the vision of the covenant, and which "burns" those who transgress against the rules. The emphasis is not on God willfully and intentionally punishing us for our disobedience. The emphasis is on relationship and responsibility. If we fail in our responsibility to God and God's creation, we and generations to come shall have to bear the consequences. It is obvious to all of us that what we decide and do today in the field of nuclear technology, ecology and genetic engineering will have consequences, good and bad, for generations to come. The reference to "four generations" places such consequences within the limits of our experience and therefore within the grasp of our imagination.

Nevertheless, the fact that God's steadfast love cannot be undone by human disobedience transcends our imagination. While judgment remains within the realm of human reason, God's mercy surpasses human imagination—"showing steadfast love to the *thousandth* generation of those who love me and keep my commandments." While we can think "four generations," God's grace is *"forever"* (Ps 136).

MESSAGE

The Struggle for Identity

While the "first word" described the uniqueness of God, the second emphasizes God's "otherness." It points to the distinctiveness of Israel's faith. While the surrounding religions and cults loved to make representations of their gods, and worship their deities in statues and pictures, in Israel there was a tendency to forbid making representations of their God.[3]

The early Christians applied this commandment to their own faith. They refused to participate in the Roman Emperor cult. Having experienced God as a savior and liberator, they refused to worship what they considered to be the "image of the beast." To many of them this brought economic disadvantages and even martyrdom (Rev 13:11–18).

During the Reformation in the sixteenth century the second commandment was quite controversial. Martin Luther agreed with the Roman

---

3. For instance Exod 20:22–23; 32:1–14; 34:17; Deut 27:15; Lev 19:4, 26:1; Hos 8:4–6; 10:5–6; 11:2; 13:1–2.

Catholic church and removed the second commandment from the list of ten by making it part of the first. Then he divided the last commandment into two in order to complete the round number. He was probably worried about some Christian enthusiasts, who would use the second commandment to come into the churches and remove all pictures and statues. His fear was not unfounded.

The congregation in Orlamünde in Germany, for instance, must have been quite surprised when they came to church one Sunday in 1523. They found that their pastor, Andreas Karlstadt, had removed from the church all pictures, ornaments, and even the organ! Similar was the emphasis of Huldrych Zwingli and the Reformation in Zürich. Even today the Reformed churches in Switzerland are fairly cold and sterile on the inside. White walls, the Bible in the centre, and the pulpit. Nothing was to detract attention from the Scriptures and from the preaching of the word of God! In Scotland in May 1559 the reformer John Knox preached a rousing sermon against idolatry from the pulpit of St John's Kirk in Perth. His listeners got so excited that they destroyed the statues, pictures and ornaments of the church and then went out to demolish the surrounding monasteries.

Today we have become a little more cautious in our judgments. We see people kneeling in deep devotion before the Black Madonna in the Benedictine monastery at Einsiedeln, Switzerland—and on the wall behind them are the crutches of those who have found healing. We see over a million Poles coming to Czestochow to celebrate a Eucharist with the Pope in the presence of the Madonna. Secular images are also quite in vogue. For some the national flag is much more than a piece of cloth. A football team has a mascot. But most importantly, did not Jesus himself speak of God not in abstract language—"God is spirit," "God cannot suffer," "God is everywhere"—but in word-pictures (parables)?

We seem to face a dilemma. We are told that as believers in the God of Israel we shall not make and worship images of our God; and yet our daily experience tells us that we can't live and, indeed, that we don't want to live without pictures, statues and images.

This tension leads us right back to the Hebrew Bible. On the one hand, there are the many prohibitions against making graven images. People who make and worship them will be punished and cursed. Our text says: "I the LORD your God am a jealous God, punishing children for the iniquity of parents, to the third and the fourth generation of those who reject me"; and when Israel had made a molten calf and worshiped it, "the LORD said to Moses, 'I have seen this people, how stiff-necked they are. Now let me alone, so that my wrath may burn hot against them and I may consume them'" (Exod 32:9–10).

Yet, on the other hand there are the very earthy ways in which the Old Testament speaks of God. God is pictured as a king, a shepherd, a father, a mother, a judge, even a man of war (Exod 15:3). God has hands and feet. He turns his face towards us. His "lips are full of indignation, and his tongue is like a devouring fire" (Isa 30:27). He has a nose to smell, and a heart to feel. He loves and hates. "I the LORD your God am a jealous God." Moreover, Israel's worship life is not all sterile and rational. There is the ark of the covenant, there is the mercy seat and the cherubim and seraphim (Exod 25:18–20; Isa 6:1–8). A man in the hill country of Ephraim makes himself a graven image of the Lord (Judg 17–18) and Moses makes a "fiery serpent" so that people who are bitten by snakes may look at it and live (Num 21).

The problem is not an easy one to resolve. We obviously have to go beneath the surface meaning of the texts and ask for their intention. Yet, so much we can say already. The alternative is not: pictures or no pictures; carved images or no carved images. The problem is what we use pictures and images for. The warning is clear: "you shall not *bow down* to them or *serve* them or *worship* them."

The idea of our text is not that Israel turned from a material to a spiritual or intellectual religion. The "second word" is not a forerunner of the European enlightenment! It wants to spell out where we can expect hope for the future and where resources for a meaningful and successful life can be found. Perhaps we can get a little closer to its meaning when we recall some experiences which we have had, or with which we may at least sympathize.

Our Experience with "Images"

Ministers of religion, like Military officials and Police officers, experience the problem of images in their own life. People categorize us. People pigeon hole us. People put a mask on our face—and they don't ask us whether we like it or not. I am at a party. People are nice, friendly, open. They joke and are not careful in their choice of words. Then comes the question: "What do you do?" "I am a pastor." And a barrier of glass is placed between us. No shady jokes anymore. I am categorized. I am made to repent for the sins of a whole professional guild and for people's experiences with its members. I can no longer be myself. The mask "minister" or "priest" is now placed on my face. Nothing new to be expected! Suddenly people know what I think! People no longer relate to me naturally. The image "minister" is now between me and my partner in conversation. He or she can no longer meet me as a living and unique person. All experiences and caricatures with "ministers" and "church" have entered our encounter. The innocence of our meeting has been distorted. My partner in conversation looks around for another group to join.

Another illustration may come a little closer to home for some of us, and at the same time it brings us right back to the second commandment. What kind of picture of God determines our life? I have met many people for whom "God" was not a good word. God was understood in terms of moral norms. And if these norms are not fulfilled, then a bad conscience results and paralyses life. The picture of God as the moral norm stands between me and God. The picture hinders me from knowing God as a liberating, forgiving, accepting, transforming personal reality!

We may also contemplate the religious scene today. Many Christians and Muslims regard each other's religion as inherently violent. The terrible acts of terror committed in the name of Allah, suicide bombers shouting "Allah akbar" ("God is great") as they murder innocent civilians, and irresponsible utterings of Muslim clerics have provided fuel for the opinion that the God of Mohammed is an angry God who justifies violence in the pursuit of their religion. Similarly, Muslims who see that the war in Iraq was started and is being waged by practicing Christians—among them the president of the United States of America, and the Prime Ministers of Great Britain and Australia—are easily convinced that the God in whom Christians believe validates war and violence in the spread of Judeo-Christian faith, often indistinguishably mixed up with Western values. Human ambition, political ideology and commercial interests have so much merged with the idea of God that the otherness of God is no longer maintained.

Our experience therefore teaches us that there can be problems with pictures and images, with masks and with categorizing people and God. Images tend to categorize. They freeze and thereby distort reality. They remove the future. To make a picture is to freeze someone into the past, taking away their future. Seeing them as we want to see them, not as they really are.

Listen to the Psalmist's description of an idol:

They have mouths, but do not speak;
   eyes, but do not see.
They have ears, but do not hear;
   noses, but do not smell.
They have hands, but do not feel;
   feet, but do not walk;
   they do not make a sound in their throat. (Ps 115:5–7)

Reason Versus Revelation

The second commandment forbids the making of carved images in order to protect the freedom, the otherness and the personhood of God who alone is the ground and well-spring of life, hope and freedom. This also has consequences for us and for our relationship to God. We are persons and we cannot meaningfully relate to a mask or a dead body or a thing. We can only meaningfully relate to a personal and living reality. So by protecting the freedom of the living God we are also protecting our freedom to relate to God as a personal reality. The commandment is therefore grounded in the reality of the liberating God: "You shall make for yourself no idol and erect no carved images or pillars, and you shall not place figured stones in your land, to worship at them; *for I am the* LORD *your God*" (Lev 26:1; also 19:4).

Here we must face a deep human irony. We know that we can't relate meaningfully relate to a lifeless body, a "thing." Yet at the same time we do all we can to remove the life, the freedom, the mystery from that which encounters us. Being children of the enlightenment, we want to *define* everything. This is part of our heritage. It has a place in science. But when it becomes the determining center of our life and removes all mystery from life, then we are the poorer for it. The passion to define everything is part of our promethean[4] attempt to understand everything on *our* terms and thus rule over it. Then we are gods!

We also like to *categorize*. All Germans are arrogant; all Americans are superficial; all English are stuffy; all Swiss are military fanatics; all Scots are stingy; and you can't trust a Russian! The mask is placed. How much does it take to remove the mask?! To discover a German who has a heart; an American who is in touch with the deep mystery of life; an English person

---

4. Prometheus is a figure in Greek mythology. He is intelligent, cunning and well disposed towards humanity. He steals fire from the gods and gives it to humans for their use.

full of creative joy; a Swiss with a commitment to peace; a generous Scot; and a Russian who can be trusted!

To define and to categorize are ways to exercise power. We try to get the other into our grasp, understand them on our terms, sort them into our vision of life. Remove the mystery, the unexpected, and with it life and freedom are gone.

Applied to our faith in God, we must seek to think and speak of God on God's own terms. We only have our human language, our human experience and our human understanding. True. We are on earth, not in heaven! But the question is whether we insist that our understanding, our language, our experience determine our perception of God, or whether we will use our language, experience and understanding to *receive* and *interpret* what God has revealed to us. Here Christians insist that God has revealed God's nature and God's will in the story of Jesus of Nazareth. The early Christians confessed: "Long ago God spoke to our ancestors in many and various ways by the prophets, but in these last days he has spoken to us by a Son, whom he appointed heir of all things, through whom he also created the worlds. He is the reflection of God's glory and the exact imprint of God's very being, and he sustains all things by his powerful word" (Heb 1:1–3).

For Christians, Jesus Christ, he and no other, "is the image of the invisible God" (Col 1:15); "in him the whole fullness of deity dwells bodily" (Col 2:9). There is a reason for these massive assertions. The uniqueness and otherness of God and of God's revelation in Jesus Christ are not arbitrary claims. They are the ground of our salvation and the basis for our hope. Only because God is *unique* and *"other"* can God break the estranging power of death and reconcile us with God: "He has rescued us from the power of darkness and transferred us into the kingdom of his beloved Son, in whom we have redemption, the forgiveness of sins. . . . in him all the fullness of God was pleased to dwell, and through him God was pleased to reconcile to himself all things, whether on earth or in heaven, by making peace through the blood of his cross" (Col 1:13–20).

Letting God be God

Perhaps we begin to understand why the word, "You shall not make for yourself a carved image," is so important. It wants to guard the mystery, the life, the personhood and transformative nature of God. That is the precondition for relating to God and discovering God ever anew as a living and liberating reality.

As Christians we perceive God's nature in the story of Jesus. He is not a carved statue. He is a person of flesh and blood. "No one has ever seen God. It is God the only Son, who is close to the Father's heart, who has made him known" (John 1:18). And the Christ in the Gospel of John announces: "He who sees me and believes in me, sees and believes in him who sent me" (John 12:44–45).

Yet—another irony in the history of the Christian church!—many Christians and churches have not been satisfied to live with God's revelation in Jesus Christ. They have wanted more. Jesus was not enough for them. They were not content with the living voice of the gospel in which Christ comes to us. They wanted more—but they got less! They wanted to know God on their terms, and they froze God into their categories.

When some reformers in the sixteenth century took down the pictures and removed the statues from the churches, they wanted to make room for the living voice of the gospel. They wanted to celebrate Jesus as the one word that we need to hear, trust and obey in life and in death. But soon others, lesser minds and lesser hearts, came along and put a book where the pictures had been. So for many Christians the living voice of the gospel has been frozen into a book, the Bible. And around the world there are many Christians who spend more time and energy fighting about the Bible than in worshipping and obeying the Christ to whom the Bible points.

The "second word" addresses the "evangelical" within us. Your Bible is the word of God if and when it points you to Christ as the Lord of your life. The Bible is a vehicle and instrument. It is an icon pointing beyond itself, not an idol pointing to itself. Like John the Baptist, its function is to point us to a living faith in Christ: "He must increase, but I must decrease" (John 3:30). When faith is directed to the Bible itself, the Bible becomes an idol, and an idol has a mouth which cannot speak, an eye which cannot see, a nose which cannot smell, and a hand that cannot touch.

The second commandment also addresses the "catholic" within us. The church is the community of God's people. Through it we receive our faith and its sustenance. The church can be the sacrament of God when it points us to Christ as the living Lord of our life. But the church, like the Bible, is not divine. When we make the church into an object of our worship or when we claim its infallibility, then we make out of a great and living community a dead idol.

The second commandment furthermore addresses the "charismatic" within us. Experience and feeling are beautiful. How can there be love without feeling? How can there be faith without experience? But when the experience itself becomes the focus of our attention, when we measure the great riches of God with the poverty of our experience, then we make our experience into an idol.

The Bible is not God; the church is not God; our religious experience is not God. They are important, just as icons and images can be important. They have their use and therefore they have their place. But the Christian who has found a living faith in Jesus Christ, who has been liberated from estrangement, who has found forgiveness for his or her sins, will not bow down or serve anything but the living God—the God revealed in Jesus Christ who becomes real to us in the power of the Spirit of God!

The same principle applies to political, social and economic movements. History is replete with dictators like Adolf Hitler and Augusto Pinochet who in the name of providence spread violence, racism, genocide and nationalism. There are dimensions in Western capitalism that convey the impression that free markets will solve the problems of the world. The war in Iraq has religious elements in that ideologues in the United States of America (the so-called neo-conservatives) really believe that what is good for America must be good for the rest of the world—and therefore can be spread with means of violence.

The "second word" reminds us that whenever we fill historical or material elements with ultimate significance we commit idolatry. We lose our bearings. We lose the grand story that is the measure of all the stories that we create here on earth. Yet the question remains: what significance do our stories, our experiences, inner-worldly realities have in the economy of God? How do we interpret the fact that a beautiful sunset or the prisoners' choir in Verdi's *Nabucco* or a worship service can lift us up and bring inspiration, courage and comfort into our lives?

From Idol to Icon

A distinction between idol and icon may help us at this point. An idol focuses attention on itself. It becomes the centre of our interest. Flags, the Bible, the church, houses, cars, sport clubs, pop singers, our country, our nationality, our tribe all have their rightful place in life, yet they become idols *if* they are expected to meet our deepest need for meaning and fulfillment.

An icon on the other hand is porous. It is like a stained glass window. It is lit from the outside, but at the same time it lets us look through it. It points beyond itself to another reality. It assigns its own norm. Take for instance a cross that many people wear around their necks. Its original meaning, its iconic character, is that it points to Jesus and his crucifixion. The crucifixion of Jesus is its ground and its norm. If a monk or a Christian aid worker or a Christian manager or a Christian politician intentionally wears the cross, then for them it serves as an encouragement and as a reminder to flesh out in their daily life what is of ultimate importance to them, their relationship to Jesus Christ. The iconic character of the cross is preserved. If, on the other hand, such a cross is worn to enhance the attraction of a woman at a socialite party, or a military general who has used his power to get rid of the opposition, or a church leader who has collaborated with the Secret police or blessed the national ambitions and the military pursuits of his government, then the icon no longer expresses what it stands for. It is being misused.

The deepest level of the second commandment is therefore the invitation to recognize that God is God and to accept God on God's terms. Only if God is other than ourselves and yet, at the same time, remains inclined towards us, can God meet our deepest needs and fuel our most earnest hopes. Affirming the godhood of God and rejecting any attempt to give divine status to inner-worldly objects or persons or institutions or movements has an emancipatory effect upon us. We are freed to become who we are. We have not been created to be gods, but to be humans. We are invited to accept our humanity and make the best of it. In a sermon Martin Luther King, Jr. encouraged people to accept who they are and make the best of it. Then he used an illustration: "When I was in Montgomery, Alabama I went to a shoe shop quite often . . . And there was a fellow in there that used to shine my shoes, and it was just an experience to witness this fellow shining my shoes. He would get that rag, you know, and he could bring music out of it. And I said to myself, 'This fellow has a Ph.D. in shoe shining.'" Then he quotes:

> If you can't be a pine on top of the hill
> Be a scrub in the valley—but be
> The best little scrub on the side of the hill,
> Be a bush if you can't be a tree.[5]

---

5. "The Three Dimensions of a Complete Life," 125–26.

Idol or Icon

By affirming the otherness of God and focusing God's revelation on the story of Jesus, we relativize the demonic and thereby remove the fear of demons and other dark forces. Anyone who has traveled widely knows the many inventive ways by which people ward off the demonic and try to pacify the divine. Offerings, sacrifices, ceremonies, liturgies and rules of morality seek to pacify transcendent forces or make them to be amiably disposed. Those who hear the message of the "second word" discover that such fear is unfounded. They have discovered with the apostle Paul, "that 'no idol in the world really exists,' and that 'there is no God but one'" (1 Cor 8:4–6).

In the West we must also gratefully realize that the scientific and technological revolution has been made possible by focusing God's revelation on Jesus Christ. Thereby nature was set free for scientific enquiry. Scientists did not have to fear encroaching upon the divine. By recognizing the difference between creation and creator and by refusing to make creation or any part of it divine, the groundwork for scientific and technological advance was laid.

Listening to the "second word" helps us to create a culture of freedom. Not fear but faith, not fate but freedom determine our lives. By focusing our life on God and refusing to expect ultimate answers from worldly things, we are paving the way for a successful and meaningful life.

"God Gave Them Up to the Lusts of Their Hearts"

The second commandment contains a strong warning. Those who make images of God and worship them are named as "rejecting God" and they will be punished. And not only they, but generations to come. The language is strong. God is pictured as a "jealous God" who punishes people for their disobedience. The language needs to be strong. If God is the giver and protector of life, then those who become servants of death must be warned that they are digging their own graves. Our focus here should not be on the way God is described but on the way humans act. By cutting ourselves off from the source of life, we shall have to live with the consequences.

The apostle Paul speaks about the "wrath of God" that "is revealed from heaven against all ungodliness and wickedness." But then he shifts the language to explain that God grants freedom which can be used or abused. In ever new formulations he says that "God gave them up in the lusts of their hearts," that "God gave them up to degrading passions," that "God gave them up to a debased mind" (Rom 1:18—2:1). That does not mean that God is cynical. It simply means that people must accept responsibility for their actions and must be responsible for the consequences.

The message is clear and relevant. Humanity today is faced with a cultural watershed. Will we seriously address the threat of climate change or will profits continue to be more important than people and their future? Will Africa be able to deal with the AIDS crisis, will Asia be able to handle ethnic and religious tensions, will the Middle East let peace and justice reign, will the West learn to solve international problems without war and violence? Will we learn to accept the authority of the United Nations and respect human rights or will we further assert that might is right and slide deeper into a politics of fear? Will we learn to share what we have and help people and nations to escape abject poverty or will we continue to protect our own markets? Will national security or global security and respect for human rights determine our political and economic and military decisions? The future looks bleak for our children and grandchildren if poverty and with it hatred and violence continue to determine large sections of our global village. That is not God's fault. It is the result of human selfishness, greed and inaction. Sandra Postel alludes to a possible epitaph for humanity with the inscription: "they saw it coming but hadn't the wit to stop it happening."[6]

The Triumph of Grace

At the same time the commandment remains true to its central message of affirming and protecting the godhood of God. While the results of human greed and inaction are serious and will in fact determine the life of generations to come, God's faithfulness cannot be undone. God will remain God. Humans may become godless, but God will remain faithful to God's promises. God will show "steadfast love to the *thousandth* generation of those who love me and keep my commandments." That is the triumph of grace. The apostle Paul says the same in different words when he confesses that in Christ, God has triumphed over the forces of sin and death: "where sin increased, grace abounded all the more" (Rom 5:20).

---

6. "Denial in the Decisive Decade," 8.

Idol or Icon

Conclusion

It is quite an achievement that the Judeo-Christian faith did not focus on the sun and the moon and the stars as the ground of salvation. The starry heavens above and the moral law within are powerful symbols that easily lend themselves to become idols.[7] The "second word" wants to protect the otherness of God because reconciliation and healing for the estrangement of our lives can only come from beyond our historical and inner-worldly reality. Real help can only come from God. For Christians "there is one God, the Father, from whom are all things and for whom we exist, and one Lord, Jesus Christ, through whom are all things and through whom we exist" (1 Cor 8:6). Anyone, anything, any movement or ideology that claims our ultimate allegiance becomes an idol from which we are encouraged to flee. With the "second word" we "turn from idols, to serve a living and true God" (1 Thess 1:9–10).

---

7. The allusion is to Kant's *Critique of Practical Reason* (1788): "Two things fill the mind (heart) with ever-increasing admiration and awe . . . the starry heavens above me and the moral law within me" (166, "conclusion").

5

A Name Is More Than a Word

The Third Word

"You shall not make wrongful use of the name of the LORD your God,
for the LORD will not acquit anyone who misuses his name."

Exodus 20:7 and Deuteronomy 5:11
Related texts: Exodus 6:2–8; Psalm 24; Jeremiah 6:13–15; 7:1–15;
Matthew 6:1–15; 7:13–23

THEOLOGICAL COMMENTS

THE MAJOR PROBLEM IS to determine the meaning of the verb. It may mean: "You shall not *swear falsely* by the name of the LORD your God." That is what we call perjury. Yahweh would then be called upon to witness a false oath (as for instance in Exod 23:1; Lev 19:12; Deut 6:13, 10:20; 1 Sam 20:42). Such a meaning would be fairly restrictive, limiting this commandment to the juridical ethos of Israelite society.

Another possibility is "You shall not *abuse* the name of Yahweh your God." This would suggest a wider application—what we generally call blasphemy or hypocrisy. God's name is then used to validate selfish or ungodly ideas and plans and activities. It may also refer to people who fail to accept responsibility for what they say. They may say "LORD, LORD," or "this is the temple of the LORD, the temple of the LORD, the temple of the LORD," or "peace, peace," but then do not implement what they have promised.[1]

A third possible meaning is "You shall not *make wrongful use* of the name of the LORD your God." People in the ancient world practiced divine

---

1. Allusions are to Jer 7:1–15 and Matt 7:21–23.

A Name Is More Than a Word

magic whereby the name of the deity was called upon to bless practices in the social, political and military arenas.

Our emphasis will be on *misusing* God's name in that we "use" and thereby utilize God to legitimate or validate our own purposes. We pray that we shall hallow God's name, but in fact we are more concerned with our own reputation.

The warning that "the LORD will not hold him guiltless who takes his name in vain" is not a sanction because what the judgment will be remains elusive. It simply underlines the seriousness of the commandment and emphasizes that life is lived in the presence of God—ultimately God is our judge.

In the later history of Israel this commandment led to the prohibition of using and announcing the name of God altogether. In some books in the Hebrew Bible—Esther, Ecclesiastes, Song of Solomon, Psalms 42–83, and in the speeches in Job—the name of Yahweh is not used at all. Designations like "heaven" or "my Lord" ("Adonai") or "the name" ("Hashem") or "God" ("Elohim") are used. But this radical prohibition probably transcends the intention of the third commandment.

The theological intention of the "third word" is related to the "second word," in which Israel was warned not to objectify God in graven images. Now they are told that they could call upon the name of the LORD, but they must be careful that they call upon God and not use God to validate their own interests. The name assures us that God is for us. Honoring God's name means properly relating to God. Nevertheless, since God is present in the divine name, therefore God's name is not to be used to validate ungodly plans and practices. God's reputation is at stake in the life of the believer and in the life of the community of faith.

Exodus 6:2–8 is instructive at this point. God reveals God's name, but at the same time God interprets that name by saying that God has a covenant with God's people and that God accepts the responsibility implied in it by liberating his people from slavery and by continuing to be their God:

> God also spoke to Moses and said to him: "I am the LORD. I appeared to Abraham, Isaac, and Jacob as God Almighty, but by my name 'The LORD' I did not make myself known to them. I also established my covenant with them, to give them the land of Canaan, the land in which they resided as aliens. I have also heard the groaning of the Israelites whom the Egyptians are holding as slaves, and I have remembered my covenant. Say therefore to the

Israelites, 'I am the LORD, and I will free you from the burdens of the Egyptians and deliver you from slavery to them. I will redeem you with an outstretched arm and with mighty acts of judgment. I will take you as my people, and I will be your God. You shall know that I am the LORD your God, who has freed you from the burdens of the Egyptians. I will bring you into the land that I swore to give to Abraham, Isaac, and Jacob; I will give it to you for a possession. I am the LORD.'"

The people of God are responsible for the reputation of God's name among the nations of the earth (Rom 2:24). Therefore when the people of God with their words and thoughts and deeds show disregard or disrespect for God, they thereby fail to honor God's name and incur God's judgment (Lev 22:32–33; Jer 34:16–17; Ezek 36:20–32; Amos 2:6–8).

MESSAGE

Being Present in a Name

When base communities in Latin America meet for worship, they call for the presence of their saints and martyrs who have shaped their communities and remained an inspiration for them. They shout their name and thereby invoke their presence: "presenté!" "Jesus is Lord!"[2] and "Come Lord Jesus!"[3] were charismatic shouts in the early churches to claim the presence of Christ in their midst.

Names have power. Somehow bearers are present in their name. Names therefore evoke responses within us: Adolf Hitler, Josef Stalin, Ayatolla Khomeni, Mother Theresa, Francis of Assisi, Rambo, Frankenstein, Marilyn Monroe, Winston Churchill, Nelson Mandela. A Methodist will mention the names of John and Charles Wesley with respect and gratitude. A Baptist will do the same with Thomas Helwys, John Smythe, Johann Gerhard Oncken and Roger Williams. Mennonites honor the name of Menno Simons; Lutherans that of Martin Luther; and Roman Catholics that of Pope John XXIII and of Pope John Paul II. While people in Europe and America hardly know the name "Gallipoli," in Australia it stands for the foundation myth of what it means to be an Australian.[4]

2. See 1 Cor 12:3; Rom 10:9.
3. See 1 Cor 16:22; Rev 22:20; Didache 10:6.
4. "Gallipoli" is the place on the Mediterranean shores in Turkey where Australian and New Zealand troops (together with British, French, Indian and Newfoundland troops) during World War I attempted to invade Turkey. The adverse terrain and bad

A Name Is More Than a Word

When we hear such names they evoke feelings within us: love or anger, admiration or disrespect. Names tease thoughts into our minds and feelings into our hearts. They are more than words. Behind a name there stands a person or an event that has given content and meaning to that name. In mentioning the name of a person or an event, the person is made present or the event assumes contemporary significance.

What thoughts are teased into our minds, what feelings are evoked in our hearts when we hear the names "God" or "Jesus Christ"? Fear or hope, anxiety or freedom, doctrines or joy, individualism or community, private spirituality or passion for peace and justice? Listening to the "third word" entails the invitation to get to know God and then flesh out what we know of God in and with our lives.

For Christians God's name is intimately tied up with the story of Jesus. We therefore baptize people in the name of the Father and of the Son and of the Holy Spirit. We find comfort and hope in the word: "In the name of Jesus, your sins are forgiven." We certainly rely on the great promise of the gospel that the "name of Jesus Christ" stands for the reconciliation of creation with its creator, "for there is no other name under heaven given among mortals by which we must be saved" (Acts 4:12). The name "Jesus Christ" stands for freedom, peace, justice and compassion. It guarantees that God's name is a *good* name.

Yes, a name is more than a word; it is more than a breath of air. The name communicates the reality of a person. In his or her name the bearer of that name is present. In 1 Samuel 25:25 we read about a person whose name is "*Nabal*" which means "fool," and the author comments: "for as his name is, so is he."

A Name Can Be Misused

We know that a name can be misused. We can take a name and spoil it. The history of the media is full of examples in which persons have been destroyed because their names have been connected with activities or with people of ill repute. Most of us have had similar experiences. A rumor is started. We are supposed to have done or said something. Whether it is true or not, the rumor is now there—and we are powerless. You can't kill a

---

military decisions led to heavy casualties. Australia alone lost 9,000 of its soldiers and had another 19,000 wounded. Their mateship and their sacrifice feed the myth to the present day.

rumor! Our disappointment, sorrow, fear, and frustration can't prevent the fact that now we are linked to something outside of our control.

Years ago, in the dark days of the iron curtain, I spoke at a pastor's conference in one of the former socialist countries. I was asked whether I believed in Satan, whether he could ultimately undo God's plans, and whether I believed in an eternal hell. I said "No" to all three—and explained what I meant. My explanation was soon forgotten, but years later, indeed decades later, I was still identified as the theologian who neither believed in Satan nor in hell. Given the theology in those countries at that time my name was seriously tarnished.

How often has God's name been misused! "In God we trust"—on a dollar note! "God with us"—on the buckle of soldiers' belts. "God can't hear the prayer of a Jew"—pronounced by an evangelical church leader! "God will punish you"—said not only as a joke! "God has sent us a Führer in this hour of crisis"—heard not too long ago even from Professors of Philosophy and Theology! "God rained bombs on Iraq"—pronounced by powerful politicians.

We have become insensitive with regard to naming God. People use God's name in the pub, and every avalanche of swear words includes the words "God" and "Christ." Even within the religious community, where God-talk seems natural and expected, I feel a certain reservation when people say "God told me this" or "God made me do that." Dietrich Bonhoeffer, an ordained pastor and theologian who was imprisoned for his opposition to Hitler, experienced such hesitancy in Tegel prison in Berlin. On April 30, 1944 he confides in his friend: "While I am often reluctant to mention God by name to religious people—because that name somehow seems to me here not to ring true, and I feel myself to be slightly dishonest (it's particularly bad when others start to talk in religious jargon; I then dry up almost completely and feel awkward and uncomfortable)—to people with no religion I can on occasion mention him by name quite calmly and as a matter of course."[5]

Why such hesitancy? Because for the believer "God" is an eminently significant word. We want it to be used sensitively and responsibly. A thoughtless use or a misuse of the name "God" grates on us. We don't like it. It offends us. We feel that somehow God's reputation is at stake in our life. We want to safeguard a responsible use of God's name.

---

5. *Letters and Papers from Prison*, 281.

A Name Is More Than a Word

Jesus knew the danger of irresponsibly using God's name: "Not everyone who says to me, 'Lord, Lord,' will enter the kingdom of heaven, but only the one who does the will of my Father in heaven" (Matt 7:21). A prophet must therefore demonstrate the credibility of his words by producing corresponding fruits: "Are grapes gathered from thorns, or figs from thistles? In the same way, every good tree bears good fruit, but the bad tree bears bad fruit" (Matt 7:15–19).

And Jeremiah, the famous prophet of old, speaks with insight and power:

> . . . from the least to the greatest of them, everyone is greedy for unjust gain; and from prophet to priest, everyone deals falsely. They have treated the wound of my people carelessly, saying, "Peace, peace," when there is no peace. They acted shamefully, they committed abomination; yet they were not ashamed, they did not know how to blush. Therefore they shall fall among those who fall; at the time that I punish them, they shall be overthrown, says the LORD. (Jer 6:13–15)

> Amend your ways and your doings, and let me dwell with you in this place. Do not trust in these deceptive words: "This is the temple of the LORD, the temple of the LORD, the temple of the LORD." For if you truly amend your ways and your doings, if you truly act justly one with another, if you do not oppress the alien, the orphan, and the widow, or shed innocent blood in this place, and if you do not go after other gods to your own hurt, then I will dwell with you in this place, in the land that I gave of old to your ancestors forever and ever. Here you are, trusting in deceptive words to no avail. Will you steal, murder, commit adultery, swear falsely, make offerings to Baal, and go after other gods that you have not known, and then come and stand before me in this house, which is called by my name, and say, "We are safe!"—only to go on doing all these abominations? (Jer 7:3–10)

How Then Can We Live?

But how then can we live? How can we believe? Do we not all use God's name in vain? Is it not our human predicament that we either don't use the name of God at all, or that we use it wrongfully? Is not our self-interest, our unbending self-will, so creative and ingenious that we use "God" to validate what serves our plans and interests? Why do nations and people think that God loves them more than others? Why do nations and people think that they are more important in the economy of God than others? Why has the name of God been invoked in every war, on all sides?

In the depth of this self-awareness, this honest self-examination, we are reminded of God's unconditional love: "thus says the LORD, he who created you, O Jacob, he who formed you, O Israel: Do not fear, for I have redeemed you; *I have called you by name,* you are mine . . . For I am the LORD your God, the Holy One of Israel, your Savior" (Isa 43:1–3). It is a call to freedom when God's name becomes inter-locked with our lives. Whether God's people are slaves in Egypt or in Babylonian exile, God's name stands for the hope of liberation.

> For thus says the LORD ("Adonai") GOD ("Yahweh"): Long ago, my people went down into Egypt to reside there as aliens; the Assyrian, too, has oppressed them without cause. Now therefore what am I doing here, says the LORD, seeing that my people are taken away without cause? Their rulers howl, says the LORD, and continually, all day long, my name is despised. Therefore *my people shall know my name*; therefore in that day they shall know that it is I who speak; here am I. How beautiful upon the mountains are the feet of the messenger who announces peace, who brings good news, who announces salvation, who says to Zion, "Your God reigns." Listen! Your sentinels lift up their voices, together they sing for joy; for in plain sight they see the return of the LORD to Zion. Break forth together into singing, you ruins of Jerusalem; *for the* LORD *has comforted his people, he has redeemed Jerusalem.* The LORD has bared his holy arm before the eyes of all the nations; and all the ends of the earth shall see the salvation of our God. (Isa 52:4–10, emphases mine)

God's name stands for God being for us. For Christians God has revealed God being for us in the story of Jesus. Christians around the world therefore pray the prayer that Jesus taught his disciples. In the Lord's prayer—Matthew 6:9–13; Luke 11:2–4—Jesus teaches his followers to take the third commandment to heart: "hallowed be your name." This prayer is a confession, a promise, and a commitment.

We confess that we have taken God's name in vain; that we have been more concerned with our own name than with God's; that our own reputation, our own plans, our own need to succeed, have distorted our commitment to Christ and our faith in God. Thus we pray from the deep: Not our name, but God's be honored!

A Name Is More Than a Word

It is also a promise. By taking us into this prayer, Jesus offers us a new beginning. God majors on new beginnings. God takes us seriously. We are free, responsible and guilty: and "the LORD will not hold him guiltless who takes his name in vain." That does not mean that God enjoys being a judge. It does mean that we are responsible and that we must accept the consequences of our actions. But by turning to Jesus we become empowered to honor God's name.

When we pray the Lord's prayer, we also commit ourselves to that new and promising reality. Knowing of our predicament, knowing that we are much more concerned about our own name than about God's name, and knowing that we take God's name in vain, we enter the pilgrimage of faith saying: not our name but your name be honored.

With the intention to honor God's name we become aware of a new beginning. God's "Yes" is greater than our "No's." The apostle Paul interprets the life of faith in Jesus Christ: "where sin increased, grace abounded all the more" (Rom 5:20). And we remember from our discussion of the second commandment that God visits the "iniquity of the fathers upon the children to the third and fourth generation . . . but showing steadfast love" to thousands of generations "of those who love me and keep my commandments" (Exod 20:5).

What Then Shall We Do?

The apostle Paul spelled it out that through faith in Christ we discover a way that does not lock us into the prison of our self-interest, but makes us open to God and to others: "it is no longer I who live, but Christ who lives in me" (Gal 2:20). Not to take God's name in vain is to accept God on God's terms. Not to carve God into an image. Not to use God to rubber-stamp our ideas. To honor God's name is to discern God's nature and God's will at the place of God's self-revelation. In Jesus Christ, in his life, death and resurrection, God has clearly spelled out God's name. To honor God's name therefore means to believe in Jesus and to follow him.

Let us once again turn to Dietrich Bonhoeffer with the question of what it would mean to honor God's name today. While in prison in Berlin Tegel in 1944, Bonhoeffer wrote an outline for a book. It was to be a short book—three chapters, about a hundred pages. The middle chapter was to be entitled "The Real Meaning of Christian Faith." The draft of that chapter includes the following:

> Who is God? Not in the first place an abstract belief in God, in his omnipotence etc. That is not a genuine experience of God, but a partial extension of the world. Encounter with Jesus Christ. The experience that a transformation of all human life is given in the fact that *"Jesus is there only for others." His "being there for others" is the experience of transcendence. It is only this "being there for others," maintained till death, that is the ground of his omnipotence, omniscience, and omnipresence. Faith is participation in this being of Jesus* (incarnation, cross, and resurrection). Our relation to God is not a "religious" relationship to the highest, most powerful, and best Being imaginable . . . but . . . a new life in *"existence for others," through participation in the being of Jesus.* The transcendental is not an infinite and unattainable task, but the neighbor who is within reach in any given situation. God in human form . . . [6]

In a proposed third chapter "consequences" (*Folgerungen*),[7] Bonhoeffer applies these theological insights to the church: "The church is the church *only when it exists for others.*"[8] And the "others" are "the outcast, the suspects, the maltreated, the powerless, the oppressed, the reviled—in short . . . those who suffer."[9] Proverbs 31:8 had become important to him: "Speak out for those who cannot speak, for the rights of all the destitute."[10]

At the occasion of the baptism of his friend Eberhard Bethge's son Bonhoeffer writes, "Our church, which has been fighting in these years only for its self-preservation, as though that were an end in itself, is incapable of taking the word of reconciliation and redemption to mankind and the world." He continues that our being Christian today will consist of two things: *Praying* and *working for justice*. "All Christian thinking, speaking, and organizing must be born anew out of this prayer and action." And then we can only patiently wait for the day "when men will once more be called so to utter the word of God that the world will be changed and renewed by it. It will be a new language, perhaps quite non-religious, but *liberating and redeeming*—as was Jesus' language . . . ."[11]

---

6. "Outline for a book," (1944) in ibid., 381 (emphases mine).
7. Not "conclusion" as it says in ibid., 382.
8. Ibid. (emphasis mine).
9. "After Ten Years. A Reckoning made at New Year 1943," in ibid., 17.

10. Letter to George Bell, the Bishop of Chichester of January 19, 1934, in *No Rusty Swords*, 259; Lectures on the Interpretation of the New Testament (1935), in Bonhoeffer, *Letters and Papers from Prison*, 325.

11. *Letters and Papers from Prison*, 300 (emphases mine).

A Name Is More Than a Word

Conclusion

The philosopher Ludwig Wittgenstein introduces (and concludes) his *Tractatus Logico-Philosophicus* (1922) with the following words: "The whole sense of the book might be summoned up in the following words: what can be said at all can be said clearly, and what we cannot talk about we must pass over in silence."[12] It is certainly difficult to talk of God and clarity in God-talk is not possible. The distance is so great. But being silent is not an alternative for the believer. The prophet Jeremiah feels the word like a fire burning in his bones (23:29), and the apostle Paul speaks of an inner necessity to witness to the gospel: "For necessity is laid upon me. Woe to me if I do not preach the gospel!" (1 Cor 9:16) Faith longs for confession. We must name the central and integrating reality of our life. But it must become clear that "God" is a good name. Christians learn from the story of Jesus what it means to honor the name of the Lord.

The "third word" invites us to use the name of the Lord by bringing comfort, consolation and forgiveness to people in need. We are invited to tell the story of Jesus in word and deed as an invitation to life. We announce the good news that we are not defined and evaluated by our achievements, but by a God who says "Yes" to us. We are encouraged to be prophets, unmasking and denouncing acts of injustice. We are called to become advocates for those who have no voice, no power and no friends. With this commandment we commit ourselves to liberate the oppressed, heal the sick, feed the poor—and announce the acceptable year of the Lord. Then our living shall not be in vain, and the name of the Lord will be honored.

> May his name endure forever,
> > his fame continue as long as the sun.
> May all nations be blessed in him;
> > may they pronounce him happy.
> Blessed be the LORD, the God of Israel,
> > who alone does wondrous things.
> Blessed be his glorious name forever;
> > may his glory fill the whole earth. Amen and Amen.
>
> (Ps 72:17–19)

---

12. *Tractatus Logico-Philosophicus*, 3 ("Author's Preface"), also 150 (§7—the final sentence in the book).

6

Celebrating Freedom

The Fourth Word

"Remember the sabbath day, and keep it holy...."

Exodus 20:8-11 and Deuteronomy 5:12-15 [1]
Related texts: Genesis 1:31—2:3; Mark 2:23—3:6; Luke 13:10-17; 14:1-6

Exodus 20:8-11

Remember the sabbath day, and keep it holy. Six days you shall labor and do all your work. But the seventh day is sabbath to the LORD your God, you shall not do any work—you, your son or daughter, your male or female slave, your livestock, or the alien resident in your towns. *For in six days the LORD made heaven and earth, the sea, and all that is in them, but rested the seventh day; therefore the LORD blessed the sabbath day and consecrated it.*

Deuteronomy 5:12-15

Observe the sabbath day and keep it holy, *as the LORD your God commanded you*. Six days you labor and do all your work. But the seventh day is a sabbath to the LORD your God; you shall not do any work—you, or your son or your daughter, or your male or female slave, *or your ox or your donkey*, or any of your livestock, or the resident alien in your towns, *so that your male and female slave may rest as well as you. Remember that you were a slave in the land of Egypt, and the LORD your God brought you out from there with a mighty hand and an outstretched arm; therefore the LORD your God commanded you to keep the sabbath day.*

---

1. In the texts the differences are highlighted with italics.

THEOLOGICAL COMMENTS

This commandment stands out:

- it is the longest of the "ten words";
- it is located at the transition of commandments that deal with the human relationship to God and those that deal with humans relating to each other;
- the versions in the books of Exodus and Deuteronomy show considerable difference, pointing to a history of expansion and situational adaptation;
- the version in Deuteronomy contains a significant social-ethical and ecological emphasis;
- it appears to be a more cultic or religious commandment in the midst of theological and moral assertions.

The sabbath was and is of tremendous religious significance for the Jewish people. Its importance calls for a little longer introduction. Sabbath observance was considered to be the measure of people's faith in God. The Rabbis therefore wanted to lead their people to a strict sabbath observance. They believed that if Israel kept two sabbaths in a row, they would be saved immediately. To provide for such a possibility, they built a fence of hundreds of rules and regulations around the sabbath. Believers were afraid that by not honoring the sabbath they were transgressing against the very being of God. In Judaism, keeping the sabbath, together with circumcision and studying and obeying the Torah (the five books of Moses), belonged to their identity marks as the people of God. The following points provide some background information.

1. The sabbath was a central religious institution in Israel. Here Israel confessed to whom they belonged, whom they wanted to obey, and whose witness they wanted to be in the world.

2. Different reasons for keeping the sabbath are given in our texts. The Exodus version grounds the sabbath commandments in the creation story. Yahweh worked for six days. "God saw everything that he had made, and indeed, it was very good" (Gen 1:31). On the seventh day God rested "from all the work that he had done" (Gen 2:2). This divine flow between doing and being, between creating and meditating, makes

the sabbath a significant event in the flux of time. The Deuteronomy version anchors the meaning of the sabbath in the great event of Israel's liberation from slavery. What they have experienced themselves should determine their vision of life. In the sabbath celebrations it must become manifest in word and deed that God is a worker for freedom and that faith in God is a liberating reality.

3. Both texts therefore emphasize that the sabbath has social-ethical and ecological dimensions. Since God's grace is equally intended for all people, therefore where that grace becomes an event—as it does on the sabbath—there all of God's creation participates in the divine rest. Equality, justice and solidarity are affirmed. Slaves and alien residents and animals are mentioned in the same breath as the patriarch and his family. This is emphasized even more in the Deuteronomy version—that "*they* may rest *as well as you*"!

4. The rhythm of seven days in a week led to other important institutions in Israel, the seventh year (Exod 23:10–11; Lev 25:3–7) and the year of Jubilee (Lev 25:8–17) which also served social-ethical and ecological goals.

5. Jesus did not show disrespect for the sabbath. But he wanted to demonstrate that the original intention of keeping the sabbath was to celebrate freedom. He wanted to reclaim the sabbath as the day when God is celebrated. And for Jesus, God is celebrated when love becomes an event, when people are liberated, and when human life is made human (Mark 2:23). Jesus therefore felt free to suspend the then current sabbath laws when it was no longer evident that they were "doing good" and "saving life" (Mark 3:4). He healed people on the sabbath even when there was no medical urgency. This was an intentional provocation. The same was true when his disciples were hungry and plucked and ate grain on the sabbath. Again Jesus said that not the laws as such but the welfare of human beings is the measure for what is right and what is wrong (Mark 2:23–28). Where love longs to become an event, there religious laws and practices must be suspended. How can the God who liberated his people from slavery and whose commandments are supposed to be structures of liberation be confined to religious rules when human life is at stake? The response of the religious people was to hold counsel as to "how to destroy him" (Mark 3:6). Jesus was charged with disrespecting the sabbath, which was one of the causes that led to his crucifixion

(see Mark 3:1–6; Luke 13:10–17; 14:1–6). Offenders against the sabbath regulations were punished heavily (including the death penalty, Exod 31:12–17; Num 15:32–36; *Jub.* 2:25, 50:8).[2]

6. Christians took up the sabbath tradition but they changed the day and interpreted it with reference to the resurrection of Jesus. Within the flux of time they celebrate not only that "long ago God spoke to our ancestors in many and various ways by the prophets," but especially, that "in these last days he has spoken to us by a Son, ... He is the reflection of God's glory and the exact imprint of God's very being" (Heb 1:1–3). Christians therefore chose the first day of the week, the Sunday, to celebrate that by raising Jesus from the dead, God had done something new, gracing our time with the promise that ultimately love will prove to be stronger than death.

7. Christians face the theological question whether keeping the sabbath falls under the cultic rules, such as fasting, washing of hands, tithing and offering sacrifices. These religious rules have been relativized by Jesus, and one could therefore conclude that also sabbath/Sunday observance is of less importance for Christians. Yet, the rest and worship motifs, and their inter-locking with the social-ethical and environmental dimensions, have maintained the importance of the sabbath, only that for Christians it is celebrated on Sunday and its content derives from the story of Jesus.[3]

8. God's *shalom* (holistic salvation) does not do away with human responsibility and with hard work, but it assigns it its place. The sabbath reminds us that our work is graced and grounded. For Christians, Sunday is the *first*, not the last day of the week. We celebrate that with the resurrection of Jesus, God has done something new and something good for God's creation. Our work is therefore grounded in God's grace. Our identity is ultimately not in what we do and can do; our identity is in what God has done for us!

We add a few exegetical comments.

2. Other texts highlighting the importance of the sabbath include Exod 16:22–27; 23:12; 31:16–17; 34:21; 35:2–3; Lev 19:3, 30; 23:3; 26:2; Neh 9:13–14; 10:31; 13:15–22; Isa 56:2–6; 58:13–14; 66:23; Jer 17:21–27; Ezek 20:12–24; 22:8, 26; 23:38; 44:24; and Amos 8:4–6.

3. There are some Christian churches, however, like the Seventh-day Adventists and the Seventh-day Baptists, who have maintained the sabbath observance on Saturdays.

"*Remember*" is often used in the Bible. It means more than the psychological activity of remembering. It is a theological word. It means that we should be aware of the fact that God invests the sabbath/Sunday with meaning and significance.

"*To keep it holy*": The grammatical form (*piel*) has the connotation of *actively making* the sabbath day what it is, *holy*. The emphasis is not on "resting" or "not working," but on actively celebrating the *difference* between the six days and the seventh day. Both versions clearly explain the difference between the "six days" and the "seventh day." The six days are related to labor and "all" your work, while on the seventh day "all" attention is to be on God and God's vision for our life.

MESSAGE

Sunday as the Celebration of Freedom

God and freedom belong together. God is the one who freed his people from slavery. This same God created the world—and it was beautiful.[4] Freedom and beauty must mark the celebration of the sabbath if it is to be a holy day. When Christians celebrate the sabbath on Sunday they do not want to negate the celebration of freedom and beauty. For them the same God who created the world and who led his people out of slavery has spoken again in the story of Jesus. And again it is a story of freedom and beauty. In Jesus Christ all the promises of God are brought to fulfillment, God has said "yes" to God's creation, and through faith in Jesus Christ people are reconciled with God (2 Cor 1:18–20; 5:17–21).

Jesus' criticism of the sabbath was not against the sabbath as such. But he was critical of the way people of his day observed the sabbath. He did not suspend the sabbath, but he made it clear that the sabbath is there to celebrate life, to make human life human.

This raises the general question of the relationship between law and truth, between law and justice. We recently witnessed the trial against the Iraqi dictator Saddam Hussein. Together with him two other men were found guilty of crimes against humanity, Barzan Ibrahim, Iraq's former intelligence chief, and Awad Hamed al-Bandar, the former head of the Revolutionary Court. These were men who were supposed to guard and execute the law! But they committed crimes against humanity. During the

---

4. For this translation—"beautiful" (Gen 1:31)—see Westermann, *Genesis 1–11*, 166–67.

Celebrating Freedom

Hitler regime in Germany 1933–45 laws were issued that discriminated against Jews, communists, Gypsies and other minority groups. At that time the theologian Karl Barth offended against the then valid law by refusing to swear an oath of unconditional allegiance to Hitler. Also Dietrich Bonhoeffer offended the then valid law by helping Jews to escape from Germany to Switzerland. Laws can further life and they can hinder life, they can be just or unjust. Just laws must demonstrate that they serve freedom and justice.

It was on a sabbath day when Jesus was met by a man with a withered hand (Mark 3:1–6). Treatment was not urgent. He had been disabled for a long time. He could have waited until the next morning. But disregarding the religious rules, Jesus demonstratively heals him on the sabbath. That was a statement! "The sabbath was made for humankind, not humankind for the sabbath" (Mark 2:27). And the great liberator, Jesus Christ himself, is Lord of the sabbath (Mark 2:28).

Two of the eight *United Nations Millenium Goals* aim at halving the number of people who go to bed hungry every day and the number of people who earn below $1 a day. The governments of the world have agreed to that—and to do it by the year 2015. Over a billion people live in abject poverty. They live under conditions that we in the West cannot understand, much less appreciate. To eliminate hunger and poverty is one of the great challenges of our time. Many people around the world wear wristbands with the inscription to "make poverty history."

One sabbath day Jesus was walking through the fields with his disciples. They were hungry. To satisfy their hunger they plucked grain to eat. In doing that they had broken the sabbath regulations several times. They walked on other people's property, they worked by plucking grain, and thereby they took what did not belong to them. The law-keepers (the Pharisees) complained. But Jesus justified their action by pointing them to their own history (1 Sam 21:1–6). When David and his friends were hungry they even "entered the house of God . . . and ate the bread of the Presence, which it is not lawful for any but the priests to eat, and he gave some to his companions" (Mark 2:23–28). That is like hungry people today entering the church and eating the bread of the Eucharist, the Lord's Supper, Holy Communion—although the amount of bread and wine offered these days in the churches would hardly quench anyone's hunger and thirst! There is nothing wrong with laws and regulations. But their legitimacy must be demonstrated by eliminating human need.

Beyond Legalism and Laxity

How then should we "observe" and "remember the Sabbath day, and keep it holy"? What rest and activity is most appropriate to make this day different to other days and to celebrate God on this day?

I still remember the days of legalism when a Christian could not play football on Sundays; or when opinionated church members would survey the beaches with binoculars to see whether any Christian dared to go swimming on Sunday. Being a pastor at a beach resort, I had to go swimming on the next beach in order not to offend the guardians of the sabbath. When we moved to Switzerland, one Ascension Day I was mowing the lawn, having momentarily forgotten that it was a Christian holiday. A neighbor came and threatened that if I did not stop immediately breaking the holy day rules she would call the police—interestingly, I never saw her showing any interest in matters related to any church while we went to church every Sunday. Ernst Käsemann tells the story about a stern Presbyterian board of deacons on Holland's Atlantic coast. A storm had assumed dangerous proportions during the night from Saturday to Sunday. It threatened to break the dykes and flood the land. On Sunday morning the Police chief called the Pastor to ask for help in placing sandbags against the rising flood. The Pastor did not want to make that decision alone, and called his deacons together. They insisted that Sunday is the Lord's day. We are not to work. If we are obedient, the Lord will save us from the flood. If he does not, it will be God's judgment upon us. In a last attempt the Pastor reminded his deacons that Jesus also broke the sabbath in order to save human life—only to hear from one of the deacons: 'I have always suspected that Jesus was a little bit too liberal.'[5] Legalism is certainly not an adequate way to celebrate Sunday.

But there is no virtue in laxity either. Lazing in bed rather than going to church on Sunday morning, spending Sunday reading the weekend edition of the *New York Times* or the *Sydney Morning Herald*, washing cars, playing golf, going shopping, mowing the lawn, or going to a football game are not necessarily demonstrations of Christian freedom. For many people, Sunday has more to do with worshipping the sun and the dollar than worshipping the Son.

Neither legalism nor laxity are proper approaches to the Sunday. What then does it mean for us to make and to "keep the sabbath day holy"?

---

5. *Jesus Means Freedom*, 16.

Celebrating Freedom

The Sabbath Graces Our Existence in Time

The "fourth word" points us to our existence in time. "Seven days"—that is the time in which we exist. Our time is made up of the rhythm of days and weeks. Each week is made up of seven days. The French and the Russian Revolutions tried to change that. They wanted to celebrate the triumph of the secular by leaving behind what they thought to be a religious invention. They wanted to get rid of the sabbath or the "Lord's Day" by creating a ten day week—but that attempt remained unsuccessful.

To celebrate the sabbath or Sunday means that we recognize the presence of God in the flux of time. When the early Christians shifted their celebration from the sabbath to the "Lord's Day" on the first day of the week, they wanted to confess that their life and their work are grounded in the grace of God. God is the giver of life and God's provision accompanies us on life's journey. That story needs to be told and it needs to be celebrated. The "fourth word" relates the celebration of the sabbath and Sunday to several dimensions of faith: creation, redemption, worship, and community.

Creation

The book of Exodus gives the following reason for celebrating the sabbath: "in six days the LORD made heaven and earth, the sea, and all that is in them, but rested on the seventh day; therefore the LORD blessed the sabbath day and consecrated it" (Exod 20:11).

On Sundays we pause and allow the word of God to remind us that we have a creator and that our life is only meaningful if we acknowledge the creator and live in harmony with God. The Presbyterians have a beautiful expression in their *Shorter* and their *Larger Catechism* (seventeenth century England). Both of them start with the question: "What is the chief and highest end of being human?" and the answer is: "to glorify God and (fully) to enjoy God forever."[6]

In one of Israel's creation stories (Gen 1:1—2:4a) we are told that in six days God created the heavens and the earth, the seas, the animals and finally humanity. We have become used to speaking of humanity as the crown of creation. But the climax of the creation story is a little different: "And on the seventh day God finished (brought to fulfillment) the work

---

6. The two Catechisms, together with the Westminster Confession of Faith make up the so-called Westminster Standards. They can be found in the Presbyterian Church's *Book of Confessions*, 227–300.

he had done" (Gen 2:2). Not humanity as the crown of creation, but the Sabbath. It does not say that on the seventh day God put the tools aside, cleaned up after his work, or put some finishing touches to creation. No, God does something different, something new: God takes a deep breath, God takes a step back, God meditates on what God had done. The outward journey issues into the inward journey.

The sabbath graces our existence in time. It adds meaning to life. God "rests." Exodus 31:17 adds that God "was refreshed." And to highlight the importance of the sabbath, God "blessed" and God "hallowed" it. Our language and the poverty of our imagination hinder our ability to understand and describe what happens here. But we are invited to entertain God's desire to restore the full meaning and the true purpose of the sabbath.

The rhythm of doing and being is clear. After God had created, after the "doing," God lets creation affect him. God has gone out to create, and now God returns and meditates on what has been achieved. God experiences the world. God lets the world with all its promises and problems affect God's very being. There is no victory of love and no selfless sacrifice that is not noted where it counts. There is no torture in Burma or in Guantanamo Bay, no killing in Darfur, no destruction of rainforests or coral reefs which do not also affect the very being of the creator.

On Sundays we remember what God is like. Sunday is not a sterile and boring day of legalism. It is not a day to do the things that we have no time for during the rest of the week. Sunday reminds us that we are gifted people. That before we work, God has shared God's life with us. That our identity is not in what we produce and consume. Our identity is in what God has done for us and in what God has given us.

Six days we work; on the seventh day we ask why we work. Six days we work, and on the seventh we thank God that we still have work. Six days we work, and on the seventh day we lean back, reflect, meditate on how we fare in our life. Six days we work, and on the seventh day we remind ourselves that life is more than work.

Sunday is therefore a healthy interruption in the flux of time. It provides occasion for self-awareness and healing for our life in time. We rest by asking ourselves what life is all about. When we go to church we allow the word of God and the community of faith to interpret our life and remind us that we "shall not live by bread alone." This is a protest against all attempts to limit life to "doing," to "producing," to "achieving," to "consuming." Sunday contains the promise that in the midst of life a God who wants the best for us does not surround us by a threatening universe. For our failures there is forgiveness. In the storms of life there are islands of rest. When we feel at an end, there are new beginnings.

At the same time, Sunday is followed by six days of work. These days are also the gift of the creator. Just as God is portrayed as a worker (creator), so human beings are called to participate with God in shaping creation. Our work has dignity and we should be proud of it. The risk is of course that we forget the difference between the first day and the six days that follow. Work is part of our human destiny. It is part of being human and being good. But it is not the ultimate. It can provide satisfaction, but it cannot meet our deepest needs. The sabbath reminds us that our deepest needs are met by faith, not by work. Faith remains even when work has to stop. In a work-and-achievement-oriented society it is often difficult for disabled and old people to feel good about themselves. They feel useless and society encourages that feeling.

For that reason it is difficult for the unemployed to celebrate Sunday. It is not true that for the unemployed every day is "Sunday." They have no Sunday, because they have been removed from the rhythm of doing and being. For them Sunday can be a terrible day, the worst day of the week—a weekly reminder that they have been excluded from the rhythm of life. They have become the modern outcasts of a society that seeks meaning only in work, achievements and profits. Therefore to honor the sabbath also means doing all we can to make it possible for people to get work. Those who hear the "fourth word" and celebrate life on Sunday will not forget the unemployed during the rest of the week. They will seek to create spaces so that those who have been excluded from the rhythm of doing and being can join in. Celebrating Sunday therefore entails social awareness and prophetic commitment that contribute towards creating a culture of freedom.

Redemption

The Book of Deuteronomy gives a different reason for celebrating the sabbath: "Remember that you were a slave in the land of Egypt, and the LORD your God brought you out from there with a mighty hand and an outstretched arm; therefore the LORD your God commanded you to keep the sabbath day" (Deut 5:15).

Israel, and by implication the church, is invited to remember their roots. We are invited to remember where we come from. Israel is to remain aware of the fact that God delivered them from slavery and oppression. When the early church celebrated the resurrection of Jesus Christ on the first day of the week, it wanted to confess that by raising Jesus from the dead, God had defeated the estranging forces of death and thereby reconciled us, indeed all of creation, with God (2 Cor 5:17–21).

Both for Israel and for the church God's liberating activity includes individual and social dimensions. For Israel the exodus motif and for the church the resurrection of Christ have become powerful symbols for salvation. Our ultimate destiny, indeed the destiny of all people, is to live in harmony with the creator. This harmony has been corrupted by human selfishness. The sabbath and Sunday are therefore the days on which the great stories of redemption and deliverance are told.

These grand stories proclaim God's passion for the weak and with it Israel's and the church's commission "to bring good news to the poor . . . to proclaim release to the captives and recovery of sight to the blind, to let the oppressed go free, to proclaim the year of the Lord's favor" (Luke 4:18–19; Isa 58:6, 61:1–2). On the sabbath not only "you or your son or your daughter" shall rest, but also "your male or female slave, your livestock, or the alien resident in your towns." This day, the Lord's Day, must become a visible symbol that the God whom we worship is passionately concerned for social justice. God feels it when the poor are exploited and the weak are taken advantage of. The prophets therefore protest against those who do not understand that the holiness of the sabbath is related to the practice of justice.

> Hear this, you who trample upon the needy, and bring to ruin the poor of the land, saying, "When will the new moon be over, so that we may sell grain; and the *sabbath*, so that we may offer wheat for sale? We will make the ephah small and the shekel great, and practice deceit with false balances, buying the poor for silver and the needy for a pair of sandals, and selling the sweepings of the wheat?" (Amos 8:4–6; also Neh 13:15–22)

The same passion for justice is related to the resurrection of Christ.[7] In what may be called a manifesto of the new reality of the resurrection of Christ the apostle Paul mentions three implications of what happens when the power of the resurrection arrives in the lives and communities of believers. The legendary barriers between Jews and Greeks will be removed,

---

7. See Lorenzen, *Resurrection—Discipleship—Justice*.

slaves will be set free, and women will be restored to an equal partnership with men (Gal 3:23-28). Where God's redemption becomes event there is no longer a need to suppress others. They are no longer a threat. Indeed, we discover that we need the other to celebrate freedom. True freedom is not an individualistic but a community experience.

This message is particularly relevant today. Racism, ethnic and religious suspicion and hatred are among the great problems of modern times. With the "two thirds" world not making much progress in escaping abject poverty, with millions of refugees and asylum-seekers looking for a space in which to live, the morality and sense of justice in the "one third" world are challenged. Globalization is a fact of modern life. The question is whether it will only serve the economic and political interests of the rich and powerful or whether it will also include responsibility for the millions of poor, oppressed and displaced people. Christians and the churches must be at the forefront of engagement to find ways of giving expression to the equality of all people, to encourage a more equal distribution of the earth's resources, and to welcome strangers into our midst. Yet many of us are apathetic and discouraged. We don't know what to do or we don't have the strength to get up and walk. There may be resources in our sabbath celebrations that can renew our vision and inspire our resolve.

Not only the social concern but also the *ecological* concern is part of the sabbath commandment: your cattle, your ox, your ass are to rest (Exod 20:10; Deut 5:14). And during the sabbath year, every seventh year, you shall let your land and your vineyard and your olive orchard rest and lie fallow (Exod 23:10-11; Lev 25:1-7).

We all know, of course, that this can't be a master plan for the social and ecological crisis in our time. Our times are so different. But it is an invitation to the best within us to use our "sabbath times" to ask what we can do to solve the social and ecological crises of our time. We are invited to honor the sabbath by leaning in the same direction as God does, to protect the garden in which God has placed us and to strive for justice so that all people can share equally in the riches of our earth.

Community and Worship

Finally, we need to say a word about Sunday and our life in the Christian community, the church. I have sufficiently emphasized that we do not want to go back to the days of legalism. Celebration needs to feed on freedom. Legalism and dogmatism is not conducive to celebration.

On the other hand, a culture of freedom needs spiritual resources and it needs points of orientation. For many countries the Judeo-Christian tradition has provided such resources and orientations. We may rightly question whether the encroaching commercialism and sport that make Sunday a day for shopping or for sport can provide alternatives to the grand stories of freedom that the Jewish and Christian traditions entail. Creating a culture of freedom must set aside times and places where people can hear, meditate and decide how and where their souls can be fed. The Epistle to the Hebrews includes the exhortation: "Let us hold fast the confession of our hope without wavering, for he who promised is faithful; and let us consider how to stir up one another to love and good works, not neglecting to meet together, as is the habit of some, but encouraging one another, and all the more as you see the Day drawing near" (Heb 10:23–25).

When the early Christians responded to the resurrection of Jesus Christ, that response of gratitude entailed two equally important dimensions: worshipping God in the community of believers in weekly worship services on Sundays; and worshipping God in the marketplaces of life from Monday to Saturday.[8] Both dimensions are held together when we "remember the Sabbath day and keep it holy."

Conclusion

In the final analysis the sabbath commandment invites us to celebrate God in the midst of life. We interrupt our work to be reminded from where we come and to whom we belong. We seek the fellowship of believers so that together we may celebrate God and at the same time hope that more and more people, yes, that even nature may tune into that celebration.

---

8. The former is described in 1 Cor 11–14, the latter in Rom 12:1–2. For details see Lorenzen, "The Centrality of Preaching in Christian Worship."

7

Generational Responsibility

The Fifth Word

"Honor your father and your mother..."

Exodus 20:12 and Deuteronomy 5:16[1]
Related texts: Mark 3:31–35; Luke 9:57–62 (Matthew 8:18–22)

EXODUS 20:12

Honor your father and your mother, so that your days may be long in the land that the LORD your God is giving you.

DEUTERONOMY 5:16

Honor your father and your mother, *as the LORD your God commanded you*, so that your days may be long and *that it may go well with you* in the land that the LORD your God is giving you.

THEOLOGICAL COMMENTS

LIKE THE PREVIOUS COMMANDMENT this word is also given special prominence in the decalogue:

- Some commence the ethical part of the decalogue with this word,[2] while others see it as the last word of the first part.[3] For the latter speaks the fact that all the "words" so far specifically mention the "LORD." On the other hand, honoring one's parents is clearly an ethical exhortation.

---

1. In the texts the differences between the two versions are marked with italics.
2. For instance Schmidt, *Die Zehn Gebote*, 97.
3. For instance Weinfeld, *Deuteronomy 1–11*, 313.

- In contrast to the other commandments—except the second one—it contains a special promise: "that your days may be long and that it may go well with you in the land that the LORD your God is giving you."

- Together with the sabbath commandment, but in contrast to Exodus 21:15 and 17 ("Whoever strikes father or mother shall be put to death"; "whoever curses father or mother shall be put to death"), the fifth commandment is formulated positively. Thereby its meaning is intensified and widened. Not punishment but promise is the underlying melody. It is a good thing to honor father and mother.

- It deals with an issue that has a high profile in the Hebrew Bible. How should the older members of the family or clan be treated when they are no longer useful and productive?[4]

At issue therefore is care for the aged and the implied responsibility between the generations. The fate of old people has been a social challenge at all times. This was especially so in times of economic hardship. It was known in the ancient world that parents were driven away from home. They could be maltreated (cursed, beaten, robbed, oppressed) and they could certainly become a burden when they were no longer productive. Such antagonism need not be rooted in ill-will. We know of hard times in the ancient world when drought, poverty and war threatened the life of the tribal families. Parents had to sell their children into slavery and they themselves became serfs (Neh 5). When parents became old, it was expected that their sons would take care of them. But when there was no food to feed the children, it was understandable that animosity was turned against those who were no longer productive. Nevertheless, ethics starts at the point of pain! There comes the time when the dignity and freedom of the parents depended on the morality of the sons to provide shelter, food, clothing and a dignified funeral.

To "*honor*" is more than to "obey" or "love." It includes the dimension of "respect," "prize highly," "glorify," "exalt." In Psalm 86:9 the same word is used for "honoring" God. Honoring transcends the emotional element of love. It includes the structural dimension of care, recognizing the contribution that parents have made in the generational chain. To honor implies

4. Relevant texts include the following: Exod 21:15, 17; Lev 20:9; Deut 21:18–21; 27:16; Prov 1:8; 15:5; 19:26; 20:20; 23:22; 28:24; 30:11, 17; Ezek 22:7; Mic 7:6; Mal 1:6; Sir 3:1–16; and in the New Testament the so-called household codes: Eph 6:1–4; Col 3:20–21.

Generational Responsibility

the respect, the hard work, the self-discipline, the creativity to protect the dignity of parents until the end of their lives.

"Your days may be long"—not only refers to chronological length, but to the welfare of senior citizens in a society where God is honored.

As we think of its relevance for today, we need to be aware of the following issues:

1. It is difficult to relate this commandment to our situation. It was originally conceived for extended families and clans, while most of us live in nuclear families; and the nuclear family has fallen on hard times. On the one hand, human rights instruments proclaim the nuclear family as the basic unit of society, on the other hand the divorce rate and family violence are increasing. The nuclear family seems to be falling apart. The question remains however: what do we do with our "parents" when they can no longer produce and look after themselves?

2. In our response we need to distinguish between the personal-ethical level at which we show respect and compassion for our parents, and the social-ethical level at which a society needs to provide social security like pensions, aged care hostels, hospices and medical care for its senior citizens.

3. This word raises the whole question of authority and responsibility, which has become a real problem today. The commandment suggests that God's covenant relationship with its reciprocal responsibility is echoed in the relationship between parents and children. But such reciprocal responsibility is questioned by many people today.

4. How can rights and responsibility be lived in a culture of freedom? Human rights emphasize the inherent dignity of people whose rights need to be protected against the arbitrary invasion of their privacy by authoritarian structures such as patriarchy, state and church. Nevertheless, freedom must also be protected against individualism and selfishness—"I want what I want, and I want it now." It is important to understand that rights entail responsibility for the welfare of the whole group.

5. A controversial issue today is euthanasia. We feel a natural sympathy when people with incurable diseases, with enormous pain and with no apparent quality of life want to end their life. At the same time, the dignity of old people is at stake in a culture that is driven by social Darwinism, economic rationalism and a profit-oriented economy. In our society (and

in our hearts, because it is very difficult not to internalize the ethos of our society) everything carries a dollar sign. We are defined not by who we are, but by what we can do and achieve and contribute. But what happens when we can no longer achieve and contribute? Having internalized the social Darwinism of our society, we often feel worthless. Whatever promises euthanasia may contain for old people, we must resist any and every attempt to make old people feel worthless and with such feeling driven towards ending their lives.

6. There is such a thing as generational selfishness. The ethos that we create will determine the context in which our children and grandchildren will live. A culture of freedom includes inter-generational generosity, compassion and care.

7. The quality of the moral ethos of a nation shows itself in how it treats its most vulnerable members.

MESSAGE

The Inter-generational Chain

All of us have parents. Many have children. We live in the flow of time with those who have been before us and those who come after us. Five generations can be present at any one time. All want to live. All have rights. Can these generations relate to each other constructively? Can they be aware of each other and learn from each other? Does our responsibility include responsibility for generations yet to come? Or must we believe those who speak not only of the clash of civilizations but of generational warfare?[5] In most Western countries too few people are being born to maintain the population balance and to pay the pensions for their parents and grandparents. At the same time, these same populations are hesitant to integrate foreigners into their social and economic networks. Here a mix is brewing that can easily explode into social conflicts. In addition, the life of future generations is threatened by global warming. The film narrated by Al Gore, *An Inconvenient Truth*, has in a methodical but dramatic way described what will happen if we don't find ways to deal with climate change.

---

5. The reference is to Huntington's influential book *The Clash of Civilizations and the Remaking of World Order*. Generational conflict is described in Schirrmacher's *Das Methusalem-Komplott*.

Generational Responsibility

The "fifth word" addresses a basic challenge of life. Just as the "fourth word" speaks to our existence in time, so the fifth commandment speaks to our existence in the chain of generations. Both our existence in time and our place in the ongoing human story belong to the basic facts of life. It is therefore not surprising that the Hebrew Bible links this word with the sabbath commandment and with God's passion for freedom: "You shall each revere your mother and father, and you shall keep my sabbaths: I am the LORD your God" (Lev 19:3).

The Addressees

In Ephesians 6:1-3 the commandment to "honor your father and your mother" is addressed to children. That is not the case in the decalogue. There it is addressed to adults, primarily to the man who is the head of the family. That may be disappointing to parents who often long for a bit of help as we enter the competition between the generations. What parent has not experienced the problem of authority? What parent would not enjoy the security of a given authority, installed by God, when they enter the struggle with their teenagers? Why should parents be worse off than bishops in the church, ministers of governments, and managers in business, who most of the time do not have to rest on their inherent personal authenticity, but who enjoy the privilege of a given authority that comes with the "office" they occupy? Parents often feel weak and frustrated and tired and helpless. Why should they not long for a little help from above or beyond?

The plea of parents is legitimate, of course. The breakdown of authority and the lack of respect for the elderly is certainly a major factor in the disintegration of our families and our society. Nevertheless, this commandment is not directed to children, but to adults. It is not part of a philosophy of bringing up children, but it addresses a social concern related to life, duty and respect for aging parents. Many parents have made an invaluable contribution to their immediate family and to society as a whole. I know parents in different cultures who have worked hard to provide for their family, who were there when their children fell ill or got in trouble with the law, who willingly made great sacrifices to provide for their children. But parents get old. What happens to them when they can no longer provide and produce? When leadership changes to dependency?

This issue has a personal-ethical and a social-ethical dimension. My children have a slogan on their window: "Be nice to your kids. They'll choose your nursing home." On a personal level we honor our parents by respecting them as bearers of tradition. Every generation must face the challenges of life anew. But a generation that ignores the wisdom and errors, achievements and failures of its predecessors is ill-prepared to face the future. Would the revolutions of Germany's youth in the 1960s and of America's youth in the 1970s have happened if their parents had talked about their war experiences and the associated horror and guilt and doubts? There is a creative tension between the generations. It happens all too often that parents impose their own problems or failed ambitions on their children and thus rob them of their own experience with freedom and responsibility. As children respect their parents, so parents must also be willing to let their children go and find their own way. In that sense what we read in the Epistle to the Ephesians can be applied generally: "Children . . . 'Honor your father and mother' . . . And, fathers, do not provoke your children to anger, but bring them up in the discipline and instruction of the Lord" (Eph 6:1–3).

Besides this personal dimension there is also a social-ethical dimension. Love and respect must also be addressed and applied to social structures in which people are protected when they grow old. Western societies are challenged to provide for their senior citizens by providing an adequate pension scheme, adequate medical care, senior citizen facilities, hospices, and a social ethos in which old people are not devalued in their dignity. We honor our mothers and fathers by allowing them to grow old with dignity and respect.

"Ageism"

Ageism, like racism, sexism, and slavery, is an ugly word. But it describes a reality that will intensify in the years ahead. It means discrimination against old people—the parent generation. The actress Doris Roberts of *Everybody Loves Raymond* fame spoke in 2002 to the United States Senate Special Aging Committee: Image of Aging in Media and Marketing.[6] The following is an excerpt of what she said:

> I'm in my seventies, at the peak of my career, at the height of my earned income and tax contribution. . . . Yet society considers me discard-able, my opinions irrelevant, my needs comical and my tastes not worth attention in the marketplace. My peers and I are

---

6. Doris Roberts, "Statement to US Senate."

Generational Responsibility

> portrayed as dependent, helpless, unproductive and demanding rather than deserving. . . . I'm here to urge you to address the devastation, cost and loss that we as a nation suffer because of age discrimination. . . . younger and younger actresses are visiting the plastic surgeon. Actresses in their twenties are getting Botox injections to prevent wrinkles from forming. Women start getting tummy tucks and facelifts in their thirties to forestall the day when the phone stops ringing. When a woman hits the age of forty Hollywood executives think she's too old.
>
> Mr. Chairman, I address you today as a person young in spirit, full of life and energy and eager to stay engaged in the world and fight ageism, the last bastion of bigotry. Its no different from sexism, racism or religious discrimination. It is a tyranny that suppresses us all at any stage and serves no one. As my late husband the writer William Goyen said, when we see infirm people, handicapped or older people, turn away from them and we take away their light. Popular culture has taken away our light. I'm here to urge you to bring it back.

It is obvious. Old people have become a problem—at least in Western societies. On the one hand they remind us incessantly that we shall all have to die. There will be no exception. The culture tries to repress that fact by glorifying youth, beauty and glamour. On the other hand, old people have become a threat. We live longer and have fewer children. The demography is clear and brutal. The old/young ratio will increase more and more in favor of the old. There will be more and more old people. They are a burden on the health and social security systems. They take our hospital beds and we have to build more and more senior citizen homes, hostels and hospices.

Old people hear and see and feel all this and internalize it. They lose their self-esteem, their self-confidence, their identity and pride. Subconsciously they begin to feel guilty for being alive.

A culture of freedom will not discard or devalue old people. Rather it will seek for and find ways to appreciate and utilize their knowledge, wisdom and competence. One of my professors once told me that in academia there should be a rule that no one should publish anything before turning fifty years of age. Konrad Adenauer was 73 years of age when he became the first chancellor of the Federal Republic of Germany and he remained in that position until he was 87 years of age. Ian Paisley became the First Minister of Ireland at the age of 81. There are artists and poets who have produced their best work after the age of sixty or even seventy. There is no reason for old people to hide. They are important players in a culture of freedom. They must assert their place, and a mature society will grant it to them. The commandment says not only to honor your father and mother, but it also contains the promise "that your days may be long and that it may go well with you in the land that the LORD your God is giving you."

Euthanasia

The above brings us directly to one of the most debated moral issues of our time, the problem of euthanasia. "Euthanasia" derives from the Greek and means "good death." Originally it had the purpose of making the dying of a person as comfortable as possible. In our society the hospice movement, palliative care, and the use of modern technology and modern medicines allow most people to die with dignity, surrounded by care, and with as little pain as possible. In most countries it is permitted to decline unwanted medical treatment and refuse "being hooked up to machines." With *active* euthanasia it is different. Active euthanasia (also called "mercy killing") is the intentional termination of a person's life to end their suffering. Many countries struggle with that issue. In Oregon (USA), the Netherlands, and Belgium active euthanasia is legal. Other countries, like Switzerland, experiment with a middle way whereby active euthanasia is forbidden while "assisted suicide" or "assisted death" is legal.

In an ideal world, many of us may like to have a doctor like Dr. Max Schur. Max Schur had become Sigmund Freud's personal physician in 1929. Freud had cancer in his mouth and nose. When they met, Freud said to his doctor: "Promise me: when the time comes, you won't let them torment me unnecessarily." Schur promised, and they shook hands on it. The time came ten years later, shortly after Freud had moved from Vienna to London. An operation had weakened him. He was over 80 years of age. "Schur, you remember our 'contract' not to leave me in the lurch when the time comes. Now it is nothing but torture and makes no sense." Freud asked Schur to "talk it over with Anna (his beloved daughter and carer), and if she thinks it's right, then make an end of it." Peter Gay in his Freud biography describes the final phase: "On September 21, Schur injected Freud with three centigrams of morphine—the normal dose for sedation was two centigrams—and Freud sank into a peaceful sleep. Schur repeated the injection, when he became restless, and administered a final one the next day,

Generational Responsibility

September 22. Freud lapsed into a coma from which he did not awake. He died at three in the morning, September 23, 1939."[7]

But we don't live in an ideal world. It is distasteful but true that materialism, consumerism, and greed can lower the moral barrier, especially when people may profit from the early death of a person. In a culture that tends to evaluate people by their ability to produce and consume, old and sick people often feel sidelined. If you add rising hospital costs, lack of sufficient hospital beds and aged care places, then old people readily feel that they are no longer of use to society and therefore are no longer worthy and wanted.

A society that rewards achievement and glorifies youth and health needs to be extra-sensitive toward old people. They have made their contribution, and now they must be made to feel that they can sit back with a good conscience. My primary reason for opposing euthanasia is the suspicion that in our success-oriented culture, with our pension funds running dry, and with the claim that the present working generation can no longer shoulder the needs of the previous generation, an ethos is wide-spread in which older people are made to feel superfluous and expendable—and when the older people themselves internalize that thinking, then euthanasia may become an attractive option.

What needs to be done, however, is to improve palliative care. Given the fact that we all have to die, we now have the know-how to make death, at least the physical side of it, relatively comfortable. It belongs among my most sacred moments to sit with my mother during the last few days and hours and minutes of her life. Holding the hand of a woman who had lived a hard but meaningful life, who had finished the course and was now ready to go, was a great and rare privilege.

The Family

Although the family is not addressed as such in this commandment, it provides the background for generational responsibility and is an invaluable institution in a culture of freedom. *The International Bill of Human Rights* recognizes the family as "the natural and fundamental group unit of society" which "is entitled to protection by society and the State."[8] Nevertheless,

---

7. Cited from Gay, *Freud*, 629–51.

8. *Universal Declaration of Human Rights*, §16:3; *International Covenant on Economic, Social and Cultural Rights*, §10; *International Covenant on Civil and Political Rights*, §23.

in many countries the institution of the family has fallen on hard times. Divorce rates are rising. Family violence, even child-abuse is not uncommon. Many teenagers in their most formative years do not experience the family as a safe space. But despite these negatives the family is an important institution for a culture of freedom. At best, the family is the space where unconditional love and trust is experienced, selfless sacrifice is practiced and where people accept responsibility for each other. This provides the context in which maturing children experience meaning, discipline and freedom.

Families are different in different cultures, and the institution is subject to constant change. In many countries the man is no longer the patriarch who provides income and security, while his wife manages the affairs at home. Children no longer blindly obey their parents. Hierarchy is being replaced by partnership. Women have become an important part of the work force, men are learning to accept responsibility at home, and children are protected "from economic and social exploitation."[9] Yet despite all the changes, the family remains the irreplaceable environment for children and their growth to maturity. So far no alternative has evolved. In a functioning family children acquire a basic trust and confidence that will be the foundation for a meaningful and successful life.

But great challenges remain. Men and women find it exceedingly difficult to be successful both at home and in their profession. Women who thrive and succeed in the professional world often discover too late that they really wanted to have the experience of motherhood. A growing individualism, increasing material expectation and a basic mistrust of intimate and lasting relationships continue to challenge functioning and successful family life. But the fact remains that so far we have not developed a better institution in which love can be guarded and in which children can be introduced to a culture of freedom.

Responsible Freedom

Being woven into the chain of generations, we realize that there is not only a selfishness of individuals. There is also a selfishness of generations. If our generation brutalizes people and nature, will our children and grandchildren not have to curse us? We have heard of the German children who criticized their fathers who fought in World War II. We have heard of the

---

9. *International Covenant on Economic, Social and Cultural Rights*, §10:3.

Generational Responsibility

American sons and daughters who could not understand how Hiroshima, Nagasaki and Vietnam could have happened. We have heard the cries and seen the scars of the children of Chernobyl.

I would like to quote here from a significant book of our time. Hans Jonas, in *The Imperative of Responsibility: In Search of an Ethics for the Technological Age*, reformulates Immanuel Kant's categorical imperative for our time:

> "Act so that the effects of your action are compatible with the permanence of genuine human life," or expressed negatively: "Act so that the effects of your action are not destructive for the future possibility of such life," or simply: "Do not compromise the conditions for an indefinite continuation of humanity on earth," or, again turned positive: "In your present choices, include the future wholeness of Man among the objects of your will."[10]

"Honoring" our mother and father protests against the selfishness of a generation. Life is more than share-value and possessing the latest gadgets. It includes respect for the wisdom of the elders. Even if our fathers and mothers have not been the best, we are still called to occupy our place in the ongoing process of human life. The verb "to honor" therefore suggests we responsibly use the freedom that God has given to us. It does not say that we are "to obey our parents unquestioningly" or that we are "to fear" or even "to worship" our parents. We are to give them the respect arising from the fact that without them we would not be here, and we are now responsible for the quality of life that we pass on to the next generation.

A "Disobedient" Son

The Jesus story includes episodes of being disobedient to his parents and of a seemingly harsh disregard for his natural family. In apparent indifference to his human mother and brothers Jesus said: "Whoever does the will of God is my brother, and sister, and mother" (Mark 3:31–35). He forbade a potential follower to fulfill his human duty of laying his father to rest (Luke 9:59–60), and he said such strong words as: "Whoever comes to me and does not hate father and mother, wife and children, brothers and sisters, yes, and even life itself, cannot be my disciple" (Luke 14:26). Can such stark pronouncements be inter-related with the word to honor father and mother, and how can we relate these demands to our faith in Jesus?

---

10. Jonas, *The Imperative of Responsibility*, 11.

Toward a Culture of Freedom

The Gospel of Luke (2:41–51) tells the story of his parents taking Jesus on a long journey to the Passover feast in Jerusalem. They traveled in a larger group, and they remained some days in Jerusalem before they commenced their return journey home. Suddenly, the parents miss Jesus. But they suspect that he is with friends and relatives and will probably turn up when they take up camp for the night. But he did not turn up. They had to return to Jerusalem and seek him. "After three days they found him in the temple, sitting among the teachers, listening to them and asking them questions" (Luke 2:46). "Son," his mother laments, "why have you treated us like this? Look, your father and I have been searching for you in great anxiety" (Luke 2:48). But Jesus speaks about another parent, another authority in his life: "Did you not know that I must be in my Father's house?" They did not understand his reply, but "his mother treasured all these things in her heart" (Luke 2:51).

This story illustrates a fundamental problem in the chain of generations. The young Jesus does not simply adopt the faith of his parents, and he does not use the word "God" to justify established customs, norms and values. He wants to find out for himself what "God" means. He goes to the center of his religion, the temple. And there he discovers that faith in God can entail a struggle with established tradition. To really honor mother and father may in certain situations mean not to fulfill their wishes and expectations. Honoring one's parents is therefore also a challenge to the parents. When children are young they need to learn and obey certain rules. They need to learn not to run on to a busy street, not to play with matches, and not to ill treat cats and dogs and birds. But such rules are transitions to maturity. As children become mature, parents must allow them to discover and exercise their own freedom and discipline.

Jesus had heard the story of faith from his parents, but now, as he is becoming an adult, the story gains its own momentum. Every person must accept responsibility for what he or she has heard and understood. Jesus honors his father and mother by letting their story rule his life, even when they don't understand. He honors them, against their understanding, by letting God be God in his life. The "fifth word" does not cancel the first and second commandment but implements them as they relate to our place in the flux of generations.

Generational Responsibility and Freedom of Conscience

On the surface Jesus disobeyed his parents. But in a deeper sense he was true to what he had learned from them. How often would he have heard from his parents that God incites ultimate commitment?

> Hear, O Israel: The LORD is our God, the LORD *alone*. You shall love the LORD your God with *all* your heart, and with *all* your soul, and with *all* your might. Keep these words that I am commanding you today in your heart. *Recite them to your children* and talk about them when you are at home and when you are away, when you lie down and when you rise. Bind them as a sign on your hand, fix them as an emblem on your forehead, and write them on the doorposts of your house and on your gates. (Deut 6:4–9, emphases mine)

Jesus lived in a patriarchal world with clear delineations of authority and power. Into that world, dominated by hierarchy and power, Jesus opens up a new vision by introducing the value of familial responsibility among the generations. Not hierarchy, but partnership among adults in a community of equals. The authority of the parent is not absolute. There comes the time when sons and daughters become adults themselves and as such must accept responsibility for their own lives. For the believer this responsibility includes the distinction between loyalty to God and respect for one's parents. There need not be a conflict. But if there is a conflict then the adult son and daughter may in good conscience disagree with their parents. How many parents have spoken of God and God's ways at home, but when their children took them at their word, they were puzzled, or even turned away in disappointment and anger.

This inter-generational tension stands behind Jesus' stark critique of cultural norms. When a potential follower wanted to fulfill his national, social and religious duty toward his parents first—"Lord, first let me go and bury my father"—Jesus replied: "Let the dead bury their own dead; but as for you, go and proclaim the kingdom of God" (Luke 9:59–60; Matt 8:21–22). Also the strong words in Luke 14:26 come to mind: "Whoever comes to me and does not hate father and mother, wife and children, brothers and sisters, yes, and even life itself, cannot be my disciple." These saying do not mean that Jesus intentionally disrespects families and family customs. They want to emphasize that there is a difference between obedience to God and family loyalty, between ultimate and penultimate commitments.[11] Jesus

---

11. See the discussion of ultimate and penultimate commitments in ch. 3.

questions the ultimate authority of the patriarch. There are limits, even to the authority of parents. There comes the time in each parent's life where they must "let their children go" and trust that they will now shape their own life in personal responsibility.

This commandment promises that if we follow the call of God in our lives, then we shall "live long in the land which the LORD your God is giving you." In that sense Jesus is the model son because he obeys God. And his mother is the model parent because although she does not quite understand, she remains open to the mysterious ways of God in her life and in the life of her son.

Conclusion

We live in a broken world. Parents and children are often at war with each other; child abuse is the order of the day; parents die as forgotten people; the traditional family does not seem to work, and yet there are no promising alternatives; authority structures are eroding. Perhaps the word to "honor your father and your mother, that your days may be long in the land which the LORD your God is giving you" can remind us that a living faith in God and respect and care for each other carries within itself the promise of the surprise and blessing of God.

Let not our freedom degenerate into individualism and selfishness. Let us, ever again, turn to Jesus Christ in faith and let that faith nourish our freedom. Then the promise at the end of the Hebrew Bible will be fulfilled: God "will turn the hearts of parents to their children and the hearts of children to their parents" (Mal 4:6).

8

Becoming Servants of Life
The Sixth Word

"You shall not kill"

Exodus 20:13 and Deuteronomy 5:17
Related texts: Genesis 4; Judges 19–21; Numbers 35:9–34;
1 Kings 21; Matthew 5:21–22

THEOLOGICAL COMMENTS

WHERE THE DECALOGUE IS understood to be written on two stone tablets (Exod 34:28; Deut 4:13, 10:1–5), "you shall not kill" could be the first saying on the second tablet,[1] paralleling "I am the LORD your God" on the first. This is an analogy to Jesus' double commandment of love: to love God and to love one's neighbor (Mark 12:28–31). The rest of the commandments on the second tablet can all be seen as illustrations of the one not to kill. Committing adultery, stealing, bearing false witness, and coveting, all lead to a diminishing of life.

The theological basis for protecting human life is that God is its creator and that God has created humans in God's own image (Gen 1:27, 9:6b). The biblical story therefore emphasizes that reverence for the creator goes hand in hand with respect for God's creation and with a special leaning towards the needy and disadvantaged. The Psalmist gathers up the tendency and the intention of the whole biblical message when he hears God speaking into his conscience: "Give justice to the weak and the orphan; maintain the right of the lowly and the destitute" (Ps 82:3). And the writer of Proverbs relates

---

1. See the introductory remarks to the previous chapter.

this directly to God's action in history: "the LORD pleads their cause" (Prov 22:22). Indeed, "those who oppress the poor insult their Maker, but those who are kind to the needy honor him" (Prov 14:31).

The main question with regard to this "word" is how to understand and translate the Hebrew verb *ratsach*. It could mean "to kill" (so the AV and the RSV) or "to murder" (so the NRSV). Taking a person's life is one thing, taking it *with intent* is quite another. The meaning of *ratsach* is controversial. It is seldom used: only 47 times in the Hebrew Bible; mostly (33 times) in connection with cities of refuge where a killer or murderer or victim of blood revenge could find refuge until proper court proceedings could be instigated.

Given the culture of the day and given the general teachings in the Hebrew Bible, originally this commandment neither referred to killings in war nor to capital punishment (Exod 21:12; Num 35:30; Lev 24:17; Deut 27:24). It also does not address the question of killing animals.

Many want to translate "you shall not *murder*." That would limit the commandment to intentional, illegal and morally depraved acts of killing. It would not cover unintentional killings, nor would it include killing by omission. However, such limitation does not work because the verb *ratsach* is used in texts that specifically refer to unintentional killing, and to providing refuge for those who have unintentionally killed (see Deut 4:41–42; 19:1–13; Num 35:11, 15; Josh 20:3). The translation "to *kill*" is therefore the more inclusive translation. It covers the following dimensions of intentional and unintentional killings:

- unintentional killings (e.g., Deut 4:41–42; Num 35:11,15; Josh 20:3);
- intentional killing/murder (e.g., Num 35:16–18; Exod 21:12; Lev 24:17; Deut 27:24; Isa 1:21; Hos 6:9; Job 24:14; Prov 22:13; Ps 94:6);
- blood revenge (Num 35:12, 19, 27);
- rape and the resultant violent death (Judg 19–21, "the killed/murdered woman" ([Judg 20:4]; Deut 22:25–26);
- Elijah uses *ratsach* to denounce King Ahab for killing Naboth. Ahab obviously misused his power and bent the law in his favor, even though he himself did not do the killing! (1 Kgs 21);
- the killing of orphans, strangers, widows (Ps 94:6) and poor people (Job 24:14).

Becoming Servants of Life

Whatever translation we use—"to kill" or "to murder"—it must become clear that this "word" seeks to protect people from acts of violence. Such violence diminishes human life and thereby disregards human dignity within a given social order. This includes intentional and unintentional killing. The covenantal context is important. It suggests that "killing" violates the ethos and structures of a given society. "Hence it means anti-social killing."[2] For us the given society is not only the country and culture in which we live but also the international community of nations. Its ethos is described in the *International Bill of Human Rights* which asserts the right to life, and then concretely spells out what that means by trying to eliminate war, resisting the death penalty, and opposing slavery, torture and child abuse. The covenantal context of the decalogue helps us to apply the commandments to our situation.

Although in its original context this "word" is not directly related to such issues as war, capital punishment, suicide, abortion and the killing of animals, we must not forget that in Old Testament days a vision of God, of the world, of life emerges which touches on these matters:

- a vision of *shalom* (all-encompassing salvation) in which swords are converted into plough shares (Isa 2:2–4; Mic 4:1–3);
- a vision in which humanity and nature are no longer adversaries (Isa 11:6–8);
- a vision of "new heavens and a new earth" when peace, justice and harmony shall reign (Isa 65:17–25).
- a vision in which death will no longer have the final say (Isa 25:6).

Both the Hebrew and the Christian Bible trace "killing" and "murder" to their roots in the "hearts" of human persons:

> You shall not hate in your heart anyone of your kin; you shall reprove your neighbor, or you will incur guilt yourself. You shall not take vengeance or bear a grudge against any of your people, but you shall love your neighbor as yourself: I am the LORD. (Lev 19:17–18)

> You have heard that it was said to those of ancient times, "You shall not murder"; and "whoever murders shall be liable to judgment." But I say to you that if you are angry with a brother or sister, you

---

2. Von Rad, *Deuteronomy*, 59.

will be liable to judgment; and if you insult a brother or sister, you will be liable to the council; and if you say, "You fool," you will be liable to the hell of fire. (Matt 5:21–22)

MESSAGE

Introduction

This commandment is also widely upheld outside the circle of Judaism and Christianity. Pacifists, vegetarians, anti-abortionists, campaigners against the death penalty, and societies for the prevention of cruelty to animals all repeat the divine word with a passion: "you shall not kill!"

We honor the apostles of life who have authentically fleshed out this commandment. Albert Schweitzer, for instance, not only spent his life to heal others but also showed his reverence for life by collecting a rain worm from the hot asphalt and placing it under the protective leaves of a bush besides the road. We esteem Francis of Assisi who embraced the flowers and the birds in his worship of God. We admire Mohandas Gandhi and Martin Luther King Jr. who have credibly demonstrated that a commitment to non-violence is not weakness but strength in the service of life. Indeed, there is an authentic ring to this commandment, sounding a chord within each one of us: "You shall not kill!" Indeed the implication is that if you are a believer in the God who sources and sustains life, then "you will not kill!"

Nevertheless, when this word comes into contact with reality things become difficult. The very commandment that is both serene in its simplicity and convincing with an inherent authenticity becomes the focus of controversy. What does "to kill" mean? Does it include killing in war? Of course not, the experts say. The Hebrew Bible is replete with stories of war, where whole nations are wiped out with divine approval. Does it relate to suicide and abortion? Of course not, others say; none of the texts that have used the verb "to kill" refer to such killings. Does it forbid capital punishment? Of course not. The Hebrew Bible is full of texts where intentional killing calls for the death penalty. Does it have anything to do with shooting animals for the pleasure of killing? Of course not, say those who like to shoot animals, and indeed the killing of animals is not forbidden in the Bible. And what about the child that dies of starvation or of preventable disease every two seconds in our world? And what about the tens of thousands who starve to death every day? Has that anything to do with killing? Of course not, we say. We did not kill them and we did not want them to die!

Thus in actual reality, where the rubber hits the runway, this "word" seems to die the death of a thousand qualifications. It remains out there in its serene beauty, but it seems to have little to do with the everyday reality of life and its challenges. It is a little like the glorification of the virgin Mary, who in her virginity and untouchable purity has become a symbol of supreme beauty and holiness, but who has little identifying power with the real women of today—the mother who does not have enough milk to breast feed her child; the wife who is regularly beaten up by her drunken husband; the single woman who has to work all day to feed her children. Or we are reminded of the minstrels in the Middle Ages who would adore a woman, compose songs and sing them to her, knowing all the time that they will never be able to touch her. Is our commandment one of untouchable beauty, or have we perhaps made it into that because we don't *want* it to touch our lives?

So here we are. We all affirm "you shall not kill," but we don't apply it to ourselves. We don't kill, and therefore this "word" is not related to our life. It may be the word of God for others—but not for us. Yet, let us look a little closer. It may yet become God's word to us.

"Killing"

We saw that the translation of the Hebrew verb used here (*ratsach*) is controversial. If we translate "to murder" then it would only refer to those killings which are intentional, motivated by hatred and revenge and forbidden by law. Murder includes the intent to kill. The text would then emphasize what we all know, what we all agree with, and what is therefore of no immediate challenge to us: "You shall not *intentionally* kill (= murder) another member of your species." Even though a different verb is used in the Cain and Abel story, Cain's murder of his brother is a salient reminder that to murder someone is wrong (Gen 4). The awful story of the gang rape and subsequent murder of a concubine, "the murdered/killed woman" (Judg 20:4), so dramatically told in Judges 19–21, is abhorrent to us. Also the judicial murder of Naboth, who wanted to defend the right to his family property even against the desires of the king, we find detestable (1 Kgs 21).

Many of us also maintain that this commandment can't be applied to killings in war and to capital punishment, because the Old Testament is replete with references to war and capital punishment. We therefore translate "you shall not murder"—thereby stating the obvious with which everyone agrees and which therefore has no moral power to impinge upon our life. We can then leave the commandment behind. It does not touch us. We are no murderers! And those who are, are taken care of by our laws and legal systems. Our commandment therefore simply underlines a basic conviction of universal morality. All people agree that murder is wrong!

But it may not be as simple as that. Perhaps we prefer that explanation because it suits us. Then the commandment is no direct challenge to our daily life, and we can keep God's claim upon us at a distance. Yet at a closer look we may have to admit that the translation "to murder" is as deficient as the translation "to kill."

It is true that the verb in our text does not refer to every kind of killing. It is also true that evil intentions often, but not always, play a role. But at the same time, there are a number of texts that specifically refer to people who have unintentionally killed another person (Deut 4:41–42; Num 35:11, 15; Josh 20:3). And there are also texts that indicate a certain leaning by specifically mentioning the killing of defenseless and helpless people, like widows, orphans, strangers and poor people (Ps 94:6; Job 24:14).

With due caution I therefore suggest that the Hebrew verb *ratsach* refers to killing—intentional and unintentional—that transgresses the community ethos. It denotes killing that arises out of selfishness and self-interest, which are often the result of excessive individualism. You should neither rape a defenseless girl, nor kill your defenseless neighbor (Deut 22:26). When Ahab, the powerful king, and Jezebel his wife had the farmer Naboth killed in order to get his vineyard, the law may be on their side, but in the community ethos they are condemned for killing a defenseless person (1 Kgs 21:19). The opposite concepts would be "to be just" and "to be true and helpful to the community." Consequently, to comprehend fully the meaning of the verb "to kill" in the "sixth word," four motifs are important:

- The killing may be intentional or unintentional. The translation "you shall not murder" is too limiting and therefore inadequate.
- Special mention is made of the killing of the defenseless and the innocent, of those who have no voice, no power, and no friends—the wretched of the earth.
- The commandment wants to break the vicious cycle of revenge. Cities of refuge were established to protect those who killed unintentionally, and also to protect people from blood revenge. Even the murderer Cain

is protected by God, because otherwise the killing would go on and on and the spiral of violence would never end.
- This commandment wants both to protect the community against the forces of death and invite members of the community to become servants of life.

If this reasoning is correct, then this word becomes highly relevant for our situation. Today we speak of the global community because all major challenges to the dignity and survival of human life—climate change, the threat of nuclear war, poverty, HIV/AIDS—are global. We must therefore ask what it means "not to kill" in our situation where we are all part of the global village. Following the barbarism of World War II, world leaders decided to lay the foundation for a future of peace and justice. The United Nations was founded and the *International Bill of Human Rights* was proclaimed to provide the structures for an ethos that would focus on peace, not war, reconciliation, not separation, justice, not social Darwinism. It is one of the tragedies of modern history that at a time when this new global ethos needed to be demonstrated, a coalition of countries under the leadership of the USA—the same USA that took the lead in establishing the United Nations and then provided the chairperson of the Human Rights Commission, Eleanor Roosevelt,which shaped the *Universal Declaration of Human Rights*—started a preemptive war against Iraq without the approval of the Security Council of the United Nations. This is a modern example of "blood revenge" in which the USA, following the awful terrorist attacks of September 11, 2001, declared a "war on terror" and initiated an attack against Iraq, even though it has been shown that Saddam Hussein had nothing to do with those attacks. The vicious cycle of violence and revenge needs to be broken. The "word" not to kill is an invitation in that direction.

"Being Angry"

Laws and rules cannot organize becoming servants of life and pursuing a culture of freedom. They arise from the depth of our being. We become aware that the desire to kill is rooted deep within us. In the book of Leviticus we read: "You shall not hate in your heart anyone of your kin; you shall reprove your neighbor, or you will incur guilt yourself. You shall not take vengeance or bear a grudge against any of your people, but you shall love your neighbor as yourself: I am the LORD" (Lev 19:17–18). Jesus universalizes this interpretation: "You have heard that it was said to those of ancient times, 'You shall not kill'; and 'whoever kills shall be liable to judgment.' But I say to you that if you are angry with a brother or sister, you will be liable to judgment; and if you insult a brother or sister, you will be liable to the council; and if you say: 'You fool!' you will be liable to the hell of fire" (Matt 5:21–22).

What is determinative for Christians—namely, the radical interpretation of Jesus—has been part of the intention of the "sixth word" from the beginning. The battle over the right translation—"kill" or "murder"—does not release us from the claim that through this word, God invites us to become servants of life. It is too narrow and too legalistic an interpretation if we only ask what the surface meaning of the Hebrew word *ratsach* is. The underlying intention of the text is to resist any attempt to violate the dignity of life and thereby transgress against the community ethos.

War

The modern nation state was founded on centering authority and power in the government. Rivaling groups in the same country had to surrender their arms to the central governing authority. Different interest groups and political parties within the same country had to learn how to solve their conflicts without the institution of war. That is the challenge for the global village today—learning to solve conflicts without resorting to war; abrogating the idea that war remains an acceptable political instrument—even if only used in what governments consider to be a last resort.

One of the aims of the United Nations is "to save succeeding generations from the scourge of war."[3] In order to facilitate that aim, "all members" of the United Nations agree to refrain "from the threat or use of force against the territorial integrity or political independence of any state . . . ."[4] That was 1945. Nearly 20 million military personnel and nearly 30 million civilians lost their lives in World War II. But such figures are too sterile to capture the bestiality and carnage of war—of each and every war. The raping of women. The brutalizing of young men and women who are taught to hate and to shoot first. Men who become killing machines, and when they return home they impose the agonies of their soul on wives and children.

---

3. Preamble to the *Charter of the United Nations*.
4. *Charter of the United Nations*, §I:2, 4.

No matter how sophisticated one's argument may be, the fact remains that soldiers are taught to kill. In war people kill and are killed. Indeed, most killings in war happen with intent. They fall under the "sixth word." Of course, we all know that war is as old as humankind. The ancient wars between nomads and settlers may be reflected in the Cain and Abel story. The Old Testament is full of war stories, wars often claimed to be commanded and validated by God. But Jesus has opened up a more radical insight into the being of God. While the original version of the "sixth word" was situated in Israel and its covenant with God, we now live in a global village searching for a universal ethos that is coherent with the nature of the God who "created heaven and earth." In addition to this universal emphasis, one of the characteristic marks of the Jesus story is Jesus' radical commitment to nonviolence, a tradition which has its roots in the Hebrew Bible where the days are foreshadowed that swords will be converted into ploughshares and God's *shalom* would cover the earth (Isa 2:2–4; Mic 4:1–3). By virtue of Jesus' resurrection from the dead, his commitment to nonviolence is given universal status and as such becomes an invitation issuing from the same God who invites people not to kill.[5]

When Christianity first came on the scene, there was a brief dawning of the vision of *shalom*. Up to the fourth century, when Christianity became the official religion of the Roman Empire, Christians largely refused to participate in war. Even in the *corpus christianum*, the marriage between state and church, theologians took over philosophical ideas and developed the so-called "just war" theory. Ethical guidelines—that a war must be declared by a legitimate authority, that civilians must be protected, that the situation after the war must be better than before the war, that the war must pursue a just cause, and be declared for the right motivation—were developed with the intention was to implement the Christian vision of life and to avoid war if at all possible. Nevertheless, against its own intention, up to the present day the "just war" theory is used by church and state to justify war. But given the modern military technology and the widespread availability of nuclear weapons, there is no justification for modern war. But, as the Iraq war eloquently demonstrates, war is still being used as an instrument of politics, ideology and economics.

Those who say that war will always be with us may need to recall some historical facts. Had we asked a Roman citizen 2000 years ago or an

---

5. I have argued this in more detail in "Waging Peace Today."

American slave-owner in Mississippi 200 years ago whether the acceptance of *slavery* would ever be consigned to history, they would have said a loud and clear "No." Slavery will always be with us! It is written into the laws of the universe. God ordains it. Our whole economy would break down without slaves. But as we all know, slavery is universally outlawed today.

Had we asked a philosopher or theologian 1000 years ago, and indeed too many people still today, whether a *woman is equal to a man*, they would have laughed. Male is spiritual, female is material; male is bound to heaven, female is bound to earth; the woman must be and always will be subordinate to the man—this is what they would have thought and said. Fortunately, at least in theory, those days are gone.

Had we asked Afrikaners in South Africa fifty years ago whether *apartheid* was doomed, they would have said "No," and they would have quoted from the Bible, which in their eyes confirmed that apartheid was an expression of the will of God. Thank God, apartheid is now history.

If slavery, apartheid and the subordination of women can be repudiated, why can't the family of nations learn to solve their conflicts without the institution of war? It certainly is a challenge to the religions of the world to refuse using the word "God" or "Allah" or "Krishna" or "Buddha" to validate violence. What a difference it would make if the religions of the world demonstrated that they are servants of life by refusing to sanction killing and by opposing modern warfare.

Capital Punishment

With the founding of the United Nations and the adoption of the *Universal Declaration of Human Rights*, a worldwide movement to eradicate the death penalty commenced. The *Universal Declaration*—"a common standard of achievement for all peoples and all nations"—asserts, "everyone has the right to life, liberty and security of person" (§3). This moral declaration is applied to the death penalty in the *International Covenant on Civil and Political Rights* (1966/1976), which has international legal status for countries that have ratified it. There the abolishing of the death penalty is encouraged. It is only permissible "for the most serious crimes" (§6). Within the European Union capital punishment has been banned altogether.[6]

---

6. This happened with the entry into force on 1 July 2003 of "Protocol No. 13 to the European Convention on Human Rights, concerning the abolition of the death penalty in all circumstances."

Yet there are still many countries—chief among them the USA, China, Iran, Singapore, Malaysia, Indonesia, Japan, South Korea and Taiwan—which use the death penalty as part of their legal and criminal system.[7] In a culture of freedom, respect for all human life is fundamental and therefore requires a clear rejection of capital punishment.

Abortion

Abortion is a very sensitive issue in many societies. It is neither helpful to criminalize nor to trivialize it. Whatever one's opinion may be, the fact is that with abortion a human life, which is growing in the mother's womb—a fetus or an embryo—is removed and destroyed. This has a tremendous effect on the mother, but beyond it, it also affects the ethos of a society in which human life is valued. The word "you shall not kill," referring to an anti-social act, therefore, applies here.

Since God is the giver and sustainer of life and since God has also provided salvation for a failed or sinful life, it belongs to the highest task of human society to protect human life. Human life, like all of life, is a process. The process starts with conception. It continues with the embryo becoming a fetus and growing in the mother's womb. Its movements can be seen and felt. The woman understands herself as "mother" and her partner as "father." They are "parents" even before the child is actually born.

In Australia, it is estimated that there are more than 80,000 abortions a year.[8] In the United States it is over ten times that number.[9] In the former USSR there were more abortions than births from 1957 to 1991.[10] A society that does not address the problem of abortion or fails to see it as a problem must be named a "sick society." Human life has become cheap and expendable. Nevertheless, the problem cannot be solved with laws and the criminal system. Governments, churches and other institutions need to find ways to create an ethos in which human life is accepted and valued, both by parents and by society as a whole. It is unfortunate that in some western countries the anti-abortion movement has become associated with the "right" (who

---

7. A complete list of countries that have either retained or abolished the death penalty can be found under http://web.amnesty.org/pages/deathpenalty-countries-eng. An important source of information and inspiration is *Amnesty International* which is engaged in a world wide campaign against the death penalty.

8. Pratt, Briggs, and Buckmaster, *Parliamentary Library Research Brief*, 2.

9. Monahan, "U. S. Statistics."

10. Johnston, "Historical Abortion Statistics, U.S.S.R."

often seem to have no problem with war) while the anti-war movement is linked with the "left" (who often seem to have no problem with abortion). A pro-life stance in a culture of freedom should help develop a climate in which both abortion and war are opposed.

This does not mean that all abortions can be avoided. In a conflict situation, where for instance one would have to choose between the life of the mother and the life of an unborn child, one may well opt for the life of the mother. Since it is vitally important that the newly born life is welcomed, accepted and loved, arguably, one should not compel a rape victim to carry her child to term against her will. But given such exceptions, the commandment "not to kill" encourages a culture of freedom in which human life in all its stages is welcomed and protected.

A Culture of Death

War, capital punishment, and abortion on demand are symptoms of a culture of death. We may add that there are 12 million refugees in our world. They are transported from camp to camp. No one wants them. They are the outcasts of modern society. Half of them are children. Every day 35,000 children under the age of 5 are dying—that is 250,000 each week, 13 million each year. Half of them could be saved with very little money and very little effort. Four simple measures would save 20,000 children each day:

- Growth monitoring (weighing and measuring the child at regular intervals until it is three years of age). This would make the parents aware of impending malnutrition.
- Oral re-hydration, which can save the lives of half a million children a year.
- Breast-feeding, which is still the best way to immunize children for the first six months of their lives against common infections.
- A five-dollar course of immunization against measles, diphtheria, whooping cough, tetanus, tuberculosis, and poliomyelitis. This could save another 25% of the children who die under the age of five.[11]

But there is no money. Governments must pay back debts and they must buy arms, and all of us profit from that. We can kill by omission. If

---

11. These measures and the preceding statistics can be found on the website of the World Health Organization, http://www/who.int.

someone is struggling in the water and we refuse to pull her out, if someone is naked or hungry and we refuse her warm clothes or bread to protect her from freezing or from starving to death, then we have killed by failing to act.

The children who die each day are innocent. They were simply born at the wrong time and in the wrong place. What kind of a human community is it that could save 20,000 children a day with what it costs to purchase seven fighter planes—but fails to do it? Has the word "you shall not kill" nothing to say to us who, with our right to vote and our taxes, allow this to happen?

In order to interpret such a situation, we have to dig a little deeper. When the texts in Pentateuch and from Jesus—see above the reference to Leviticus 19 and Matthew 5—suggest that killing includes not only the outward action but also the inward motivation, and when the verb *ratsach* also includes unintentional killing, their intent is not to make us feel bad. They intend to shake us into awareness and make us face reality. Of course, none of us is a murderer by intention. Indeed, most of us, I would assume, are very nice people who would not want to harm anybody. But, do you think that this word speaks only to the few murderers in our prisons or to the warlords in our world? Who is responsible for the killing fields in our world—in Iraq and Sudan and the Congo and Afghanistan and East Timor and in Myanmar? Is it really always the "others"? Or could it be that what goes on in the world is the outward manifestation of what goes on in our hearts?

Erich Fromm once said:

> man differs from the animal by the fact that he is a killer; he is the only primate that kills and tortures members of his own species without any reason, either biological or economic, and who feels satisfaction in doing so. . . . It is this "malignant" aggression that constitutes the real problem and the danger to man's existence as a species . . . .[12]

That applies to all of us. Need we be reminded of the old biblical sayings that "the inclination of the human heart is evil from youth" (Gen 8:21) and that "the wages of sin is death" (Rom 6:23)? Death is the reality that determines our life. Our hating and unconcern and killing are manifestations

---

12. Fromm, *The Anatomy of Human Destructiveness*, 24–25, compare also 148, 251, 294.

of death. Whether we like it or not, we are all servants of death: the death of economic exploitation; the death of social unconcern; the death of seeing the worst rather than the best in others; the death of passive spectatorship. Sin is to be and to remain a servant of death. Sin is the despair we feel in the face of the powerful instruments of killing in our world. Sin is the sloth that keeps us calm and collected in the face of injustice and the rape of human beings.

The Promise of Life

But listen to the basis for hope! Although God knew that "the inclination of the human heart is evil from youth . . . the LORD said in his heart, 'I will never again curse the ground because of humankind'" (Gen 8:21). The apostle Paul joins in: "the wages of sin is death, but the free gift of God is eternal life in Christ Jesus our Lord" (Rom 6:23). To hear the word "you shall not kill," as a word from God is to hear God's protest against death and its many servants. This protest of God against death has been firmly implanted in our history by the resurrection of Jesus Christ.

The resurrection of Jesus Christ is God's defeat of and protest against the reign of death. The apostle Paul says, "We know that Christ, being raised from the dead, will never die again; death no longer has dominion over him" (Rom 6:9). And the risen Christ invites us to a life of faith, to join the community of the servants of life: "I am the resurrection and the life. Those who believe in me, even though they die, will live, and everyone who lives and believes in me will never die" (John 11:25–26).

On the basis of the resurrection of Jesus Christ and our faith in him, we ask with the apostle of old, "Where, O death, is your victory? Where, O death, is your sting?" and we join the answer with conviction, "Death has been swallowed up in victory . . . thanks be to God, who gives us the victory through our Lord Jesus Christ" (1 Cor 15:54–57).

Structures of Life

We may say, "That is all too religious and too individualistic. What difference does it make?" These texts are normally read at funeral services! Little do we realize that it is we who have removed the potency from the message of the resurrection and made it into a private religious affair. In fact, however, the resurrection is God's protest against death and its many messengers, against oppression and exploitation. The Swiss poet and theologian, Kurt Marti, captures it well in the following funeral oration:

> it might readily suit many lords of this world
> if everything were settled at death
> if the dominion of the lords
> and the servitude of the slaves
> were confirmed forever
>
> it might readily suit many lords of this world
> if in eternity they remained lords
> in expensive private tombs
> and their slaves remained slaves
> in rows of common graves
>
> but a resurrection is coming
> quite different from what we thought
> a resurrection is coming which is
> god's rising up against the lords
> and against the lord of lords—death[13]

If the resurrection life of Christ is real, if it becomes real in our life, then the structures of life will make inroads into the realm of death. The word "you shall not kill" is not a law to apply to others or to make us feel guilty. It is God's invitation to become a servant of life by resisting the forces and inroads of death. Killing and hating, and its manifestations from war to abortion, from suicide to the death of innocent children, are not part of God's plan. But that is our world, a world we have created! Into this our world, the gospel speaks a message of realistic hope. We have been invited to become witnesses to that hope. The Spirit of God wants to empower us to become servants of life.

Although the structures of death are strong and powerful, the sixth "word" invites us to join the tradition of St. Francis, Albert Schweitzer, and Mother Theresa, to become evangelists telling by word and deed that the God of the Decalogue and the God of Jesus affirms life and invites us all to join God's passion for life.

How did St. Francis teach people to pray?

> Lord, make me an instrument of your peace.
> Where there is hatred, let me sow love,
> where there is injury, pardon,

---

13. Marti, "Leichenreden," 153 (my translation).

where there is doubt, faith,
where there is despair, hope,
where there is sadness, joy.

O Divine Master,
grant that I may not so much
seek to be consoled, as to console,
to be understood, as to understand,
to be loved, as to love.
For it is in giving that we receive,
it is in pardoning that we are pardoned,
it is in dying that we are born again to eternal life.

In joining that prayer, we become servants of life and we begin to understand that the God who has freed us from selfishness, estrangement, and despair, calls to us, "you shall not kill!"—or, even better, as servants of the living God, "you will not kill!"

9

Love and Its Protection

The Seventh Word

"You shall not commit adultery"

Exodus 20:14 and Deuteronomy 5:18
Related texts: Genesis 2:15–25; 39:1–12; Mark 10:2–12; 12:18–27
(Matthew 22:23–33; Luke 20:27–40); Matthew 5:27, 31–32; 19:3–12;
Luke 16:18; John 8:1–11; 1 Corinthians 7; Ephesians 5:22–33

Exodus 20:14	Deuteronomy 5:18
"You shall not commit adultery."	"*Neither* shall you commit adultery."

THEOLOGICAL COMMENTS

THE HEBREW VERB *na'ap* means "to commit adultery." This commandment was originally spoken in the context of the extended family, which in Israelite society was the social and economic center of life. The family provided shelter, produced food, offered security, passed on the community traditions, and assured the survival of the clan. It was a patriarchal society. The man was the head of the clan. He had one or more wives as well as servants and slaves. Besides his wives, female slaves and servants were also sexually available to him. But men were forbidden to interfere with the marriage of other men. In those days only a man could violate another man's marriage; a woman could only disrupt her own marriage. "Committing adultery," therefore, originally referred to interfering sexually with another man's marriage, including his time of engagement.

This was not merely a private and personal matter. Any instability of marriage and family had social and economic consequences for the clan and the surrounding society. The following text underlines the seriousness of the issue:

> If a man is caught lying with the wife of another man, both of them shall die, the man who lay with the woman as well as the woman. So you shall purge the evil from Israel.
>
> If there is a young woman, a virgin already engaged to be married, and a man meets her in the town and lies with her, you shall bring both of them to the gate of that town and stone them to death, the young woman because she did not cry for help in the town and the man because he violated his neighbor's wife. So you shall purge the evil from your midst.
>
> But if the man meets the engaged woman in the open country, and the man seizes her and lies with her, then only the man who lay with her shall die. You shall do nothing to the young woman; the young woman has not committed an offense punishable by death, because this case is like that of someone who attacks and murders a neighbor. Since he found her in the open country, the engaged woman may have cried for help, but there was no one to rescue her. (Deut 22:22–27; similarly Lev 20:10)

Although the commandment is mainly addressed to men, the involvement of women, willing or unwilling, is also recognized. It is to be expected that a patriarchal society leans in favor of the male. Nevertheless, the intention of forbidding adultery was to protect the marriage and with it to assure the survival and smooth functioning of the wider family. This was seen to be the will of God. Therefore to commit adultery was a sin against God. The seriousness of this commandment is underlined in the texts above where transgressing against it is punished with the death penalty. Such punishment was not a private matter of revenge. It was decided in the village gate and took place through stoning in public. The punishment demonstrated that the protection of marriage and family was important for sustaining a healthy social ethos.

Today our situation is quite different. The equality of male and female is not only an essential part of the Christian ethos but it belongs to the core of human rights: "All human beings are born free and equal in dignity and rights."[1] The extended family has become the nuclear family. Slavery has

---

1. *The Universal Declaration of Human Rights*, §1.

Love and Its Protection

been outlawed and few families have servants. Also the sanctions (stoning) are unacceptable today—at least in Western countries influenced by the Judeo-Christian tradition. And most importantly, since the Enlightenment and Romanticism, marriage is more than duty and child-bearing. Love, sexuality, and enjoyment are expected to be the foundation of a modern marriage.

Still, the family remains important, and marriage is considered sacred. Partners promise publicly that they will be faithful to each other. Functioning marriages and stable families are central to a culture of freedom. It is within the family that the new generation learns what it means to trust, love, and obey.[2] There the important tension between freedom and responsibility is intuitively acquired. Although in some circles adultery has become socially acceptable, the "seventh word" is a salient reminder that adultery is not conducive to furthering love, trust, and freedom.

The following theological emphases should be kept in mind as we discern the claim that this commandment may have on our life:

1. Marriage and family are important social institutions. They are seed beds for a culture of freedom. Christians believe that they are part of God's provisions for structuring human life in community. "He who finds a wife finds a good thing, and obtains favor from the LORD" (Prov 18:22).

2. These structures change in form as times and social situations change. Their aim remains, however, to protect the commitment of partners to each other, and to safeguard the family as the basic unit of society.

3. Life in these structures is part of one's faith in God (cf. Gen 39:9; 2 Sam 12:13; Ps 51), therefore both obedience to God as well as forgiveness and renewal from God are possible.

4. In the Hebrew Bible divorce was possible for the man (Deut 24:1)—except when the man led the woman astray as a virgin (Deut 22:28–29) or when the woman was falsely accused as not having come into the marriage as a virgin (Deut 22:13–19). Deuteronomy 24:1—"Suppose a man enters into marriage with a woman, but she does not please him because he finds *something objectionable* about her, and so he writes

---

2. The *Convention on the Rights of the Child* stipulates "that the child, for the full and harmonious development of his or her personality, should grow up in a family environment, in an atmosphere of happiness, love and understanding" (Preamble).

her a certificate of divorce, puts it in her hand, and sends her out of his house"—has been interpreted in various ways in the Jewish tradition. For some rabbis the "something objectionable" refers to adultery, while for others it can include insignificant things like burning the dinner or seeing a prettier woman. In fact, however, divorce occurred infrequently, because the man would have to return the dowry and it was believed that divorce was against the will of God (Mal 2:16).

5. Jesus and the New Testament assign high dignity to marriage and recognize divorce as an unfortunate compromise. Adultery is considered a serious offense, whereby Jesus emphasizes not only the act but also the motivation: "You have heard that it was said, 'You shall not commit adultery.' But I say to you that everyone who looks at a woman with lust has already committed adultery with her in his heart" (Matt 5:27–28).

6. Since the church has such a bad record with regard to appreciating sexuality as one of the greatest gifts and joys of life, we must give some special attention to the sexual dimension of human life.

MESSAGE

Introduction

The story is told among rabbis that God reduced the commandments to ten—but that the seventh is still among them! Adultery then and now seems to be such a frequent and even popular practice that it is always good for a joke. And yet, for those who are immediately affected, it can mean the shattering of life.

Our situation is quite different from the time when the commandment was first spoken. Then there was no equality between male and female. The woman was basically defined through running the home, and bearing and rearing children. She was under the authority of the man. Hierarchy rather than partnership was the model. Yet the exhortation not to commit adultery remains as important now as it was then.

Sex as the Language of Love

This word recognizes that sexuality permeates and shapes intentional and lasting partnerships and marriages and wants to protect them against outside intrusion. At best sexuality is the language of love. At the same time, the "seventh word" is down to earth in that it recognizes sexuality as a frail and vulnerable reality. It can easily be used for selfish aims. It can destroy marriages and families. The same passion that belongs to the greatest experiences a person can have can also be degraded to violate human dignity and diminish human life. Sexuality needs to be joyously affirmed as being fundamental for a successful and meaningful life. At the same time it needs to be protected against human selfishness and exploitation so that it can become, ever anew, the language of love.

Sexuality is difficult to describe because it determines our *whole being*. We cannot take a position outside of it and then analyze it. We are sexual beings. Sexuality shapes our thinking, dreaming and acting. Believers joyously accept their sexuality as a gift of the creator. Indeed, it is unfortunate that religion in general and the Christian religion in particular have often had a negative attitude toward human sexuality. There is a longstanding religious tradition that devalues the body in favor of the soul. Many Christians have seen sexuality as a kind of necessary evil. Indeed, some Christians have even understood sexual intercourse as the gateway by which sin and evil is passed on from generation to generation.

We need to emphasize that sexuality is an ever-present and important reminder that for a fulfilled life we need the "other." We are *relational beings*. We are not created to live alone but to live together with others. We find human fulfillment, not alone, but together in friendship, partnership, or marriage. In one of the creation stories the man erupts into a chorus of joy when a partner is given to him (Gen 2:23). Not in aloneness, but in togetherness do we become who we are meant to be. Not as individualists but in community do we walk toward the fulfillment of life. An ancient wisdom saying captures this well:

> Two are better than one, because they have a good reward for their toil. For if they fall, one will lift up the other; but woe to one who is alone and falls and does not have another to help. Again, if two lie together, they keep warm; but how can one keep warm alone? And though one might prevail against another, two will withstand one. A threefold cord is not quickly broken. (Eccl 4:9–12)

Only in recent times—since the Enlightenment and with the help of the feminist revolution—have we begun to realize that mature and life-enhancing relationships call for *equality*. By women experiencing liberation and claiming their equality the male has also gained in quality and depth of life. It was at this point that Christianity brought a significant difference into the ancient world. Christians interpreted the subordination of women as the consequence of selfishness and sin. Faith in Christ restores the original intention of equality between male and female—"God created humankind . . . male and female" (Gen 1:27)—so that in the community of faith this equality is affirmed and implemented. It belongs to the tragedies of the history of the Christian church that in many Christian churches the full equality between male and female is still not recognized.

The creation story also contains the exhortation to "be fruitful and multiply" (Gen 1:28). A partnership of love contains the desire to share. It longs to go beyond itself and find continuity in children. Marriage as the most intense form of love between a man and a woman therefore aims at *creating a family*. The family does not only guarantee the continuation of society, but it is also the place where unconditional love is experienced, where compassion is shown, where nearness and intimacy provide a safe space, and where responsible freedom is practiced.

But since in some Christian traditions procreation is seen as the only justification for having sex, it must be emphasized that sexuality *has its own value*. It is tragic when women abstain from sex after children have been born, or when they are ridden by guilt because they enjoy having sex. Sexuality is to be enjoyed. It enriches life. True sexuality is different from lust, but it contains the dimension of *eros* (desiring the other) and *agape* (being willing to give oneself unreservedly to the other).

This commandment, then, encourages us to build a protective fence around meaningful, serious and lasting human relationships. For that reason it wants to emphasize the sanctity of marriage. It wants to protect the dignity and promise of love. It aims to safeguard the institution of marriage and family against outside and destructive interference. It also seeks to protect both partners in a marriage against getting bruised. It assigns the proper context for sexual intercourse. It challenges us to understand sex as the language of love; therefore, intentional and committed love is the proper context for sexuality.

The intention of this commandment is utterly positive. It does not present God as a spoilsport of life. God is the "living" One who affirms life in its fullness. "I came that they may have life, and have it abundantly," Jesus said, fleshing out the nature of God (John 10:10). The word "not to commit adultery" is not against love, and it is not against sex. But, it places sexuality within the framework of love.

Love and Its Protection

Love

Sexuality without love degenerates into lust. Apart from a relationship of love, the "other" is merely used for one's own gratification. Lust lacks respect for the other and violates his or her dignity. Its extreme form is rape. What then is love?

In the experience of love, two people no longer want to understand themselves apart from each other. They want to be *together*. They want to celebrate life together. Their individualism and their personal identity is not negated or limited. It is transformed into a richer reality. They look into each other's eyes and this look signifies something new. Theologians mislead us and cause us to feel guilty when they differentiate between divine and selfless *agape*-love and human sexual *eros*-love. Lovers desire each other. Their looks are erotic. But the difference from lust is that at the same time and with the same passion lovers also want to give themselves to each other. The desire to have and the longing to give become one in the event of love.

This creates something *new*. The modern Western understanding of love contains the element of surprise and newness. We generally do not decide with our will that we want to love this or that person. In most Western countries, partners are no longer chosen by their parents. We "fall" in love. In a community of life and intimacy, we discover a new dimension of life. We need the other for the experience of love.

This discovery *enhances* life. Persons who fall in love are renewed. Unpoetic persons are suddenly able to write poems. Unmusical people suddenly enjoy singing. Flowers suddenly look more colorful. Indeed, love changes things. It transforms reality. "Love is strong as death" (Song 8:6).

Love cannot rape. It can have nothing to do with coercion or violence. Therefore it is powerless. Lovers are *vulnerable*. They live with open arms rather than with clenched fists. They give themselves to each other and thereby open themselves to be enriched or hurt. They take that risk because apart from this surrender to each other, they will not discover that in giving themselves they receive more than they give. This is illustrated in Eccl 4:9–12, where the "two" form a "threefold" cord. In the encounter of love there is always a surplus.

Although love is vulnerable, it is not weak. It has an *inner strength* that keeps going when difficulties arise. It is much more than romantic feeling. It is patient and kind. It has the strength to sacrifice. "It bears all things, believes all things, hopes all things, endures all things. Love never ends"

(1 Cor 13:4–8). It faces the future with openness and courage. "There is no fear in love, but perfect love casts out fear; for fear has to do with punishment, and whoever fears has not reached perfection in love" (1 John 4:17–18). Love therefore is the substance of life. It assures that at the center of life there is freedom, compassion and hope. That is a gift! "We love because he first loved us" (1 John 4:19).

Marriage as the Protection of Intimate Love

In a marriage sermon written by Dietrich Bonhoeffer from his prison cell in May 1943, he said, "It is not your love that sustains the marriage, but from now on, the marriage that sustains your love."³

Love is vulnerable. It needs to be protected. For an intentional partnership with the prospect of founding a family, the best protection is marriage. Not only the divorce statistics but also our own experiences tell us that our love is often frail and our good intentions weak. When friendship becomes love between two people, this love needs to be protected against temptations from the inside and from the outside. In marriage two people promise to each other publicly that they want to live their life together and thereby start something new.

Marriages are threatened from within and from without. Jesus was perceptive when he located the threat to marriage in the look of the eye: "You have heard that it was said, 'You shall not commit adultery.' But I say to you that everyone who looks at a woman with lust has already committed adultery with her in his heart" (Matt 5:27–28). With Adam and Eve this look is known to all of us (Gen 3:1–7). But the look can be resisted. Love provides the resources to say "no" and thereby affirms that trust, loyalty, and commitment are important ingredients of a successful marriage. But marriage is not only threatened from within. A "James Bond morality" has invaded many hearts, and the attempt to repeat in the bedroom what we see on movie screens or in women's or men's magazines has brought a performance ethos into our marriages that is more related to consumerism than to the enjoyment of sexuality. When in the sexual revolution we tore away the "fig leaves" and "loincloths" of shame (Gen 3:7), we failed to realize that they were not the symbols of a conservative culture, but that they represented the realization that our freedom is threatened and needs discipline and protection.

3. Bonhoeffer, *Letters and Papers from Prison*, 43.

Love and Its Protection

The experience of love can be likened to a river and its course. The river breaks forth from the ground and then begins to shape its bed in which the water flows. Tributaries join it and increase the amount of water which makes it even more necessary to have strong river banks to keep the water flowing in the right direction. The river banks are necessary to keep the water from dissipating into the landscape.

The relationship of love can also be likened to the creation of a work of art. The artist has the foundational experience of wonder and intuition. The discovery occurs; it is like falling into love. The vision is there. But it is a long and stony road until the work of art is ready. Blood, sweat and tears, discipline and sleepless nights will mark the journey until the vision has resulted in a reality. Marriage is the work of art on which two people who have fallen in love work for the rest of their lives.

When two people experience the reality of love, in this experience there are the seeds of *exclusiveness* and of *eternity*. It is with this particular person that I want to experience and experiment the mystery of love, and it is with this person that I want to remain together for the rest of my life. We now want this love to shape our lives. We want to honor each other through thick and thin. We do not want to hurt each other, because love is patient and kind (1 Cor 13:4–7). We want to protect the depth of our love against the fleetingness of our own moods, against the instability of our own emotions, and against the unpredictability of our own feelings. In the budding experience of love we have felt the exclusiveness of our allegiance and we have felt a touch of eternity. This is what we want to guard, and therefore we promise allegiance to each other,

> for better for worse,
> for richer for poorer,
> in sickness and in health,
> to love and to cherish,
> until we are parted by death.

Just as a river needs banks to keep the water flowing in orderly ways, and just as a highway needs guardrails to guide traffic, so also love needs guardrails and banks to protect it against the storms of life.

Marriage is not the fortress into which a man drags his wife to be her master for the rest of her life. Marriage is not the safe haven in which a wife can rest secure for the rest of her life. Marriage is an intentional partnership to protect the reality of love against the stirrings and temptations of the moment.

Modern marriage therefore contains the following elements:

- It is part of *God's provision* to provide context and structure for the survival of the encounter and experience of love between two people—"what God has joined together, let no one separate" (Mark 10:9; see also 1 Tim 4:3–4). At the same time, marriage is an institution for this world and this life. It shapes human life under the condition of selfishness. In the kingdom of God such provisions are no longer necessary (Mark 12:18–27).

- Many men and women who try out the single lifestyle experience what is well formulated in one of the biblical creation accounts: "Then the LORD God said, 'It is not good that the man (we would add today 'or the woman') should be alone; I will make him/her a helper as his/her partner'" (Gen 2:18). Marriage is the *partnership* in which intimacy, security, and sexuality find their context of trust. Such partnership is an end in itself. It is not simply there to serve a certain purpose, whether to produce children, or to multiply riches, or to have a sexual partner readily available at all times. Human beings are created to shape life together: "God created humankind . . . male and female" (Gen 1:27). If this togetherness is only there to perform certain functions, then when these functions are fulfilled, the marriage is over. Many divorces happen when the children leave home or when a partner is no longer sexually attractive or sexually available. But when people marry they do so not to discharge certain duties or functions but to celebrate life together. They resolve that in their togetherness they deepen and widen their experience of life more than they would be able to do alone.

- This promise that together in marriage people experience *more* than they would experience alone points to the *mystery* of marriage. Even the great skeptic, Friedrich Nietzsche, wrote in *Thus Spoke Zarathustra*, "Marriage: Thus I name the will of two to create the one that is *more than those who created it*. Reverence for each other, as for those willing with such a will, is what I name marriage. Let this be the meaning and truth of your marriage."[4] This "more" in *being* together, rather

---

4. Nietzsche, *Thus Spoke Zarathustra*, 182 (emphasis mine). See also comments above about the text in Eccl 4:9–12.

than merely fulfilling certain functions, calls for a lasting commitment: "Therefore a man leaves his father and his mother and clings to his wife, and they become one flesh" (Gen 2:24, cited in Mark 10:7–8; Matt 19:5; and Eph 5:31).

- Because marriage is an end in itself and not merely a means to an end, it is destined for the *whole of life*, "until death do us part." If partners are to experience total openness, intimacy and trust, this is only possible in monogamy and life-long relationship.

- The high expectations related to marriage call for *monogamy*. Partners who are in love with each other meet as equals. This equality is diminished if their lifelong commitment to each other were to be shared with others. Even in the Old Testament, where both polygamy—mainly for the rich and famous (Judg 8:30–31; 2 Sam 5:13; 1 Kgs 11:3)—and the duty and utilitarian character of marriage is known, there is a clear tendency towards monogamy: "a man leaves his father and his mother and clings to his wife, and they become one flesh" (Gen 2:24). The symbolic power of monogamy was such that it could serve as a parable for God's relationship to Israel (Isa 54:4–8; Jer 2:1–2; Hos 1–3) and for Christ's relationship to the church (Eph 5:22–33). Adultery was seen as a transgression against one's partner and against God (Gal 5:19). This does not mean, of course, that marriage partners do not experience the desire for sexual variety. But like freedom, genuine love has its own discipline. It needs to be preserved by being willing to say "no" to oneself and to others.

- When the dignity and mystery of marriage has been recognized and accepted as an end in itself, *then* we can also speak of *procreation*. Love transcends. It entails the desire to share widely what partners have with each other. This is the basis for wanting to have children and found a family. When that happens, joy widens, potential pain deepens, and their accountability increases. Now partners are not only responsible for each other but they must also provide a secure home and a compassionate environment for their children.

Although I have spoken here about the nature of marriage, it must be emphasized that sexuality is not only genital, it is not limited to marriage. There are many people who choose to remain single or who have not found the right partner for a marriage. Sexuality is a pervasive reality that allows single as well as married people to live a successful and meaningful life.

Love as the Protection of Marriage

The greatest danger for modern marriage is probably that partners take each other for granted and get bored with each other. When the children leave home, when their function as parents is over, when the sexual drive lessens, a new challenge arrives: does love provide resources to sustain the promise that it is better to be together than to be alone?

Not only our love, but also our marriage needs protection. Marriage protects our love against the many winds of change and storms of temptations. In turn, our marriage is protected by the firm decision to shape our life with this one partner. This firm decision finds its expression in the commandment, "you shall not commit adultery." You shall not transgress against your own promises, and you shall not break into the marriages of others.

Neither Jesus nor God, who gave the commandment not to commit adultery, want to make us feel bad. They do not want us to feel guilty. They do not want to condemn us. They simply want to remind us of the responsibility and discipline of freedom. They encourage us to be true to ourselves and to our promises. What is true for marriage is true for all human relationships: be true to yourself; be true to your promises; do not use your partner for your selfish desires; do not exploit the weaker partner in a relationship; do not break into another relationship to fulfill your own desires.

Sex Outside of Marriage

Traditionally the churches understood sexuality solely in terms of procreation. They, therefore, limited sexual intercourse to marriage and forbade sex outside of marriage. They wanted to protect marriage and family and provide a safe space for children. A significant change in attitude came with the rise of the so-called New Morality.[5] With the erosion of parental and church authority, the rise of birth control technology, and the general tendency of a consumer-oriented generation to seek immediate satisfaction for their natural inclinations, many singles and unmarried couples no longer accept the constraints of tradition in church and culture. Sociological

---

5. See Fletcher, *Situation Ethics* and Fletcher, *Moral Responsibility*.

Love and Its Protection

investigations, like the famous Kinsey reports in the late 1940s and early 1950s,[6] have shown that sexual activity outside marriage is much more prevalent than people had thought. Today, even in faith communities, many couples live together before they are married.

Since our faith in God is voluntary, intentional, and encompasses all areas of life, one cannot simply accept that whatever is widely practiced is as such right, healthy, and helpful. If "right" or "wrong" is established by what people do, then we have no argument against inequality, violence, and war. In that sense many Christians are correct when they insist that the word of God, not the practice of people, establishes ethical norms and that, therefore, irrespective of what people do, sexual intercourse should only be practiced within the confines of marriage. Nevertheless, times change and one cannot simply ignore the practice of people, especially of those who maintain the sincerity of their faith and yet decide to engage in sex outside marriage. We need to seek a way beyond traditionalism and situationalism.

We have to admit that sexuality in the Bible and sexuality today are not the same. The romantic view of sexuality is a fairly recent phenomenon. A re-reading of 1 Corinthians 7 reminds us of Paul's low view of sexuality. Sex seemed to be a necessary evil. In response to a question from the Christians in Corinth, Saint Paul wrote,

> It is well for a man not to touch a woman. But because of cases of sexual immorality, each man should have his own wife and each woman her own husband. . . . To the unmarried and the widows I say that it is well for them to remain unmarried as I am. But if they are not practicing self-control, they should marry. For it is better to marry than to be aflame with passion. (1 Cor 7:1–9)

This view has greatly influenced the thinking and the practice of churches and Christians through the ages. Although Paul in this chapter distinguishes between his own opinion and words of the Lord, and also differentiates between concession and command (1 Cor 7:6), in general his negative view of sexuality has been pervasive in the history of Christianity. At this point we need to correct Paul and try to develop a view of sexuality that affirms its beauty, and at the same time warns against its misuse.

With regard to sexuality in the lives of singles and of unmarried partners, we need to affirm that sexuality is more than sexual intercourse. We

---

6. See two books by Kinsey, Pomeroy, and Martin: *Sexual Behavior in the Human Male* and *Sexual Behavior in the Human Female*.

also need to understand sexuality as a process. When teenagers become sexually aware, masturbation is not uncommon. It would be silly to deny or condemn it. It is part of the process of becoming a mature person. At the same time one has to differentiate between sexual encounters that continue in the vein of masturbation and serve only to satisfy one's sexual desires and those that take place within an intentional, caring and long-term partnership.

Churches must also learn to get rid of their negative disposition towards sexuality and trust their members to act responsibly. Most people in faith communities affirm traditional values like friendship, trust, love and partnership even when they differ in their sexual practice. When people decide on their sexual practices I would suggest the following guidelines.

- Be honest with yourself and decide what you are going to do and how far you are going to go *before* you get into the actual situation. I like Paul Lehmann's formulation: "The sexual act is no more and no less open to . . . freedom in obedience than is any other human action. But the Christian Church . . . has lacked the faith, the imagination, and the boldness to include the sexual act among the risks of free obedience." The challenge is not to put constraints upon sexuality, but "to offer a context within which sexual intensity can be creatively related to sexual sensitivity because sexuality itself has been transformed from a biological to a human fact." And again, "The course of faithfulness is not the course of safety through conformity but of the risk of obedience in faith and hope and love."[7]

- The fact that "every one does it" is no reason for you and me to do it. Strength of character can be shown by swimming against the stream! (Many teenagers regret that their first sexual intercourse happened during a rite of passage party when the alcohol flowed freely.)

- Do not use others to satisfy your own lust and don't exploit the feelings or dependency of others.

- Do not risk having an unwanted child.

- Growth toward becoming a mature person includes not only respect for the other but also the discipline of waiting.

---

7. Lehmann, *Ethics in a Christian Context*, 138–39.

Love and Its Protection

Singles and Sexuality

We have seen that the Bible and Christian tradition have a *high view of marriage*. The "seventh word" is a warning not to invade the marriage of others. At the same time I have emphasized that our views of sexuality have changed over the years. We now know that sexuality affects our *whole being*. Everyone therefore, married or single, has to deal with it. It is part of the process of becoming a mature person.

I hesitate to say anything about singles and sexuality because I am not single myself. But since I have argued for a holistic view of sexuality and since more and more people live, intentionally and unintentionally, as singles I cannot ignore the subject in a discussion on sexuality.

Much of what I said in the previous section would also apply to singles. When we realize that sexuality is more than sexual intercourse then a wide range for meaningful relationships opens up in which dimensions of love, friendship, and compassion fall under a holistic understanding of sexuality. Whether and how singles engage in overt and intimate sexual activities needs to be a decision of each person as part of their obedience of faith.

Masturbation

A widespread and normal part of a person's sexual development is masturbation. The Bible does not address this issue and one wonders why it has been frowned upon, and why to the present day the Roman Catholic church considers "masturbation . . . an intrinsically and seriously disordered act" and names it a "grave moral disorder."[8] This verdict is probably based on bad science which used to suggest that all potential human life is contained in the male sperm, which therefore must not be wasted. While we should not make people, especially young people, feel guilty for practicing self-eroticism, we must say at the same time that masturbation should be seen as a transition to healthy sexuality that is not self-oriented but takes place in responsible relationships.

Homosexuality

Although the question of homosexuality is not directly addressed by the "seventh word," in our contemporary situation the issue cannot be avoided in any discussion of love and sexuality. While secular society in the West

---

8. Sacred Congregation for the Doctrine of the Faith, *Persona Humana*, Declaration on Certain Questions Concerning Sexual Ethics (1975) §IX.

has "more or less" come to terms with the presence and partnerships of gay and lesbian people, most faith communities have not yet seriously listened to homosexuals and so far have failed to give them a voice. Indeed, churches that have faced the issue, like the Uniting Church in Australia, are torn apart by it and are seriously hampered in their mission. Many conservative churches like the Roman Catholic church, Baptists, and charismatic churches deny or repress the issue, although it is widely known that a number of their ministers and members are homosexual. On the global scene, those churches that try to face the issue, like the Anglican and Lutheran world communions, have been unable to reach a consensus.

Most churches affirm that marriage between a man and a woman is the proper place for intimate sexual activity. There is also widespread agreement that homosexuals should be welcomed in the churches—although many churches expect them not to engage in sexual practices. In most churches homosexual people cannot be married or ordained. Homosexuals experience that as discrimination and rejection. At the present time there is a deadlock and no one knows a way forward. We therefore have to tread softly and invite serious and concerned people to enter the discussion with a sense of compassion and a longing for truth and justice. In this context it is not possible to do justice to this important issue. On the other hand I do not want to ignore it either. All I can do is to offer a few guidelines, indicate where I stand at the moment, invite people to consider the arguments, and then form their own opinions.

Firstly, I would like to repeat that the "seventh word" encourages us to affirm the importance of marriage and family for a culture of freedom.

Secondly, when we think and speak of homosexual people and their relationships, we must apply the same presumptions and expectations as we do for heterosexual people. It would be unfair automatically to associate gay and lesbian people with seedy bars, one-night stands, and ostentatious street parades. Not lust or "degrading passions" (Rom 1:26) but love, friendship, commitment, caring, compassion, respect for the "other," as well as discipline, are signs of maturity for both heterosexual and homosexual relationships.

Thirdly, we are confronted with the question as to what norms we accept for our ethical reflection. We must also be willing to question our own personal likes and dislikes. These are related to our particular history and psychology. It would be unfair to make our likes and dislikes the norm for the sexuality of others. Indeed I suspect that much rejection of homosexuals has more to do with psychology than with theology or charity.

If we seek the verdict of *tradition* the answer is fairly clear. Homosexuality has, for the most part, been seen as a sexual perversion. This is still the view of many people, especially in faith communities.[9] We need to say, however, that such rejections evaluate homosexuality as a general phenomenon. They do not take into consideration the stories of homosexual people and they do not distinguish between homosexual promiscuity on the one hand and mature and responsible relationships of gay and lesbian people on the other.

If we follow the laws of *nature*, the answer is less clear and indeed quite controversial. When homosexuality was named "unnatural," such thinking was often been based on the misunderstanding that the male sperm was the sole carrier of life and that the female womb was only the breeding incubator. There was no perception of female ovulation and that the female egg was necessary for reproduction. Since sexuality was traditionally seen only in terms of procreation, the "wasting" of male sperm (as in masturbation or homosexual acts) was seen as an offense against the rules of life.

So far the natural and psychological sciences have failed to provide a reliable verdict on whether homosexuality is inherited, acquired, or chosen.[10] In any case, even though many people consider homosexuality to be "unnatural" and the Roman Catholic church even ascribes normative status to natural law, in fact nature does not supply reliable answers. From "nature" one could also argue for the inequality of males and females and for the legitimacy of war and violence. In 1 Corinthians 11:14, "nature" teaches that men must not wear long hair.

We also have to recognize that during the last couple of centuries the "romantic" dimension of sexuality has been emphasized in Western countries. It is possible for both heterosexual and homosexual people to live in long-term, caring and non-exploitative relationships.

---

9. To illustrate the point, the Roman Catholic Church declares "that homosexual acts are *intrinsically* disordered and can in no case be approved of." (Sacred Congregation for the Doctrine of the Faith, *Persona Humana*, Declaration on Certain Questions Concerning Sexual Ethics [1975], §VIII [emphasis mine]). For the Anglican Communion see the *Lambeth Conference* 1998, Resolution 1.10—Human Sexuality.

10. For a survey see Clarke, "Scientific Reason and Homosexuality," and Mullen, "Science and the Meaning of Homosexuality."

Even the *Bible*, the main source for ethical decision-making in Christian communities, is not clear on the question of homosexuality as we understand it today. It is a marginal issue in the Bible. Jesus and the Gospels don't mention it and many texts that are used by antagonists—like the gang rape in Sodom (Gen 19)—don't really deal with homosexuality.[11] The following texts are important (always keeping in mind that it is not a central issue in the Bible):[12]

In Leviticus 18:22 and 20:13 a man lying with "a male as with a woman" is named an "abomination" to be punished with the death penalty. But we must immediately note that the same punishment is meted out for "giving their offspring to Molech" (Lev 20:2–5), for witchcraft (Lev 20:6) and for cursing father or mother (Lev 20:9). If we condemn homosexuality on the basis of these texts, then we must also condemn eating blood (Lev 17:12), sowing two kinds of seeds in our garden or wearing a garment made of two kinds of yarn (Lev 19:19), eating pork or rabbit (Lev 11), and declaring women during their period "unclean" (Lev 12). And for Christians it is of course decisive that with Mark 7:15 Jesus suspends the whole cult system of Leviticus: "there is nothing outside a person that by going in can defile, but the things that come out are what defile."

Turning to the New Testament we have already noted that neither Jesus nor the Gospels address the issue. The "immorality" (also translated as "fornication") that Paul and the Pauline tradition condemn in many places applies both to heterosexuals and to homosexuals and it is mentioned together with many other vices: "impurity, licentiousness, idolatry, sorcery, enmities, strife, jealousy, anger, quarrels, dissensions, factions, envy, drunkenness, carousing, and things like these. I am warning you, as I warned you before: those who do such things will not inherit the kingdom of God" (Gal 5:19–21). The references to "male prostitutes" and "sodomites" in 1 Corinthians 6:9–10 and 1 Timothy 1:9–11—mentioned in the same breath as stealing, drunkenness, greed, lying, murder, slave-trading—may refer to a perversion of homosexual practices but certainly do not have caring, lasting, and non-exploitative relationships in mind. That leaves us with Romans 1:24–28 where the godlessness of heathens is described: "Their women exchanged natural intercourse for unnatural, and in the same way

---

11. Dunnill, "Homosexuality in the Old Testament," 49–53.

12. From the voluminous literature I mention only two articles that provide a balanced summary: Dyer, "A Consistent Biblical Approach to '(Homo)sexuality," and Wink "Homosexuality and the Bible."

also the men, giving up natural intercourse with women, were consumed with passion for one another." Again Paul is not referring to a responsible friendship or partnership between two males or females. He is referring to the well-known orgies in the ancient world where people followed "the lusts of their hearts" and "to a debased mind" leading to do "things that should not be done."

We must therefore conclude that while the Bible condemns sexual perversions and moral corruption, it does not speak to the question whether homosexual relationships that are based on love and mutual consent, and are not exploitative, are moral or immoral. While I agree with the Bible when it criticizes homosexual excesses and perversions I would caution against applying such text to homosexuality in general and to responsible gay and lesbian relationships in particular.

If we agree that the Bible is not a book of laws and rules and that for Jesus and Paul the law is summarized in loving God and neighbor, then we are challenged to deliberate our response in light of the Spirit of God who has spoken the story of Jesus into our conscience. I suggest that we affirm gay and lesbian people and challenge them to express their sexuality with the same sensitive discipline as we would expect from heterosexual people.

This leaves us with the much-debated question of gay and lesbian marriage. I think that civil contracts in which gay and lesbian couples make a legal pledge to each other before the law are in order. They provide security and fairness for a committed and long-term relationship. Marriage, howeve, is another matter because it entails the desire for a family. I think that every child has the right to experience the life-shaping presence of a mother *and* a father. The rights of a child precede the rights of gays and lesbians because the child is the more vulnerable part in the relationship.[13]

---

13. Both biblical narratives and the human rights instruments show special interest in protecting vulnerable people in general and children in particular. The "Universal Declaration of Human Rights" postulates that "All children, whether born in or out of wedlock ... are entitled to *special* care and assistance" (Office of the High Commissioner for Human Rights, "Universal Declaration of Human Rights (1948)," §25:2, emphasis mine). The "Convention on the Rights of the Child" insists that in "all actions concerning children ... the *best interest* of the child shall be a primary consideration" (United Nations General Assembly, 44th Session, "Resolution 25 (1989) Convention on the Rights of the Child," §3, emphasis mine). For further details consult Lorenzen, *The Rights of the Child*.

Conclusion

The word not to commit adultery wants us to relate the freedom we have found in Jesus Christ to our experience of love. When two people encounter each other in love, their life is enriched, even renewed. They experience a new reality. Their eyes have been opened by love and they no longer want to be apart from each other. By looking into each other's eyes they desire each other. This is why Jesus sees already "in the look" the seed of adultery. Adultery means that I take the intentional "look" from my partner and look around for other sexual partners.

"You shall not commit adultery" is the fence surrounding the garden of our sexuality, love, and marriage, protecting us against the many ways to destroy them. Just as Joseph said "No" when his master's wife "day after day" wanted him to "lie with her" (Gen 39:1–12), because he did not want to betray his master's trust and he did not want to "sin against God," so each one of us can make a resolves not to violate the marriage and family of others.

At the same time, if our love and marriage has failed and our lives are shattered, even then the God who is the source of love and who affirms marriage provides the possibility of a new beginning. Jesus addressed a woman caught in adultery, saying to her: You are free! Live your freedom, go and sin no more (John 8:1–11).

10

The Right to Be Free
The Eighth Word

"You shall not steal"

Exodus 20:15 and Deuteronomy 5:19
Related texts: Exodus 22:21–27; Galatians 3:23–28;
Ephesians 4:25—5:2; Luke 4:16–21, 19:1–10

Exodus 20:15	Deuteronomy 5:19
"You shall not steal."	"Neither shall you steal."

THEOLOGICAL COMMENTS

"You shall not *rob*" may be a better translation. The Hebrew verb *ganav* includes the dimension of aggression, even violence. Robbing someone creates pain and loss. It is an invasion into the life and freedom of a person and a group.

Beyond the obvious stealing of *money* and *property*, the history of the commandment also includes the stealing of *persons*.[1] In the Hebrew Scriptures such stealing was punished with the death penalty.

> Whoever steals (kidnaps) a person, whether that person has been sold or is still held in possession, shall be put to death. (Exod 21:16)
>
> If someone is caught stealing (kidnapping) another Israelite, enslaving or selling the Israelite, then that kidnaper shall die. (Deut 24:7)

---

1. This is the case in three out of 55 occurrences in the Hebrew Bible.

Joseph, being imprisoned in a dungeon interprets a dream for the chief cupbearer and then reminds him: "... in fact I was stolen out of the land of the Hebrews; and here also I have done nothing that they should have put me into the dungeon" (Gen 40:15).

Since God is a God who loves freedom, the taking away of a person's freedom through slavery or serfdom or as booty is a serious offence. Although neither the Hebrew Bible nor the New Testament questions the institution of slavery as such, whenever the topic is raised in the Hebrew Bible, it is always to ease the burden of the slaves (Lev 25:39–46; Deut 15:12–17; 23:15–16). For the early Christians a new era had been ushered in with the resurrection of Christ. This new era is marked by freedom in which the end of slavery, patriarchy, racism, and inequality is announced. In the realm where Jesus Christ is heard, believed, and obeyed "there is no longer Jew or Greek, there is no longer slave or free, there is no longer male and female; for all of you are one in Christ Jesus" (Gal 3:28). It is a tragedy, however, that it took the church 1800 years to understand the simple fact that faith in Christ entailed the abolition of slavery.

MESSAGE

Introduction

The exhortation "you *shall* not steal," or the indication, that as the people of God, who have experienced divine liberation, "you *will* not steal," is all inclusive. It has no direct object because there are many ways and means to rob and steal. There are many ways of limiting or taking away people's freedom. In the Hebrew Bible reference was made to the stealing of animals (Exod 21:37; 22:11–12), of objects and money (Gen 44:8; Exod 22:2; Josh 7:21), and also to the kidnapping of people.

Jesus and the earliest Christians knew this commandment (Mark 10:19; Matt 19:18; Luke 18:20). They respected it. Not to steal was part of the new way of loving God and neighbor (Rom 13:9). Hearing and obeying this word was also important for the reputation of the Christian community (1 Pet 4:15). Thieves are challenged to give up stealing and find honest ways to live and to share their lives (Eph 4:28).

The great Christian reformer, Martin Luther, commenting on this commandment over 400 years ago, saw the inter-relationship between personal and social ethics:

stealing is not just robbing someone's safe or pocketbook but also taking advantage of someone in the market, in all stores, butcher shops, wine- and beer-cellars, workshops, and, in short, whenever business is transacted and money is exchanged for goods or services.... The poor are defrauded every day, and new burdens and higher prices are imposed. They (the merchants) all misuse the market in their own arbitrary, defiant, arrogant way, as if it were their privilege and right to sell their goods as high as they please without any criticism.[2]

Luther touches on two dimensions by which this commandment touches our life. Both have to do with stealing people's freedom! People's lives are diminished by taking away their belongings, their property, be it land or money, bicycles or cars. At the same time, people's freedom is stolen by selling them into slavery and by keeping them captive in an unjust world. A world too often controlled by greed, corruption and injustice. Human lives seem cheap when profits and power are at stake. We miss all that, we miss this revolutionary demand of God upon our lives, if we only think of stealing apples and bicycles and cars, however annoying that may be.

Widening Our Horizons

Most of our thinking remains at the *personal level*. When we find a purse on a park bench, we bring it to the police station, rather than keeping the money. We do not want to disadvantage the community by withholding information from the tax office or by "tailoring" our tax returns. We certainly do not steal in the supermarket or the department store.

But there is another level of morality. It is called *Social Ethics*. It recognizes that most of our life is determined by structures and institutions. As citizens we are part of a society and as such pay our taxes and keep the respective laws and customs. We are embedded in a global network in which economic and military decisions taken far away have immediate consequences for our savings and our security. We are also interwoven into nature so that the food we eat, the water we drink and the air we breathe affect our well- or ill-being.

For instance, for poverty to become history and for seemingly damned people to receive some realistic hope, it is one thing to respond at the *personal* level. We give our $10 or $100 or $1000 a month to a credible aid organization. On our home turf we vote for the party that promises to give

2. Martin Luther, *The Large Catechism* (1529), 416 and 418.

priority to debt-relief and poverty-reduction. All that is important. It shows that we feel a sense of global responsibility. Yet alongside this personal engagement we also need to be aware of the importance of *structures*. To really help the poor of the world, structures need to be changed. World trade needs to be directed to give a "fair go" to developing countries. Corruption in high places needs to be stopped. Personal ethics, therefore, needs to be inter-related with social ethics. And with it, we need to develop the awareness that by trying to help others we are in fact helping ourselves. Being interwoven into an all-encompassing network of relationships, ultimately we are all in the same boat.

Our personal engagement therefore needs to be complemented in two ways. Firstly, we need to sustain the conviction that we are not damned or fated. Things *can* change, and we can develop the personal and political will to *change* things. We cannot afford the luxury of despair or withdrawal from responsibility. Secondly, for change to become effective, we require not only personal but *corporate responsibility*. All major problems today are global problems. We need to wage a change of consciousness whereby governments not only seek their national well-being, but also contribute to the welfare of the global community. Corporations must be compelled to make the struggle for human rights and ecological sustainability part of their cost and profit analysis. We need to create structures and institutions like the United Nations and invest them with authority to help with the elimination of poverty and the pursuit of peace and justice. We cannot leave the future of the world in the hands of some anonymous fate. We humans have created a world of violence and greed. It is up to us to change it! And for such change to succeed we need to operate both on a personal and on the corporate level.

The present United Nations Millennium Development Goals (MCD's) are a good example for the challenge of change on all levels. All 191 member nations of the UN have promised to meet the following goals by the year 2015:

- Goal 1: Eradicate extreme poverty and hunger; and as such, by the year 2015, to halve the proportion of people whose income is less than $1 a day, and to halve the proportion of people who suffer from hunger.
- Goal 2: Achieve universal primary education; and as such ensure that by 2015 children everywhere, boys and girls alike, will be able to complete a full course of primary schooling.

- Goal 3: Promote gender equality and empower women. Also eliminate gender disparity in primary and secondary education, preferably by 2005, and in all levels of education no later than 2015.
- Goal 4: Reduce child mortality; and as such reduce by two-thirds the under-five mortality rate by 2015.
- Goal 5: Improve maternal health; and as such reduce by three-quarters the maternal mortality ratio by 2015.
- Goal 6: Combat HIV/AIDS, Malaria and other diseases.
- Goal 7: Ensure environmental sustainability by:
    » integrating the principles of sustainable development into country policies and programs and reverse the loss of environmental resources;
    » halving, by 2015, the proportion of people without sustainable access to safe drinking water and basic sanitation;
    » achieving by 2020 a significant improvement in the lives of at least 100 million slum dwellers.
- Goal 8: Develop a global partnership for development by:
    » furthering an open, rule-based, predictable, nondiscriminatory trading and financial system (including a commitment to good governance, development, and poverty reduction both nationally and internationally);
    » addressing the special needs of the Least Developed Countries (including tariff- and quota-free access for Least Developed Countries' exports, enhanced programs of debt relief for heavily indebted poor countries and cancellation of official bilateral debt, and more generous official development assistance for countries committed to poverty reduction);
    » addressing the special needs of landlocked developing countries and small island developing states (through the Program of Action for the Sustainable Development of Small Island Developing States and 22nd General Assembly provisions);
    » dealing comprehensively with the debt problems of developing countries through national and international measures in order to make debt sustainable in the long term;

> developing and implementing, in cooperation with developing countries, strategies for decent and productive work for youth;

> providing, in cooperation with pharmaceutical companies, access to affordable essential drugs in developing countries;

> making available, in cooperation with the private sector, the benefits of new technologies, especially information and communications technologies.[3]

For this challenge to succeed, our governments need both to be supported and to be held accountable. Each one of us can tune into this global movement. We can vote for parties committed to implementing these goals. Christian aid organizations have created the *Micah Network* and the *Micah Challenge* which seek to inform and inspire Christians and churches worldwide to put this struggle onto their theological agendas.[4] They seek to influence politicians to remain aware of the promises of their governments so that these promises will indeed be kept. A failure to do so would mean that "millions of lives that could have been saved will be lost; many freedoms that could have been secured will be denied; and we shall inhabit a more dangerous and unstable world."[5] Let us therefore widen our thinking and become aware of how "stealing" and "robbing" are practiced and experienced today.

TAKING HOSTAGES

Since the Iraq war started we are confronted regularly with the dreadful agony of women and men being kidnapped and often killed in the Middle East. Horrendous events like the hijacking of a *Lufthansa* plane to Entebbe in 1976, or of the cruise ship *Achille Lauro* in the Mediterranean in 1985, or the "Black September" taking of nine Israeli athletes hostage during the 1972 Olympics in Munich, constitute only the surface of what happens daily to individuals around the globe. They are the reminders that humans and their freedom are traded for commercial, criminal, and political gain. There is now an *International Convention Against the Taking of Hostages*

---

3. See United Nations, *The UN Millennium Goals*.

4. For more information about the Micah Network and Micah Challenge see http://en.micahnetwork.org/ and http://www.micahchallenge.org/.

5. The former UN General Secretary, Kofi A. Annan, in his foreword to the UN's *The Millenium Development Goals Report 2005*.

The Right to Be Free

(1979), inviting the global community to unite in its efforts to affirm and implement people's right to be free.

SEXUAL EXPLOITATION

Two World Congresses *Against Commercial Sexual Exploitation of Children* have recently been held in Stockholm (1996) and Yokohama (2001). They lamented the stealing of freedom from millions of children around the world: 300,000 child prostitutes in the USA, 700,000 in Zambia, 200,000 in Thailand, 40,000 in Venezuela, 20,000 in the Dominican Republic, 500,000 in India, 5,000 in Britain.[6] A brief quotation from the official UNICEF website names the tragedy: "Trafficking in children is a global problem affecting large numbers of children. Some estimates have as many as 1.2 million children being trafficked every year. There is a demand for trafficked children as cheap labor or for sexual exploitation."[7] David Batstone, in his recent report on human trafficking, tells the horrific stories of the sex trade in South East Asia and in Europe.[8]

STOLEN CHILDREN

In Australia thousands of indigenous children were forcibly removed from their parents in order to assimilate them into the white Anglo-Saxon culture.[9] Stories of horror have emerged. At best, the "stolen children," robbed of their parents and culture, not being allowed to speak their language and make contact with their families, suffer a life-long feeling of loss, separation, and crisis of identity: "Why me; why was I taken away? It's like a hole in your heart that can never heal."[10] At worst they were beaten, sexually abused, and destroyed in body and soul. Like the girl in South Australia who was taken away from her mother as a young child and placed in a home. When she became a teenager, she was sent to serve in a white family for the summer vacation. She was sexually abused by the man of the house. When she returned to the home and told the matron her mouth was washed out with soap. Although she pleaded not to be sent back to that place, next

6. United Nations Children's Fund, *Child Protection from Violence, Exploitation and Abuse*.

7. Ibid.

8. Batstone, *NOT for Sale*. See especially chapters 1 and 4.

9. See Human Rights and Equal Opportunity Commission, *Bringing Them Home*. Also Manne, "Aboriginal Child Removal and the Question of Genocide, 1900–1940."

10. Human Rights and Equal Opportunity Commission, *Bringing Them Home*, 177.

summer she was sent back there. This time she was raped and became pregnant. When her child was delivered, it was immediately taken away from her and the young mother never saw it again.[11] These are not only barbaric facts, but here we witness a modern, democratically elected government that blatantly disregarded human rights. "The Australian practice of Indigenous children removal involved both systematic racial discrimination and genocide as defined by international law."[12]

Child Labor

A report from a matchstick factory in Sivakasi, India contains this description: "Dust from the chemical powder and strong vapors in both the storeroom and the boiler room were obvious . . . We found 250 children, mostly below 10 years of age, working in a long hall filling in a slotted frame with sticks. Row upon row of children, some barely five years old, were involved in the work."[13]

Millions of children are forced to work, most of them in South East Asia. In Africa, every third child has to work and in Latin America it is every fifth.[14] They are bonded out for life, squatted, day in and day out, on narrow planks in Morocco, Pakistan, Iran, and India knitting carpets. They are working in mines underground, hewing and picking coal for many hours each day in Colombia. They populate the so called "sweat shops" in Taiwan, Hong Kong, New Delhi, Bombay, and Bangkok weaving, connecting wires, sowing. Their pay is minimal; they are stunted in their physical development; they are denied an education; they lack the family care to develop a healthy self-image; and they are deprived of a healthy moral and spiritual development. And we buy the goods they make!

Of course, we say that child labor is not our fault, but we mostly do not even know under what circumstances goods have been produced, and it abhors us to hear such things. Indeed these facts are so terrible that we all develop mechanisms to keep them at arm's length from us. But we are,

---

11. This story was told to me by Sir Ronald Wilson, President of the Human Rights and Equal Opportunity Commission, a national independent statutory body of the Australian Government.

12. Human Rights and Equal Opportunity Commission, *Bringing Them Home*, 266.

13. United Nations Children's Fund, *The State of the World's Children 1997*, 17.

14. For information and statistics about child labor see International Labor Organization, "Child Labour," and Human Rights Watch, "Children's Rights."

whether we like it or not, part of a system that robs children, men, and women of their freedom and their future.

One need only consider the economic reality in our global village. Two factors are determinative: *profit making* and *competitiveness on the national and international markets*. Both forces call for the best product at the cheapest price. The price and the quality of a product determine whether it can survive in a very competitive world market. The established economic structures encourage child labor and poor working conditions. Child labor is cheap, and children have no voice and no power to protest. Parents are forced into submission because the family cannot survive without the income of the children. At the same time, the fathers of these children are denied their right to work and the pride of caring for their family. Many lose their sense of self-worth. This in turn often gives rise to aggression, alcoholism, crime, and child and spousal abuse, all of which destroy the human environment so necessary for the healthy development of a child.

It is indeed a vicious circle. Where child labor is the strongest, unemployment is the highest. More child labor will keep the wages low, the working conditions poor, and the social security inadequate. It thus intensifies the exploitation of the whole work force, and the poor will ever become poorer.[15]

The future does not look promising for children in the two-thirds world. Governments in their countries have tremendous debts they need to repay in order to maintain enough credibility to qualify for new debts. Many of them are engaged in internal and external strife and therefore have ever-increasing defense budgets. Where is the money for interest repayments and weapons taken from? Is it from the health and education budgets which are supposed to pave the way for a better future? It is difficult to avoid the impression that children and future generations are sacrificed on the altar of the self-interest of the present generation.

Do we have anything to do with stealing children's future from them? Whether we like it or not, we are part of a system that tells us to buy the best carpet and the best video recorder and the best computer and the best silk shirt for the cheapest price—and thereby we facilitate stealing freedom from some children somewhere in the world.

---

15. For the correlation between unemployment, poverty, and child labor see the many examples and vignettes in Schmitz, Traver, and Larson, *Child Labor*.

Child Soldiers

We have seen them in documentaries about struggles in Africa, Asia, and the Middle East. Children with guns. They are taught to hate and to kill. They see and they commit atrocities that are hard to believe. In addition to fighting, girls also have to provide sexual favors for men and boys. These boys and girls have no education and they experience no love. They will be psychologically damaged for the rest of their lives.[16] Community movements and governments that seek to solve problems with war and violence steal the future from these children.

Global corruption

Corruption is rampant worldwide, in places high and low. Whether one thinks of the United Nation's "oil for food" program for Iraq, the $3.2 trillion worldwide construction industry, the industrial military complex, or the global health systems and their need for drugs, everywhere, in high places of governments and industry, and in low places of consultants, police, customs officials, and public servants, the welfare of people is undermined by corruption. The annual Global Corruption Reports list example after example of how stealing has become an acceptable practice in places high and low.[17] Millions of dollars were paid by the Australian Wheat Board to maintain its business with Iraq as part of the UN "oil for food" program. This money flowed via Jordan to Iraq to keep in power the man against whom the Australian government joined a coalition to start a preemptive war—Saddam Hussein. Australian commercial interests supported a regime against which Australian soldiers later had to risk their lives.[18]

The story is told about a Mt. Everest expedition who on their last stretch to the top passed one and then another two mountain climbers who were in obvious difficulty, cowering in the snow, close to death. No word was exchanged, no food, water, or oxygen offered. Eisuke Shigekawa, Hiroshi Hanada, and their Sherpas (who in strict mountaineering discipline must follow the commands of their leaders) walked passed. On the way back, one climber was dead, one had disappeared, one was still alive. Again, they

---

16. Batstone tells the story of the child soldiers in the "Lord's Resistance Army," a militia group mainly made up of boys and girls in Uganda (*NOT for Sale*, ch. 4).

17. The Global Corruption Reports are easily accessible at www.globalcorruptionreport.org and www.transparency.org. See also the readable account of global corruption by Ziegler, *Die neuen Herrscher der Welt und ihre globalen Widersacher*.

18. News Limited, "AWB Kickback Scandal."

walked passed, leaving the climber freezing to death. In a subsequent interview Eisuke Shigekawa said that above 8000 meters there is no room for morality.[19] That seems also to be the attitude in big business and government. Above a certain "height" there is no longer room for morality.

COLONIALISM

It must have been one of the greatest acts of robbery in the history of humankind when in the twilight of the nineteenth century Africa was colonized. Belgian King Leopold's exploits in the heart of Africa had raised the awareness and subsequent jealousy of other leaders in Europe. The then chancellor of Germany, Otto von Bismarck, was asked by Portugal to host an Africa conference. From November 15, 1884, to February 26, 1885, fourteen European nations plus the USA met in Berlin. Before the conference 80% of Africa was under African self-control; after the conference and the subsequent grab for a piece of Africa, over 90% was under foreign ownership. Major colonial holdings included:[20]

- Great Britain desired a Cape-to-Cairo collection of colonies and almost succeeded through their control of Egypt, Sudan (Anglo-Egyptian Sudan), Uganda, Kenya (British East Africa), South Africa, Zambia, Zimbabwe (Rhodesia), and Botswana. The British also controlled Nigeria and Ghana (Gold Coast).

- France took much of western Africa, from Mauritania to Chad (French West Africa), Gabon and the Republic of Congo (French Equatorial Africa).

- Belgium and King Leopold II controlled the Democratic Republic of Congo (Belgian Congo).

- Portugal took Mozambique in the east and Angola in the west.

- Italy's holdings were Somalia (Italian Somaliland) and a portion of Ethiopia.

19. "Mt. Everest, 1996: Zwei Mal an Sterbenden vorbeigegangen?" A contrasting example is given by an American and British group. They met the Australian Lincoln Hall who had been thought dead and then left behind by the Sherpas near the Summit of Mt. Everest. They found him alive and stayed with him until a team of Sherpas came up to rescue him. This meant that they had to abandon their own attempt to reach the summit. One of them thought later: "How in any way is a summit more important than saving a life?" (Bearup, "Left for Dead," 24).

20. Rosenberg, "Berlin Conference of 1884–1885 to Divide Africa."

- Germany took Namibia (German Southwest Africa) and Tanzania (German East Africa).
- Spain claimed the smallest territory—Equatorial Guinea (Rio Muni).

All these European countries claim Christian tradition as formative for their respective cultures. They knew the ten commandments. But they ignored the reality that colonialism was transgressing against the eighth commandment.

Modern slavery

Most of us think that slavery is gone. It is a tragedy that it took the church 1800 years to understand the simple fact that in Christ there is "no longer slave or free" (Gal 3:28). Today the *Universal Declaration of Human Rights* states once for all: "No one shall be held in slavery or servitude; slavery and the slave trade shall be prohibited in all their forms" (§4). There is a whole human rights machinery to implement the abolition of slavery. Nevertheless, The International Labor Organization in a recent report and David Batstone in his recent book, *NOT for Sale: The Return of the Global Slave Trade—and How We Can Fight It*, have demonstrated that the modern slave trade is still a billion-dollar business in which millions of women, men, and children are deprived of their right to be free—not only in Africa and Asia, but also in the West.[21] In the USA alone, 17,500 new slaves are smuggled into the country every year.[22]

Ecology

"Ecocide is homicide."[23] The ecological crisis is beginning to enter the human consciousness, but the structures, the powers, the systems of the world are pervasive—and so far they prevail. Ecological disasters loom on the horizon. The tsunami at Christmas 2004 and the terrifying earthquake at the break of winter 2005 in the mountains of Pakistan are reminders of the forces of nature. Too often economic and national interests collide with ecological concerns—it is the latter that often lose. That is suicidal. Nature is not merely our environment. It is our destiny. We are part of it. For too long our thinking has been dominated by history and progress. Now it is time

---

21. See International Labor Organization, *A Global Alliance against Forced Labor* and Batstone, *NOT for Sale*.

22. Batstone, *NOT for Sale*, 3.

23. Rasmussen, "Human Environmental Rights and/or Biotic Rights," 39.

to change our ways. In 1992 Sandra Postel alluded to a possible epitaph for humanity: "They saw it coming but hadn't the wit to stop it happening."[24] With our continuing disrespect for nature, we are stealing the future from our children.

The preceding paragraphs have made it obvious that stealing has become an integral part of our way of life. At the personal level we are confronted with the stealing of bicycles and cars. At the corporate level, there is greed and corruption. And even governments, the very institutions that we elect to uphold the law, are involved in stealing freedom and the future from people.

What God Has Done

Can an ethos of stealing be transfigured into an ethos of giving? Can "you shall not steal" become "I would like to share"? Can we point to a reality that promises freedom rather than slavery and servitude? Can we be part of the gentle revolution that creates spaces of freedom and safety for those who have been cheated and bruised?

Realistic Hope

Realistic hope is grounded in two assertions. Firstly, that God has done something to make possible the transfiguration of selfishness to selflessness, of greed to generosity, of sin to forgiveness, of sloth to vigorous commitment to justice. Secondly, that we, individually and as a community, can hear God's invitation to faith and obey God's call by turning around and tuning actively and creatively into the story of liberation.

Let us remind ourselves that this commandment already contains a promise. In light of the introduction to the decalogue—"I am the LORD your God, who brought you out of the land of Egypt, out of the house of slavery" (Exod 20:2)—we may also interpret "you *will* not steal." The people of God, liberated by their God from slavery, are being told that part of their faith, part of their experience of liberation, is that they will not steal the freedom of other human beings. This word interprets their life under God. It spells out the structures of their liberation. They whose freedom was stolen from them, they who were slaves in Egypt will, given their own experience of liberation, not steal freedom from others. Part of their faith in God is to assert the right for all people to be free, and therefore to grant

---

24. Postel, "Denial in the Decisive Decade," 8.

this right of freedom to others. "Remember," the people of God are told again and again, how they were slaves in Egypt, how the LORD led them into a broad place where they could breathe, how the LORD sent Moses to lead them into freedom, how the LORD helped them to throw off their shackles. This experience of slavery and liberation must now shape their life. They who have experienced liberation can never be part of robbing the freedom of others.

> You shall not wrong or oppress a resident alien, *for you were aliens in the land of Egypt*. You shall not abuse any widow or orphan. If you do abuse them, when they cry out to me, *I will surely heed their cry*; my wrath will burn, and I will kill you with the sword, and your wives shall become widows and your children orphans. If you lend money to my people, to the poor among you, you shall not deal with them as a creditor; you shall not exact interest from them. If you take your neighbor's cloak in pawn, you shall restore it before the sun goes down; for it may be your neighbor's only clothing to use as cover; in what else shall that person sleep? And if your neighbor cries out to me, *I will listen, for I am compassionate*. (Exod 22:21–27, emphases added).

Jesus tunes into this tradition and the early Christians pick up the tune. In a beautiful passage the evangelist Luke composes this overture to Jesus' life:

> When he (Jesus) came to Nazareth, where he had been brought up, he went to the synagogue on the Sabbath day, as was his custom. He stood up to read; and the scroll of the prophet Isaiah was given to him. He unrolled the scroll and found the place where it was written:
>
>> "The Spirit of the Lord is upon me,
>> because he has anointed me to bring good news to the poor.
>> He has sent me to proclaim release to the captives
>> and recovery of sight to the blind,
>> to let the oppressed go free,
>> to proclaim the year of the Lord's favor."
>
> And he rolled up the scroll, gave it back to the attendant, and sat down. The eyes of all in the synagogue were fixed on him. Then he began to say to them, "Today this Scripture has been fulfilled in your hearing." (Luke 4:16–21)

Confronted with the gospel of Christ, neither fear nor guilt is the appropriate response. God has created us to be free. The early Christian confession that "Christ died for our sins" means that God has made it possible to escape selfishness and greed and claim the right to be free. With our faith we remain dependent on the one who has given us that right; and we are not to forget that God has given that right to *all* people. The more we share our freedom with others, the more we shall free ourselves. As free persons we will not steal freedom from another, but we will contribute to each other's freedom.

While in the secular world this longing for freedom and equality remains a hope and a dream, those who have faith in the God of Moses and Jesus know of spiritual resources that will fuel the journey of freedom. For them the word "you shall not steal" is an invitation to make room for the God of freedom to continue the story of liberation. It is a wonderful privilege and a sobering responsibility to be part of that story.

God Is Involved in World Affairs

Our faith in God cannot be reduced to a private and personal affair. God is not only part of our personal life. God is the creator and also the sustainer of heaven and earth. That means that God is involved in world affairs—and God seeks partners in implementing the divine vision. Hidden in the letters of the apostle Paul is this wonderful little affirmation that we are "God's fellow workers" (1 Cor 3:9). Protestant theologians tend to overlook or downplay this saying. They feel that human life and work receive too much theological attention. That is a misunderstanding of God's economy. God's grace does not bypass us. It is spoken into our conscience to empower us to join God in God's passion for the world.

We are, therefore, invited to tune into the process of liberation for all people. We may not be Moses, or Jefferson, or Mandela, or Gandhi, or Xanana Gusmao, or Aung San Suu Kyi. But when God and our love for people have opened our eyes and our ears and our hearts, we shall receive the ability to see and the courage to take little steps in the right direction. There is an increasing community of pilgrims from all nations who work and pray that people may be delivered from the vicious cycle of bondage and despair. Are we willing to join hands with the messengers of freedom? Can we do any other? If we believe that our God has liberated people from slavery and has forgiven our sins, then we will do all we can so that others do not have their freedom stolen from them.

Toward a Culture of Freedom

What We Can Do

On the basis of who God is and what God has done, we are invited to stop and turn around the vicious spiral of robbing and stealing. Let us hear some stories, stories of faith, courage, and generosity that may make us aware of and invite us to join the soft revolution of granting freedom to others.

Zacchaeus—a Counter Paradigm to Stealing

In the Gospel of Luke we have this delightful little story of what happens when a person who is used to an ethos of stealing comes to a personal encounter with the living God (Luke 19:1–10). We have to realize of course that this story, like all stories in the Bible, is more than a historical narrative. When the early Christians told the story of Zacchaeus' life-changing encounter with Jesus, for them Jesus stood for God and Zacchaeus could be any one of them.

Zacchaeus was rich. His riches had come from a tax-collecting business that he had leased from the government. There was plenty of opportunity to overcharge people and pocket the rest. Stealing from others had made Zacchaeus rich. But Zacchaeus was hated because he embodied another, a more subtle way of stealing freedom from people. People did not like tax collectors because they collected taxes on the soil that God had given to the Jewish people and then gave the taxes to a Gentile government that had occupied their land. Collecting taxes was seen as collaborating with the oppressor. Some people, the so-called Zealots, refused to pay taxes and openly fought those who compromised with the Romans.

People were suspicious when Jesus focused on this despised tax collector: "Zacchaeus, *hurry* and come down; for I *must* stay at your house *today*" (v. 5). Note the urgency of the invitation. For Zacchaeus this encounter became an unexpected surprise of joy. Rather than turning away, he turned to Jesus and joyously accepted the consequences: "Look, half of my possessions, Lord, I will give to the poor; and if I have defrauded anyone of anything, I will pay back four times as much" (v. 8). This is a paradigm change. This is a transfiguration of reality. An ethos of stealing was transformed into an ethos of regret and generosity. And it was God who made that transfiguration possible.

The Right to Be Free

THE POWER OF SAYING "SORRY"

In response to the stolen children inquiry in Australia and given the fact that the Howard government (1996–2007) refused to recognize the damage that official policy had done to thousands of children and their families, the church could not remain silent.[25] The Howard government spoke of "*practical* reconciliation" with the implication that the problems of removal and assimilation could be settled with policies and money.[26] It failed to recognize the ancient insight that "one cannot live by bread alone" and that the body will remain frail and vulnerable unless the soul experiences healing.

The church in which I was a pastor in those days (1995–2005) worked through the issues. We studied the history that Australian children never learned in school. We had Aboriginal speakers and we exchanged stories with the local Aboriginal community. After a two-year process our church came to the conviction of needing to offer an apology. This is what we said:

> We (the Canberra Baptist Church) confess that we have sinned before God and against you. We acknowledge that the churches played a role in the administration of the laws and policies under which indigenous children were forcibly removed from their parents. Your families were dislocated and generational links were severed and we, as silent observers, have passively contributed. We have not honored your culture, religion and heritage. We have failed to recognize your prior presence in the land. This land to which you belong was occupied and claimed without fair and just negotiations and we have profited from those acts of dispossession. We recognize with deep regret that we have been blind to our governments making laws, and other public institutions and churches adopting policies and practices that violated fundamental human rights and contravened the United Nations *Convention on the Prevention and Punishment of the Crime of Genocide* (1948, entered into force 1951).
>
> We recognize and confess our failure to see that what has been done to you, denied our common humanity, and degrades us all. We acknowledge the prophetic and compassionate intentions of many missionaries and Christian workers. At the same time, Christian churches, in bringing the Gospel to Australia, often failed to acknowledge that God was already present in this land, and often failed to distinguish between its own "Western" culture and the good news of Jesus Christ. We acknowledge that the

---

25. See above, pp. 137–38, and the report mentioned in fn 9.
26. Howard, "Towards Reconciliation."

continuing social dislocation, loss of personal identity, and high rate of imprisonment is often a direct result of children having been separated from their parents.

For all this we are truly sorry and apologize unreservedly.

The apology was generously accepted. It meant a small advance in the story of freedom.

Statement of Awareness by the European Baptist Mission

Another institutional response to becoming aware of robbing people of their freedom and identity is how a modern missionary society working in Africa is addressing the context there. We have seen how the colonialization of Africa was one of the greatest acts of robbery in the history of humankind. No one who works or ministers in Africa can ignore that tragedy. Here is what the *European Baptist Mission* declared in Berlin 2004, the same place in which Africa was carved up in 1884/85.

> As European Christians who follow the example of Jesus Christ, we must confess that we have profited from the inequality of nations and markets. We must confess that we are a part of a system that has for too long accepted these past and present injustices without resistance; and that has pocketed these profits for itself and its own prosperity without a guilty conscience. We confess that we stand in the debt of our African neighbors in many regards, and that we owe them more than the promise of a future work in partnership.
>
> At the same time we ask our African partner churches for forgiveness for allowing the spirit of colonialism to make a mockery of the spirit of Christ. We ask for forgiveness for the lack of fraternalism and simple partnership, which regularly comes to light in the joint activities of the European and African churches. We also ask for forgiveness for the events of the past, which we recognize today as being contrary to the spirit of Christ. . . .
>
> We support the challenge for a "New Berlin Conference," which has been raised several times, especially by Nigerian president Obasanjo since he took office in 1999. As member churches of the European Baptist Mission we call upon our governments to immediately stand up for the convening of this type of a truly "new" conference.
>
> We do, however, look to the future and vow to devote our energy toward the goal of having peace and justice prevail in all levels of our shared lives: church, society, economics and politics. We do this in accordance with the words of our Lord: "Blessed are the

peacemakers." We vow to learn from the 1884 Berlin Conference to strive for a world where justice prevails.[27]

WILLIAM KNIBB IN THE CARRIBEAN

History is replete with stories of women and men who have risked their lives to gain freedom for others. The Anglican William Wilberforce (1759–1833), the Quaker Granville Sharpe (1735–1813) and the Methodist John Wesley (1703–1791) fuelled the anti-slavery movement towards the end of the eighteenth and beginning of the nineteenth centuries by realizing that their faith in Jesus Christ included opposition to slavery. The famous porcelain manufacturer Josiah Wedgwood produced a medallion which portrayed a slave in chains, naked, kneeling, lifting up his hands and pleading: "Am I not a Man (human being) and a Brother?" It became the logo for the anti-slavery movement in Great Britain.

In 1988, at the 150th anniversary of the abolition of slavery in the Caribbean,[28] the British Baptist Missionary, William Knibb (1803–1845) was granted Jamaica's highest civil honor, *The Order of Merit*. Only one other non-Jamaican, and no white person, shared the honor at the time. The inscription reads:

> For Knibb's work as liberator of the slaves.
> For his work in laying the foundation of Nationhood.
> For his support of black people and things indigenous.
> For his display of great courage against tremendous odds.
> For being an inspiration then and now.[29]

He was only 42 when he died. But his name, like the names of Adoniram Judson in Myanmar, William Carey in India, and Hudson Taylor in China are remembered with reverence and gratitude to the present day. For them, preaching the gospel of Christ and engaging in the struggle for liberation from slavery and oppression and helping people to shape their cultural identity was one and the same thing. A modern theological statement, the *Micah Declaration*, says it this way:

---

27. European Baptist Mission, "The 'Berlin Conference' 1884."

28. The slave trade in the British Empire was officially prohibited in 1807. Then again in 1833 slavery was officially abolished in the British colonies. But it took until 1838 for the abolition to be effectively implemented in the Caribbean.

29. Jackson, "William Knibb."

Integral mission or holistic transformation is the proclamation and demonstration of the gospel. It is not simply that evangelism and social involvement are to be done alongside each other. Rather, in integral mission our proclamation has social consequences as we call people to love and repentance in all areas of life. And our social involvement has evangelistic consequences as we bear witness to the transforming grace of Jesus Christ. If we ignore the world we betray the word of God which sends us out to serve the world. If we ignore the word of God we have nothing to bring to the world. Justice and justification by faith, worship and political action, the spiritual and the material, personal change and structural change belong together. As in the life of Jesus, being, doing and saying are at the heart of our integral task.[30]

The Story of a Shipping Clerk

May I introduce you, finally, to Edmund Dene Morel. Morel was a shipping clerk at Elder Dempster, a shipping line based in Liverpool, England. We are at the end of the nineteenth century. He would never have graced the pages of history books. But Edmund Dene Morel had conscience and courage and he used it to fuel the anti-slavery movement, bringing freedom to slaves in the heart of Africa.

The famous Anglo-Polish novelist Joseph Conrad wrote the novel *The Heart of Darkness*. It is about the darkness of greed and imperialism and fate in the Congo during the nineteenth century. The Belgian King Leopold had made an early claim in the 1870s to the Congo River and its wealth in diamonds, ivory, and rubber. He became the first of the greedy colonialists exploiting Africa to increase their wealth and power in Europe. He did it under the guise of opening up the heart of Africa for missionaries and capitalists.

In Europe, at that time the first bicycle tire was inflated. Rubber was in demand. Before the time of rubber plantations, wild rubber was found as long creeping vines deep in the forests of the Congo. Leopold enslaved men and sent them into the forest to get rubber, which he then shipped with Elder Dempster ships to Belgium. The wives and children of the slaves, separated from their husbands and fathers, starved. This unleashed one of the greatest tragedies in Africa, with possibly 10 million women, children, and old people dying.

---

30. Micah Network, "Micah Declaration on Integral Mission." The Micah Network is a coalition of evangelical churches and aid agencies from around the world committed to integral mission.

The Right to Be Free

Edmund Morel was sent to Antwerp to inspect the Elder Dempster ships, their loadings, and documents. He soon noticed that the consignment records were falsified. Ships that arrived in Belgium with rubber were sent back with soldiers, guns, and ammunition. He recorded it. Slavery, exploitation, and murder could be the only conclusion. Here are Morel's own words: "I was giddy and appalled by the cumulative significance of my discoveries. It must be bad enough to stumble upon a murder. I had stumbled upon a secret society of murderers with a King for a croniman."[31]

Morel took his heart into his hands and protested. He became one of the finest investigative journalists, a beacon in the struggle against slavery. An ordinary citizen, like you and me, he had his eyes opened and accepted responsibility for what he saw.

Conclusion

"You shall not steal" is the invitation to a new lifestyle inspired by an intentional faith in the God who wants all people to be free. There is a soft revolution around the world, engaged in setting people free. We can all join in. David Batstone has started his own organization and lists many other movements that invite people to join them so that stealing people and their freedom may indeed become history.[32]

---

31. Hochschild, *King Leopold's Ghost*, 181.

32. Batstone's organization is found under www.notforsalecampaign.org/ and www.NotforSaleFund.org. The addresses and websites of other organizations that pursue the same purpose are found in *NOT for Sale*, 283–93.

11

Speaking Truth in Public
The Ninth Word

"You shall not bear false witness against your neighbor."

Exodus 20:16 and Deuteronomy 5:20
Related texts: Deuteronomy 19:15–21; Exodus 1:15–19; 1 Kings 21;
Micah 3; Matthew 5:33–37; James 3:1–12

Exodus 20:16	Deuteronomy 5:20
You shall not bear false witness (*ed shaqer*—"*lying witness*") against your neighbor.	*Neither* shall you bear false witness (*ed shaw*—"*witness of emptiness/nothingness*") against your neighbor.

THEOLOGICAL COMMENTS

THE ORIGINAL SCENE IN ancient Israel is the court of law at the city gate where the free men and the elders deliberate a case and thereby engage the help of witnesses. A "witness" can also be the "accuser." If persons witness something that is not right, they must bring it to the attention of the elders and accept personal responsibility for the factuality of their claim. Ignoring injustice or remaining silent when witnessing something that is wrong is not an option. "When any of you sin in that you have heard a public adjuration to testify and—though able to testify as one who has seen or learned of the matter—*does not speak up*, you are subject to punishment" (Lev 5:1, emphasis mine). The sin of omission is as serious as the sin of commission.

Speaking Truth in Public

Two different Hebrew words are used for "false witness." One emphasizes the truth/lie problem (Exod 20:16), the other suggests that a lie has no ground (Deut 5:20). It is built on nothingness. It is empty.

Witnesses can be true or false. "A truthful witness saves lives, but one who utters lies is a betrayer" (Prov 14:25). "Like a war club, a sword, or a sharp arrow is one who bears false witness against a neighbor" (Prov 25:18; see also Deut 19:18; Prov 6:19). A true witness saves and enhances life, while false witnesses stand in the service of death. Indeed, Israelites were constantly concerned about their reputation—"A good name is better than precious ointment" (Eccl 7:1)—and they lamented it when false witnesses rose up against them (Pss 27:12; 35:11). The criteria for being true or false relate to the saving or enhancing of life on the one hand and its diminishing or destruction on the other.

There are two ways in which Israel tried to deal with the problem of false witnesses. They are listed in Deuteronomy 19:15–21. Two or three witnesses are better than one. And, if witnesses are proven wrong, then they shall receive the punishment that was due to the potential offender.

"Neighbor" refers to "the broader sense of 'fellow human being.'"[1] This is underlined by the fact that the translators of the Hebrew Bible into Greek (the so-called *Septuagint*) used the term *plēsion* which refers to all human beings "regardless of their national and religious ties."[2] This wide meaning is grounded in the theological conviction that "God's revelation . . . is intended for the whole world."[3]

Israel's prophets were aware that justice was being diverted in high places.

> Your princes are rebels and companions of thieves. Everyone loves a bribe and runs after gifts. They do not defend the orphan, and the widow's cause does not come before them. (Isa 1:23)

> Ah, you who are heroes in drinking wine and valiant at mixing drink, who acquit the guilty for a bribe, and deprive the innocent of their rights! (Isa 5:22–23)

> Listen, you heads of Jacob and rulers of the house of Israel! Should you not know justice?—you who hate the good and love the evil, who tear the skin off my people, and the flesh off their bones; who

---

1. Kühlewein, "רֵעַ," 1244. See also Kellerman, "רֵעַ," 526–27.
2. Ibid.
3. Kellerman, "רֵעַ," 531.

eat the flesh of my people, flay their skin off them, break their bones in pieces, and chop them up like meat in a kettle, like flesh in a caldron. (Mic 3:1–3)

The ninth commandment aims at protecting a basic right of Israelites, their reputation. To lose one's reputation means the diminishing of life. With our words and with our silence we can enhance or destroy the lives of others and we can advance or hinder the cause of justice in our midst. We are responsible for our neighbor in the public place.

As is often the case, Jesus radicalized this word. For him the neighbor includes the enemy (Matt 5:43–48) and one's language must be radically related to telling the truth: "Let your word be 'Yes, Yes' or 'No, No'; anything more than this comes from the evil one" (Matt 5:33–37). In the parable of the good Samaritan Jesus makes clear that it is not we who define who our neighbor is but the "other," any other, the unlikely other, who determines to whom we are called to be the neighbor (Luke 10:29–37). For Jesus, worshipping God and loving one's neighbor belong together (Mark 12:29–31).

MESSAGE

Introduction

As I have been emphasizing, the "ten words" are not laws to restrict our freedom. They are guidelines to discipline our freedom so that our freedom may be a worthy reflection of the God who has given it to us and a helpful reality to shape the culture in which we live. "You shall not bear false witness against your neighbor" challenges us to live responsibly in the public arena. We have heard previously about protecting one's parents, about not stealing freedom from people, about not killing. Now the emphasis is on protecting our neighbor's dignity and reputation. We are to confess the God who has liberated us from the chains of self-interest and who has freed us from spiritual sleepiness by living truthfully in the public place. People who believe in God will honor those whom God has created. They will show their faith in God by protecting the dignity and reputation of their neighbor. Such respect for one's neighbors, whoever they may be, builds trust and therefore contributes to a culture of freedom.

Speaking Truth in Public

A "Lying Witness" Is a "Witness of Emptiness"

The Exodus version of this commandment reads literally, "You shall not testify against your neighbor as a *lying witness*." The Deuteronomy version is a little different: "You shall not speak against your neighbor as a witness of *nothingness (emptiness)*." This small difference is suggestive. The arena is the public, the market-place of life. The original scene is the village community, which solves its legal, social and criminal problems in that male citizens meet at the gate of the city and deliberate about justice. A testimony can mean freedom or condemnation for a potential suspect. Witnesses therefore have the lives of other people in their hands. The witness can influence decisions of life or death for the accused. To protect the dignity of the accused, the witness must tell the truth. A "lying witness" will cause harm to another person and thereby do injustice to one of God's creatures. Such witnesses have no respect for life, its dignity and freedom. Their words are empty, grounded not in truth but in *nothingness*.

There are many ways in which people can become "lying witnesses" or "witnesses of emptiness." There are occasions when our lives are in the hands of others, when we depend on others to defend us and to guard our honor and reputation. This commandment spurns us to unmask false witnesses, to name those aspects of our life and our society that harm people because spin and dishonesty have become more important than commitment to the truth.

Today we live in a global village. Every other human being is our neighbor. However limited our exposure to the world may be, our responsibility is global. And, if in addition we realize that moral responsibility is not to justify what is comfortable and convenient but to unmask what is wrong, to name it, and to suggest ways to change things in the direction of peace and justice, then this commandment speaks directly to our situation.

Reputation and Honor

There are cultures in which it is common for people to commit suicide if they "lose face." Honor and reputation is more important to them than life. We also hear of families in which a person is killed if she or he steps outside accepted social mores. A Moslem woman, for instance, who fell in love with a Christian man and wanted to marry him, was killed by her brothers. They felt that the reputation of their family and their religion was at stake. Indeed, "honor killings" is a major problem in many countries. As I am writing (April 2007) the news comes through from Ramle, Israel that in the Abu Ghanem family in the past six years eight women have been murdered to maintain the "family honor." Last year a young woman—Reem Abu Ghanem, 19 years old—sought the protection of her brother, a pediatrician, because she did not want to marry the man whom the men of the family had chosen for her. But instead of protecting his sister he smothered her with anesthetic chemicals and then handed her over to her other four brothers who "buried" her while still alive in an old well. This year another girl—Hamda Abu Ghanem, also 19 year of age—was shot in the head nine times by her own brother.[4]

These extreme examples remind us of the universal human reality that no one likes their honor and reputation destroyed. There is, of course, no justification for the above. Indeed according to universal moral standards found in many human rights instruments, it is the brothers, not their sisters, who destroyed the honor of their family. Nevertheless, it is to criticize people behind their backs and thereby suggest that we are better than they are. Professional jealousy erodes trust because people are suspicious of false witnesses. This word therefore challenges us to protect the dignity of people and enhance their freedom by telling and living the truth. The Psalmist reminds us: "Who shall ascend the hill of the LORD? And who shall stand in his holy place? Those who have clean hands and pure hearts, who do not lift up their souls to what is false, and do not swear deceitfully. They will receive blessing from the LORD, and vindication from the God of their salvation" (Ps 24:3–5).

Responsibility in the Public Arena

Many have experienced the hurt, the damage, and the destruction which a false testimony can cause. No one would want to curtail the freedom of the press. How would we otherwise unmask and discover the political intrigues, the injustice, and the misuse of power in high places? But freedom demands a commitment to truth, otherwise it becomes an instrument of nothingness. A journalist, by bending, slanting or withholding truth, can destroy a person by publishing a false or slanted report. Once in the public arena, a story, true or untrue, cannot be untold. Nothing is more difficult to kill than a rumor!

---

4. Hardaker, "Women Break Silence on Honour Killings."

Speaking Truth in Public

In the Epistle of James (3:1–12) the tongue is given a significant role in ruling one's life. It is like "bits in the mouths of horses" by which we can guide "their whole bodies." It is like a "very small rudder" by which a captain can guide a large ship through strong winds and waves. Like a "small fire" it can set great forests ablaze. With the tongue "we bless the Lord and Father, and with it we curse those who are made in the likeness of God." The tongue demonstrates who we are. "Can a fig tree, my brothers and sisters, yield olives, or a grapevine figs?" To be truthful and not damage the reputation of others is essential for our own well-being.

It is very possible that telling lies or starting rumors about others mostly results from a sense of anxiety. Being aware of our own limitations, we may become jealous of others and then seek ways to drag them down. We start rumors or encourage innuendos about our colleagues at work to advance our own career. We are silent when others tell untruths in order not to get involved or to look after our own interests. Committing ourselves to the truth of the "ninth word" will improve our mental and spiritual health. It makes us agents of life, rather than servants of death.

Telling the Truth

I remember an experience from the end of World War II. My father was on active duty. My mother and we three children lived with our grandparents in Güstrow, Mecklenburg (a small town halfway between Hamburg and Berlin), because our apartment in Hamburg had been destroyed during the carpet bombings in July/August 1943. In Güstrow we lived at the edge of the town adjoining the forest where, towards the end of the war, at the beginning of 1945, the battle between Germans and Russians was being fought. The noise of gun and cannon shots came closer and closer. My grandfather took us all into the cellar of the house. We were huddled together, frightened.

Then there was a knock on the door. My grandfather shouted, "who is there?" A German voice pleaded for someone to open the door. He opened the door and there stood two frightened teenagers in uniform. They were fleeing from the Russians and asking us to hide them. What to do? The propaganda had made quite clear that whoever hid German soldiers would be shot on the spot. My mother took over. She told the two frightened boys that they must leave again as soon as possible—and then hid them in a cupboard.

We huddled back in fear and panic. Then came another knock. Firm. Demanding. It was the first wave of Russian soldiers who tried to capture fleeing German soldiers. To our total surprise they were kind and polite. They offered us children candies and asked the adults whether they were hiding any German soldiers. My grandfather said that we had not seen any. They searched through the house. They did not find the soldiers, and then they left. We breathed a deep sigh of relief. Immediately after the Russians left, my mother told the German teenage-soldiers that they must leave. She pointed them to a safe way into the forest that was right near our house. They left, and I have often wondered what became of the two young soldiers.

The question is whether it was right to tell a lie in order to save the lives of these teenage soldiers—and our own! A simplistic and legalistic interpretation of the truth/lie challenge would say that one must never tell a lie. But if the truth/lie question is related to the demands not of a law or a principle but of the living God, and therewith to the enhancement of human life, then the matter becomes more complicated. My grandfather was right to tell a lie, indeed one might consider it the will of God in that situation to tell a lie, because he saved human life. In that situation, telling a lie was the real truth, because it saved life. Otherwise he would have been a false witness.

We may also recall the interesting little story of the Pharaoh's midwives who were supposed to kill all male children of the Israelites, lest they became too numerous and powerful. But Shiphrah and Puah who were committed to the service of life could not agree to become servants of death. When questioned, they told a lie and thereby became witnesses to the truth: "the midwives feared God; they did not do as the king of Egypt commanded them, but they let the boys live" (Exod 1:15–19).

"History Wars" in Australia

In Australia we are witnessing a "history war."[5] It is a conflict about the interpretation of history. Prime Minister Howard, elected in 1996, did not only have a political and economic program. He also had a cultural agenda. It has to do with the beginnings and the progress of British/European

---

5. The relevant literature is extensive. Much of it is mentioned in the review article by Bonnell and Crotty, "An Australian 'Historikerstreik'?" See also MacIntyre and Clark, *The History Wars*, especially chapters 1 and 8; and Attwood and Foster, *Frontier Conflict: The Australian Experience*, 1–30. A concrete example is provided by Ryan, "Waterloo Creek Northern New South Wales, 1838."

settlement of the Australian continent. Among the foundational questions, relating of course to the identity of Australia as a people and a nation, is whether a spirit of genocide with regard to Australia's indigenous people has to be acknowledged as part of Australia's history and identity.

This basic question centers around two topics. The first is the extent of racially motivated massacres and other aspects of intentionally dispossessing Aboriginal people, taking their land and destroying their social fabric. The other is the intent and extent of forcibly removing "half-caste" children from their mothers in order to breed the aboriginality out of them and assimilate them into "white" society.[6]

Those historians—and it is the vast majority of respected historians—who insist that those aspects of Australia's history must not be denied, but must be addressed, are accused of having a "black armband view of history."[7] The government, on the other hand, with the help of some historians, insists that atrocities are exaggerated, that many can be explained, that massacres have been fabricated, that stolen children were removed for their own well-being, and that the aboriginal people "must get on with life." The help offered for "getting on with life" is called "*practical* reconciliation." Saying "sorry" is considered to be superfluous and emotive. By wanting to maintain a positive view of history, the government and its conservative supporters fail to realize that some wounds cannot be healed with money. We cannot undo or redo history, but at the same time, any government— e.g., the German government with regard to the Jews, Gypsies (Romanies) and communists; the US government with regard to slaves and Native Americans; the Canadian government with respect to the First Nations people, etc.—should be concerned about healing the past. And although total healing is not possible, it is imperative that the stories be heard with open hearts, that a genuine confession of guilt and an apology be made, and that compensation be offered. Otherwise we bear false witness against our neighbor.

---

6. Both issues are discussed in the volume of essays edited by Moses, *Genocide and Settler Society*. With regard to massacres and a "genocidal spirit" see especially the articles by Kociumbas, Reynolds, Evans, Watson, Bartrop, and Haebich. For the "stolen generations" see especially Manne. The controversy about frontier massacres is well described and analysed in the articles in Attwood and Foster, *Frontier Conflict: The Australian Experience*.

7. The "black armband" metaphor was coined by the historian Geoffrey Blainey in 1993, and then taken up by Prime Minister Howard (see Attwood and Foster, "Introduction," *Frontier Conflict: The Australian Experience*, 28–29n39).

Lying in High Places

Prime Minister John Howard and his government in Australia had been in office since March 1996. Two elections had been won, and the third was called for on November 10, 2001. The Opposition (the Labor Party) was doing well in the run-up to the election. Then three major events happened. They caused the election to be dominated by the issues of terrorists, asylum-seekers and refugees—all related to the issue of security. Mr. Howard was able to convey the impression of being tough on security, and the majority of people, having become unsure and feeling unsafe, re-elected his government. It was a "dark victory."[8] These three events were:

- *September* 11, 2001 with the terrorist attacks on the World Trade towers and the Pentagon in the USA. Prime Minister Howard happened to be in Washington at that time which gave a personal dimension to his response to that tragedy.

- *The Tampa affair.* During the last days of August 2001 the Norwegian freighter, *MV Tampa*, at the initial request of Australian rescue authorities had taken on board 438 mostly Afghan refugees from an overloaded Indonesian boat, *KM Palapa I*, that was in danger of sinking. Although the Tampa was in Indonesia's sea-rescue zone, it was closer in distance to the Australian territory of Christmas Island. Captain Arne Rinnan requested entrance into Australian waters to bring the refugees to Christmas Island. The request was denied. He was told to take the refugees to Indonesia or Norway. Nevertheless, it being an emergency situation—the Tampa was a cargo ship, not a passenger liner!—Rinnan, following two medical "Mayday" calls that remained unanswered, decided to enter Australian waters and sail to Christmas Island. There he was boarded by Australian SAS military troops and ordered to go back. He refused. The government tried to push through a "Border Protection Bill 2001" that would have allowed them—retroactively—to use military force to turn the ship around, which would have made it impossible for the refugees to apply for protection in Australia. The bill was defeated in the Senate. Finally, when its popularity sank in the polls, when the Refugee High Commissioner, Mary Robinson publicly criticized the Australian government, and when there was a worldwide outcry, the

---

8. So the title of a book by Marr and Wilkinson who set out in great detail the "Tampa affair" and the "children overboard" deception, both just before the election in 2001.

Howard government caved in. But, rather than taking the refugees on Australian soil, it exploited the economic needs of Nauru—after East Timor had refused to cooperate in this manner—took the refugees on to the Navy vessel, *HMAS Manoora*, and took them to Nauru for detention and processing.[9]

- *The Children overboard affair*.[10] With the "Tampa affair," the issue of "refugees" was in the air; then came the "Children overboard affair." In the beginning of October 2001, a month before the election, the *HMAS Adelaide* intercepted *SIEV 4* (Suspected Illegal Entry Vessel 4) near Christmas Island. It had 187 Iraqi asylum-seekers on board. The *HMAS Adelaide* fired warning shots to hinder the boat from entering Australian waters. People were frightened. Some jumped ship. Others held their children in the air to demonstrate their vulnerability. The *HMAS Adelaide* took the refugee boat into tow to take it back into international waters. A day later the ship began to sink. Women, men, and children were in the water. They were all saved by the crew of the *HMAS Adelaide*. Misreading a communication from the *HMAS Adelaide*, government officials and, on the officials advice, ministers of the government accused the refugees of throwing children overboard. The then Minister of Immigration Philip Ruddock proclaimed, "I regard this as some of the most disturbing practices I've come across in public life . . . People would not come wearing life jackets unless they planned action of this sort."[11] Melbourne's biggest selling newspaper, the *Sun Herald*, "quoted an 'angry' John Howard saying, 'I don't want people like that in Australia. Genuine refugees don't do that . . . They hang on to their children.'"[12] The controversial pictures taken were of the refugees who were in the water as the boat was sinking and as they waited to be picked up by the crew of the *HMAS Adelaide*. The matter was intentionally left unclear until after the election. A Senate report from 2002 demonstrated that the government knew that the claim of "children overboard" was false.[13] Two years later a senior public servant confirmed that he

9. The Tampa Affair is detailed in Marr and Wilkinson, *Dark Victory*.
10. See pictures and various opinions in "The Unthrown Kids."
11. Marr and Wilkinson, *Dark Victory*, 186.
12. Ibid., 189.
13. Parliament of Australia, Senate, Select Committee for an Inquiry into a Certain Maritime Incident.

had spoken to the Prime Minister three times and told him that there was no evidence that children had been thrown overboard. The phone calls took place three days before the election. The Prime Minister and several ministers knew the truth, but they decided not to reveal it.[14] It was lying in high places.

Something similar happened on the world stage when the USA and Great Britain needed to justify commencing a pre-emptive war against Iraq without the mandate of the United Nations Security Council. In February 2003 the then Secretary of State of the USA, Colin Powell, addressed the UN Security Council, backing up his speech with satellite pictures, claiming that there was no doubt in his mind that Saddam Hussein possessed weapons of mass destruction. Two years later he publicly admitted that there was no truth to that statement. The then Prime Minister of Great Britain, Tony Blair, expressed the same convictions and even announced that Saddam Hussein could deploy his chemical weapons within 45 minutes. It is recognized in many circles today that the Iraq war is a disaster. Political expediency, ideological pragmatism, and economic benefit drove the agenda more than bringing peace and democracy to the Middle East or security to the rest of the world. A proverbial saying is that the first victim in any war is the truth.

Underlying Racism

Societal leaders like politicians and journalists can bear false witness against people and thereby spread racism, mistrust, and cynicism in any society. In 1996 the conservative Australian politician, Pauline Hanson, made her maiden speech in the federal parliament. She denounced an immigration policy and multiculturalism that has caused Australia to "being swamped by Asians," and she called on the government to discontinue the "privileges Aboriginals enjoy over other Australians."[15] This attitude persists in certain circles and is given voice by influential radio commentators. It spreads hatred and suspicion. Was Hanson speaking truth in the public arena? Or was

---

14. One is reminded of Kant's famous essay *Perpetual Peace*, in which he says, "All actions affecting the rights of other human beings are wrong if their maxim is not compatible with their being made public" (126). Nevertheless, Kant issues a realistic caution right at the beginning of his essay: "The practical politician tends to look down with great complacency upon the political theorist as a mere academic" (93).

15. Hanson, "Pauline Hanson's Maiden Speech."

she a "witness of emptiness" that increased the racism in Australian society and hindered the process of reconciliation with the indigenous people?

Prophetic Preaching

In the story about the king and his wife who wanted to acquire Naboth's vineyard, we have a good illustration of true and false witnesses (1 Kgs 21). In order to get what does not belong to them, Jezebel, Ahab's wife, employs two "scoundrels" as witnesses. In a public assembly they witness against Naboth—"you have cursed God and the king"—and thereby provide the legal legitimacy to have Naboth stoned to death. The prophet Elijah is a witness to the truth. He names the injustice—"Have you killed, and also taken possession?"—and then pronounces God's judgment upon Ahab.

Like the Hebrew prophet, the Christian preacher is also called to be a public witness to the truth. One of his or her responsibilities is to claim language for the truth. He or she has twenty or thirty minutes of uninterrupted time to deal with an issue. Given that most issues are complex and that generalities are boring—all people prefer peace to war and love to hate—the preacher must accept the risk and the danger of being specific and proclaiming the will of God in a certain situation. Otherwise they risk being witnesses of emptiness and prefer spin to truth.

Authentic witnesses accept responsibility for what they see and say. The English word "witness" comes from the Greek *martys* which is related to "martyr." Martyrs give their lives for what they consider to be the truth. They stake their life on the truth. For them truth is more important than life. People like Jeremiah, Jesus and Paul named what they saw and did not withdraw when life became difficult. Suffering became a distinctive mark of their life-story. Not because they sought suffering. They did not have a so-called martyrs' complex. They were suffering prophets because they wanted to be witnesses for the truth.

Forgiveness

The fact is that with all our determination not to be false witnesses against others, with all our commitment not to twist language and thereby hide rather than reveal, with all our resolve to speak truth rather than to use spin, we still fail. We miss the mark and thereby we become divided within ourselves. The story is told that at the end of a talk by the Dalai Lama, someone from the audience asked, "Why didn't you fight back against the

Chinese?" The Dalai Lama looked down, swung his feet just a bit, then looked back up and said with a gentle smile, "Well, war is obsolete, you know." Then, after a few moments, his face grave, he said, "Of course the mind can rationalize fighting back . . . but the heart, the heart would never understand. Then you would be divided in yourself, the heart and the mind, and the war would be inside you."

When we are divided within ourselves we need healing. Otherwise anxiety will grow within us and we shall feel the need to compensate for it by becoming false witnesses against others. Faith in Christ carries with it the promise that we are saved by grace, not by works. Such faith reduces anxiety—"there is no fear in love" (1 John 4:18)—and therefore takes away the temptation to use lies, spin and rumors in order to justify or exalt ourselves.

Conclusion

Speaking and living the truth in public is not easy. It has never been easy. There were times when bearers of bad news were slain although their message was true. At the courts of nobility during the Middle Ages, there was, besides the minstrels and poets and knights, the court jester. He was the fool. No one took him seriously, but no one wanted to miss him. He alone could tell the truth to everyone. A truth which could then be laughed away.

In our time we have experienced eloquent witnesses to the truth. Nelson Mandela, for instance, who, for the sake of truth, endured 27 years in prison and thereby unmasked the blasphemous claim of government and church to act in the name of almighty God. And who will not want to mention the prophets of the Old Testament, the apostles of the New Testament, and the martyrs of the Christian church who, because of their commitment to truth, had to bear the marks of the Crucified in their own bodies and souls?

And what about him who uncompromisingly fleshed out truth? Not like the Greek philosopher walking the halls of learning, trying to approach the truth by question and answer. No! Concretely by restoring the dignity of the wretched of the earth. A man of sorrows, he was named. His crown was a crown of thorns. And the symbol of truth came to be a cross.

Truth seems to have a difficult time in our lives. Our faith in the God of Moses and Jesus will set us free to celebrate life and grant us the resources of courage and conviction to speak the truth in the public place.

12

Who or What Occupies Our Conscience?
The Tenth Word

"You shall not covet"

Exodus 20:17 and Deuteronomy 5:21
Related texts: Genesis 3; 2 Samuel 11–12; 1 Kings 21; Matthew 5:21–22

Exodus 20:17	Deuteronomy 5:21
You shall not covet (*chamadh*) your neighbor's *house*; you shall not covet (*chamadh*) your neighbor's *wife*, or male or female *slave*, or ox, or donkey, or anything that belongs to your neighbor.	Neither shall you covet (*chamadh*) your neighbor's *wife*. Neither shall you *desire* (*avah*) your neighbor's *house*, or *field*, or male or female *servant*, or ox, or donkey, or anything that belongs to your neighbor.

THEOLOGICAL COMMENTS

THE EXODUS VERSION PLACES the reference to the "wife" after the "house," thereby giving the impression that the wife is simply part of the other belongings of the patriarch. In Deuteronomy the "wife" is given a more prominent status: she is mentioned first, and different verbs are used for coveting the neighbor's wife and coveting the neighbor's house. It is not clear whether anything could or should be made of the different verbs in the Deuteronomy text. For some they are synonymous,[1] while others see a "significant distinction" between them: "The emphasis of

---

1. Mayer, "אוה," 135.

chamadh falls on an emotion which often leads to a commensurate action, whereas the focus of *avah* rests much more on the emotion itself."[2] For our discussion this would mean that the longing for the neighbor's wife is more intense with the desire to possess than it is for his other possessions. The valuing of the woman in Deuteronomy can also be observed in other Deuteronomic texts:[3]

- In contrast to Exodus 21:2–11, Deuteronomy 15:12 makes specific mention of the "*Hebrew* woman," implying that by that time she may have acquired some rights for herself.

- In variation to Exodus 22:16–17, Deuteronomy 22:28–29 specifically stipulates that a man who has had illegitimate sex with a virgin must not only marry her, but "because he violated her he shall not be permitted to divorce her as long as he lives."

The Roman Catholic Church and some Protestant churches (e.g., Lutherans) divide this word into two, one dealing with coveting the "neighbor's house," the other with coveting the "neighbor's wife."

"House" refers primarily to the dwellings and the land surrounding them. This was the basis for being a free and responsible citizen. Then, in addition, "house" can also refer to the wider family. An eighth-century prophetic text illustrates both meanings:

> Alas for those who devise wickedness and evil deeds on their beds! When the morning dawns, they perform it, because it is in their power. They *covet* fields, and *seize* them; houses (i.e., dwellings), and *take them away*; they *oppress* householder and house (i.e., family), people and their inheritance. (Mic 2:1–2)

This text also illustrates that the verb, "to covet" (longing, lusting, desiring), includes motivation (thinking, willing, scheming, manipulating) and its consequences (taking what one desires, acting). The same togetherness of "wanting" and "taking" in the verb "to covet" is found in Exodus 34:24 where people are assured that during their pilgrimages when, three times a year, they are away from their homes "no one shall *covet* your land when you go up to appear before the LORD your God." Coveting therefore

---

2. Childs, *The Book of Exodus*, 427.

3. For the place of women in the Deuteronomy see Frymer-Kensky, "Deuteronomy," 52–62.

describes a basic attitude to life. Not what can I give, but what can I get. Not what can I do for others, but what I can make others do for me.

This commandment is intended to protect the marriage, family, and property of people from an invasion of their "neighbors." It is therefore closely related to the previous words: the sixth (taking life), seventh (invading another's marriage), eighth (taking people's freedom) and the ninth (spoiling one's reputation). The question arises whether the tenth word adds anything to the preceding commandments. It can be seen as a kind of summary.

- It is radical in the sense that the root cause for killing, stealing, adultery, and false witness is named as coveting.
- This includes "legal" ways of coveting. A person may decide, for instance, to lend someone money although he knows that the debtor will not be able to pay back his debts. This would allow the creditor to take the debtor and his family into serfdom or slavery.
- It covers the whole belongings ("anything") of the person.
- It refers not only to the actual deed, but also to the motivation leading to the deed.

MESSAGE

Introduction

Coveting has to do with what moves us at our deepest level—our conscience. The conscience is the most valuable and the most vulnerable dimension of our life. It designates our personal identity. It determines who we are. It was an important step in the evolution of modern humanity. People began to recognize that they have inherent dignity and with it the responsibility to shape their life. The modern journey of freedom includes the claim of many parts of the Reformation in the sixteenth century, and then the Enlightenment in the seventeenth and eighteenth centuries, that our human dignity is not granted by the state or the church, but it is a given and it can be claimed. Freedom of conscience is now recognized as a core human right. It corresponds to the deepest longings of the human person.

> As a deer longs for flowing streams, so my soul longs for you, O God.
> My soul thirsts for God, for the living God. When shall I come and behold the face of God? (Ps 42:1–2)

> How lovely is your dwelling place, O LORD of hosts!
> My soul longs, indeed it faints for the courts of the LORD; my heart and my flesh sing for joy to the living God. (Ps 84:1–2)

> I long for your salvation, O LORD, and your law is my delight.
> Let me live that I may praise you, and let your ordinances help me. (Ps 119:174–75)

In a positive sense we are created to covet. To covet life. At best our conscience is not the moral spoil-sport of life. It is our orientation towards God, our longing for the God who liberates us to become who we were created to be.

The last commandment brings us back to the beginning. The ten words started out with the invitation to believe in the God who sets us free from estranging claims and forces, and brings us back to where we belong—a meaningful relationship with God. So now, in the final word we are asked whether it is really God who is determining us at our deepest level—in our conscience.

For Christians the challenge is to make faith in Christ our ultimate concern. Jesus Christ has set us free to worship God, accept ourselves, love our neighbor, care for the garden in which we have been placed and participate responsibly in the affairs of the world. In the church, for instance, where the Gospel of John was written, Jesus Christ is portrayed as the true fulfillment of our human longing. He is the "bread *of life*" (6:35, 51), the "*good* shepherd" (10:11, 14), the "*true* vine" (15:1, 5), the "light of the world" (8:12), the "resurrection and the life" (11:25), the "way, the truth and the life" (14:6). A conscience focused on Christ promises the fulfillment of life.

Coveting

"Coveting" is normally used in a negative sense. It means that our innermost drive for life has gone wrong. We all want to create and we want to relate. Focusing beyond ourselves constitutes our human identity. We are created to worship God, love our neighbor, partake of the fruits of the earth, and participate creatively in society. Our personal identity is therefore not only the life that has been given to us but also the way we use it by relating to life around us. Who we are is to a large extent shaped by the way we relate and include the "other" into our own journey.

This openness toward the "other" becomes distorted if we exploit the "other" for our own purposes. Rather than enjoying a relationship with another person, we want to use that person to fulfill our own plans and dreams. Rather than sharing the joy of friends having a new car or a new house, we become jealous and want to have what they have. Rather than worshipping God for God's own sake, we use "God" to validate our self-interested schemes and ideologies. Rather than enjoying the garden into which God has placed us, we so often use natural resources for selfish gain.

We all know what it means "to covet." The inner longings that issue into looks of desire, lust, and greed, seeking and finding ways to get what we want. It is the longing to seek our own advantage at the expense of others. It is one of those human characteristics that is evenly spread among the good and the bad, the rich and the poor, the educated and the uneducated. And often coveting is done within the parameters of legality. The law, which is designed to implement fairness and to spread justice, can be used against its own intention. Every lawyer knows that the law does not always serve truth and justice. Sometimes we use the law to escape the responsibility of freedom. Privileged persons might, for instance, employ expensive lawyers to change council regulations so they can buy the beach in front of their houses for their exclusive use, the beach which for decades has been used by the locals to fish and play. People invade the partnerships of others, claiming that it is not against the law. One can be an upright and law-abiding citizen yet "covet" what belongs to one's neighbor. And if one covets what the neighbor has, then one can no longer freely relate to that person and one's own freedom is curtailed.

Coveting is seated in the human heart. Jesus says in the Gospel of Mark, "there is nothing outside a person that by going in can defile, but the things that come out are what defile" (Mark 7:15). The same point is made in the Sermon on the Mount: "You have heard that it was said to those of ancient times, 'You shall not murder'; and 'whoever murders shall be liable to judgment.' But I say to you that if you are angry with a brother or sister, you will be liable to judgment" (Matt 5:21–22).

This also has social, political, and economic dimensions. How many million laborers, including children, are exploited in our world in the pursuit of profits for the few? There is not only coveting of the individual but also of nations. One may recall the colonial history of many European countries in the nineteenth century. And today's globalization does not bring unfettered bliss to developing nations. It is the strong who write the rules of trade, and if there is a conflict of interest, then it is clear that economic and national interest precede a commitment for a sustainable future for all humanity.

Motivation and Action

Coveting has to do with motivation and with action. We may have to update the objects of desire—car for an ox; employee for slave—but otherwise the objects of our desire sound rather modern. With a divorce rates reported as high as 40–50% in western countries and extra-marital affairs being widely accepted as normal, coveting the neighbor's wife (or husband) is well known to us. The desire for private property is also one of the accepted values of many cultures.

What is out of date—fortunately!—is that the neighbor's *wife* is mentioned in the same breath as his house, his fields, his servants, and his animals. Indeed, in the Exodus version, the wife is even mentioned *after* the house. It reminds us of those days when the wife was the property of her husband. He could domineer over her and use her. He could divorce her if he saw a more attractive woman or if she had burned his dinner. And for many women in our world, those days are not yet gone! We hear worldwide reports of wife beating, disadvantaged female children, female genital mutilation, and sexual violence. But for most of us in the West, the commandment seems dated and reminds us of days and social conditions that will hopefully never return and will soon be gone for all women.

In order to deepen and widen our understanding of coveting, let us recall some biblical stories which illustrate what it means "to covet." Perhaps we shall find our place in one or another of them.

Eve (Genesis 3)

There is the story of Eve in the garden of paradise. Into her life of dreaming innocence there comes the moment of temptation. The tempter begins to whisper to her, to deposit thoughts into her mind, to sow seeds into her heart. He does not say, "I am the tempter, and I want to talk to you about the pleasures of sin." Eve would have run as fast as she could; she would have hidden behind the next tree; and the conversation would never have taken place.

Who or What Occupies Our Conscience?

The tempter talks about God, and, using God's name, he sows a seed into Eve's heart. Is *everything* in the garden yours? Can you eat of *all* the trees in the garden? "Yes, of course I can," she assures herself. "I am free to do what I like! Freedom is part of God's beautiful creation."

But wait, there is *one* tree that I am not supposed to touch, and from which I am not supposed to eat. It is the tree of universal knowledge, the knowledge of good and evil. It is the symbolic reminder that we are human, we are not God. We are creature, not creator. It is the tree that stands for the fact that humans are finite beings and that there are limitations to human striving. It is the tree that points us to our place in creation, that we belong to God, and that God will reveal to us what is good and what is bad for us. It is the tree that shows us that there is a difference between God and humanity. Otherwise, all the garden and all the trees are there for Eve. There is enough space and time and food for everyone.

But the seed of longing has been sown into Eve's heart—and Eve stands for all of us. It is the seed of the desire to be in charge. To be independent. To know everything. The seed will now want to sprout and to blossom. Eve surveys the garden, all the trees, and all the freedom. Like the butterfly which hovers over its territory and settles down on one tree, Eve now focuses all her attention on one tree—and we all know which one it is, because we all know what it means "to covet." Does God want to hold something back? Perhaps God does not want me to be free? Perhaps God is afraid that I may become like God in power and glory.

Eve is all of us, with an unquenchable quest for knowledge and independence. Neither knowledge itself nor the search for knowledge is the problem. The problem is the demand to make ourselves the judge over good and evil and thereby to subject the rest of the world to our vision of life.

The flower is dependent on the sun, because it is the sun that guarantees its survival. The flower may not like that dependence. It may choose the eternal night, not realizing that the disappearance of the sun means the disappearance of life.

Little may we realize that by placing ourselves in the center of reality and allowing no room for the tree that is off limits, we question God's good plan for us and we remove mystery from life. We fail to recognize that we are relational creatures, created to worship God, love each other, and look after the garden in which God has placed us. To opt out of that relational existence leads to a distortion of life. Coveting is therefore very deceptive.

It promises the enrichment of life, but in fact it brings isolation, loneliness, and death.

David (2 Samuel 11–12)

David was an honorable man. A leader, a charismatic figure, a person with integrity. People trusted him. It was good that he was commander in chief. He was a good example. Men would leave wife and family and fight for their country because they trusted David.

And then he sees her. Bathsheba was her name, and Bathsheba was beautiful. Her husband was on the frontline risking his life for his country. David knows that. But coveting is powerful. It is a seemingly irresistible force. David sees her, and then he wants her, and with the power he has, he gets her. She conceives!

What do we do now? The spiral of coveting begins to turn. Evil begets evil in the attempt to cover one's tracks. David sends for her husband, Uriah. Having been starved of love and comfort on the battle front, Uriah would seek the warmth of his wife's body and then he would think that the child is his. But Uriah was an honorable man. He had been on the front, he had been in the company of mates whose lives were difficult. He needed and he deserved to lie with his wife. But no! "While my friends are sacrificing, should I have pleasure?" He slept with the servants at the king's house. David tries again. Covetousness is inventive. He invites Uriah to a feast. They eat and drink and get drunk. But even being drunk, the soldier shows more character than the king: "he went out to lie on his couch with the servants of his lord, but he did not go down to his house."

David has offended against the rules of life, and now he wants to cover his tracks. The spiral of injustice keeps turning. One deed calls for the next and the next. Uriah must die! David instructs the military commander to send Uriah and others into a heavy battle and then leave them without backup. So it happened. Not only Uriah, but his friends died with him. It was bad military strategy, but all that David is interested in is the message, "Uriah the Hittite is dead." That is all that counts. No matter how bad the strategy and how many men lost their lives, all that matters was that the king could take Bathsheba and have the child born.

One day the prophet Nathan tells David the story about a rich man who had everything, and a poor man who had nothing—except one little lamb. Like Eve, who among the many trees wanted the one, so the rich man was not satisfied to look at his riches, be grateful for them, and use them wisely. No, like a zoom lens in a camera, his greed focuses on the one lamb he did not have. And he took it! He had the power not only to covet but also to get what he wanted.

David listens, but he fails to make connections. He is incensed. "As the LORD lives, the man who has done this deserves to die," he cries out. Then Nathan turns to David: "You are the man!"

This story is not against sex. But it reminds us that sex becomes deformed if used to gratify one's own selfish desires and use other people in the process. David lives in all of us.

Ahab (1 Kings 21)

Ahab was the king of Samaria (1 Kgs 16:29). He had a palace and he had land and he had riches. But his mind zeroed in on the little vineyard next to his palace. He wanted it for his vegetable garden. The vineyard belonged to Naboth. Indeed, it had belonged to Naboth's family for generations. It had become part of the family's identity; and out of loyalty for his family tradition, Naboth was not going to sell it or exchange it for another vineyard. He had a right to keep it according to the law of the land.

But Ahab was not satisfied. All the land and all the riches and all the power he had were not enough. He wanted the little vineyard to make it into a vegetable patch.

A political intrigue was instigated. Jezebel, Ahab's wife, had Naboth killed and Ahab took the vineyard. Ahab coveted by doing nothing! When he could not get what he wanted, he sulked and went to bed. That is also a decision, a decision to escape moral responsibility and let other people do the dirty work. But when the dirty work was done he got up out of bed and took the vineyard. And the word of the LORD came to him through the prophet Elijah: "Thus says the LORD, 'You have killed, and also taken possession?' . . . 'In the place where dogs licked up the blood of Naboth shall dogs lick your own blood.'"

Ahab wanted what did not belong to him, and Ahab lives in all of us.

Sharing

What do Eve and David and Ahab have in common? What do they have in common with all of us? The fact that the desire for intensifying life can go wrong. That it can become distorted and therefore hurt rather than help people.

Every quest for knowledge, every encounter of love, every extension of our possibilities has the desire to intensify and extend life. The temptation is that we focus the search for life on ourselves, we seek resources only within us rather than in the "in between" with the "other," we forget we are communal beings and need the community for our own happiness and fulfillment, and we want to use others for our own ends. We forget the basic principle that the only way to increase happiness is not to take things from others but to share life with others.

How often do we seek knowledge, not to enhance our community, to display solidarity, and to create ways to heal the sick and feed the hungry, but to protect our own interests? How often do we engage in sex, not as the language of love and the enriching of partnership, but merely using the other for our own pleasure? How often do we use our power, not to help those who cannot help themselves, but to acquire more and more for ourselves?

Let us list some elements that make up coveting:

- Placing ourselves at the centre of reality rather than seeing ourselves as part of a diverse and colorful complex of relationships.
- Using others for our own purposes and desiring what they have.
- As the stories of David and Ahab readily demonstrate, it is often the weak and vulnerable who are being taken advantage of. The rich and powerful exploit or bypass the poor and thereby fail to understand that a just and resilient society is measured by the way it looks after its most vulnerable citizens.
- Not being satisfied merely to think or express a wish to have something, but then actually scheming to get it.
- Coveting does not deliver what it promises. We deceive ourselves. Every new car creates the desire for a better one. The grass always looks greener in the neighbor's backyard. We shall never be satisfied.

It may be helpful to remind ourselves of Dietrich Bonhoeffer's distinction between ultimate and penultimate commitments. They are interlocked, but they are not the same. Our ultimate commitment is to God through faith in Jesus Christ. Only that commitment will bring true and lasting fulfillment to life. But since that commitment is to Christ, whose

Who or What Occupies Our Conscience?

being is a being "for others," therefore "it would be blasphemy against God and our neighbor to leave the hungry unfed while saying that God is closest to those in deepest need." Feeding the hungry does not mean salvation for them. It is penultimate. But it is related to the ultimate by preparing the way of the Lord.[4] Only God can satisfy our deepest longings.

The challenge is whether a lifestyle of coveting can be transformed into an ethos of sharing. To do that we need to be honest with ourselves and diagnose our situation. Why do we feel the need to covet? It is often because deep down we feel unsure about life. We are anxious. We are afraid that we are not really in charge. We think that we might I miss out. The grass always seems to look greener in my neighbor's backyard. Such anxiety makes us dissatisfied with life. We want more because we think that by getting more we intensify life and thereby gain the happiness that we seek. There is nothing wrong of course with wanting more. But we need to seek in the right direction! Just as the flower needs the sun to become what it is, so we need the "other" to become who we are. By focusing all attention on the self, we functionalize others and thereby fail to recognize that only in relationship with others can we access the resources of life, joy and happiness.

The Need for a "New Heart"

Since coveting is seated in and arises from the human heart, we begin to appreciate the biblical promise that it is possible for God to liberate our conscience from the unbending will to self and give us a new heart. The prophet Jeremiah promises: "this is the covenant that I will make with the house of Israel after those days, says the LORD: I will put my law within them, and I will write it on their hearts; and I will be their God, and they shall be my people" (Jer 31:33). Similarly the prophet Ezekiel: "A new heart I will give you, and a new spirit I will put within you; and I will remove from your body the heart of stone and give you a heart of flesh. I will put my spirit within you, and make you follow my statutes and be careful to observe my ordinances. Then you shall live in the land that I gave to your ancestors; and you shall be my people, and I will be your God" (Ezek 36:26–28).

The early Christians picked up that promise and experienced its fulfillment when God, through the death and resurrection of Christ, created a new reality in which people can participate through faith and baptism. To the learned Nicodemus who comes to Jesus out of the night of his life

---

4. Bonhoeffer, "Ultimate and Penultimate Things," 163.

and asks him what is ultimately true and lasting, Jesus says, "You must be born anew" (John 3).[5] By following Jesus, the believer experiences the joy of belonging ("you shall be my people, and I will be your God") and thereby is freed from seeking life in oneself for celebrating life together with others in the context of space (environment) and time (history).

The negative example is the man who came to Jesus on "a journey" (Mark 10:17–31; Matt 19:16–30; Luke 18:18–30). He approaches Jesus with the question of ultimacy. His manner (running, kneeling) and his language ("good teacher") suggest expectancy. Jesus' presence issues the promise of being able to deal with ultimate questions. Jesus at first points to the traditional answer of *morality*. He cites from the decalogue. The man's reply is revealing. He has fulfilled the moral claims of his religion, but his longing for a fulfilled life, for God, has not been satisfied.

Now comes the crunch point. Who or what will be ultimate reality for him, who or what will be "god" in his life? Before the challenge is posed, the text makes clear that not morality but the abundant life is the driving motivation: "Jesus, looking at him, *loved* him."

Jesus diagnoses the man's conscience and then names the challenge: "go, sell what you own, and give the money to the poor, and you will have treasure in heaven; then come, follow me." This challenge touches the foundations of his life. The choice is clear. Will Jesus ("follow *me*") be more promising in the quest for the fulfilled life ("treasures in heaven") than possessions?

One can virtually feel the tension. The choice has to be made. Unless he transfigures his dependence on possessions into a new lifestyle of relationships, he will never understand what Jesus and God are on about. This is the only place in the Christian Bible where someone refused the invitation to follow Jesus—and it was because of material possessions. In a money-mad, consumer-crazy world, we must feel the "shock." Will Jesus or money be the focus of our conscience?

The "Neighbor"

The neighbor whose belonging we may covet is not only the person next door. Today we are woven into a global community. The neighbor is the child in Iran who may have knitted the carpet that graces our floor; the fisherman in Vietnam or Thailand who caught the shrimps that we eat; the

---

5. Similar texts emphasizing a "new birth" are Titus 3:5–7 and 1 Peter 1:3.

factory worker in Bangladesh who made the football with which we play; the woman in a sweat shop in China who made the shirt that I wear.

By not coveting we freely and voluntarily commit ourselves to include these neighbors into our decision-making. By engaging ourselves for debt relief for the poorest of the poor, supporting the struggle against the AIDS epidemic, helping in the movement to make poverty history, joining the peace movement we help to change a culture of coveting into a culture of generosity.

Women

The decalogue is addressed to men. It was a patriarchal society. Women and slaves had no dignity on their own. They are therefore named in the same breath as the rest of the household, including the farm animals. We have already said that in the Hebrew Bible there is a tendency to ease the lives of women and slaves and other disadvantaged groups like widows, orphans, and aliens. This tendency was intensified with the coming of Jesus. He had female disciples (Luke 8:1–3), and when the power of his resurrection became manifest in the Christian community, the barriers of race, gender, and class were broken down (Gal 3:28). Indeed, in the early church there were female apostles (Junia; Rom 16:7). Several churches, which in those days met in peoples' houses, were led by women. We read of Phoebe (Rom 16:1), Nympha (Col 4:15), Lydia (Acts 16:14–15, 40), Mary, the mother of John Mark (Acts 12:12), and Priscilla, who is often mentioned before Aquila (Rom 16:3, 5a; Acts 18:18, 26; 2 Tim 4:19). Again, it belongs to the tragedies of the church's story that in many traditions the full equality of male and female is still not realized or even recognized.

Conclusion

For Christians it is good to know that in Christ "we do not have a high priest who is unable to sympathize with our weaknesses, but we have one who in every respect has been tempted as we are, yet without sin" (Heb 4:15). And, the text includes the invitation: "Let us therefore approach the throne of grace with boldness, so that we may receive mercy and find grace to help in time of need" (Heb 4:16). By believing in Jesus Christ we participate in his obedience to God and his openness to others. We no longer need to dethrone God and put ourselves in God's place. We no longer need to expand our own life at the expense of others. We can be free toward

God, free toward others. In that freedom of faith we will not "covet the neighbor's wife and the neighbor's goods," because we no longer feel the need to do it. We discover our real freedom and the fullness of life in our faith in Jesus Christ.

Conclusion

WE ARE LIVING IN threatening times. People everywhere seek orientation, meaning, and certainty. Traditional values and institutions face radical questioning and are undergoing radical change. Concerned people are looking for spiritual visions and moral values that can provide the foundation for shaping a meaningful life, a civil society, and a promising future. On the global level there are many and diverse efforts being undertaken in the search for universal values that can guide the human family towards a just and peaceful future.[1] In such a search—and it is a necessary and important search!—we must not forget the history that shaped our culture and brought us into the present. We should not idolize the past. But if we refuse to digest it and learn from it, we forego important resources for paving a creative and constructive way into the future.

Some years ago, in 1991, following the fall of the Iron Curtain, and at a time when Russian society was in the process of reconstruction, a delegation of Christians met with some Russian leaders. Among other things, they visited the KGB headquarters and spoke with its vice-chairman, General Nikolai Stolyarov. One of the visitors asked General Stolyarov whether he would comment on the Gulag, the infamous Corrective Labor Camps in Russia, made known by the three volume work of Aleksandr Solzhenitsyn (*Gulag Archipelago*). He responded, "I have spoken of repentance. This is an essential step . . . . There can be no perestroika apart from repentance. The time has come to repent of the past. We have broken the Ten Commandments, and for this we pay today."[2] Even within a socialist and secular context there remained the consciousness that the *ten commandments* stand for a kind of universal morality which one disregards at one's peril.

---

1. The *United Nations* (1945) and the *International Bill of Human Rights* (1948 and 1966/1976) are themselves part of that search. This effort is continued by organizations such as the Parliament of World Religions (www.cpwr.org) and the Global Ethics Foundation (www.weltethos.org).

2. Cited from Yancey, *What's So Amazing About Grace*, 127.

Toward a Culture of Freedom

I have endeavored to retrieve the importance of the "ten words," remain faithful to the intention of the texts, and explore their relevance for today. Biblical illustrations have shown how the "ten words" addressed issues that are also found in other parts of the Bible. References to past and present incidents and events have demonstrated their relevance and universal application. The "ten words" have unmasked ideas and practices that contain no promise, and at the same time they show the way towards a better future which we have named a "culture of freedom."

We saw that the decalogue supplies its own key of interpretation by grounding the "ten words" in the God who created a "beautiful" world and who liberated God's people from slavery.[3] It is a popular misunderstanding to qualify the "ten words" as "laws" or "commandments" and then contrast them with "faith" and "grace" in the New Testament. Such a contrast between the Old and New Testaments cannot be maintained. It is false to say that the God of the Hebrew Bible is a God of law and war, while the God of the Christian Bible is a God of grace and peace. The intention of the "ten words" is misunderstood if they are separated from the God who "speaks" and "liberates." If one separates the "ten words" from the liberating presence of God, then we are left with moral principles. The intention of the "ten words" is to be more than moral principles. At the same time, if we divorce the "ten words" from our understanding of God, then an abstract and faceless God remains. Therefore, like in a good opera, the overture about the God who speaks and acts and the "ten words" that follow belong together—in that order, with a procedural priority for the overture!

For Christian believers and Christian communities the "ten words" are part of the Holy Scriptures which all churches accept as the authority for their faith and practice. Yet the Holy Scriptures need to be read and interpreted. We find a plurality of voices in the Bible. Among the many words, we must seek, ever again, the one word that we need to hear, trust, and obey. This process of interpretation in which texts are applied to ever new and changing situations is already evident in the Old Testament. In Deuteronomy, for instance, the "ten words" are given a more prominent place than in Exodus. Both books narrate the story that Moses destroyed

---

3. For a translation of Gen 1:31 that includes "beautiful" see ch. 6, p. 72n4. Brueggemann says it this way: "Command is rooted in theophany. The juxtaposition of theophany and command asserts that, for Israel, there is nothing more elemental or fundamental (even primordial) than the commands that intend to shape and order the world according to the radical and distinctive vision of the God of the exodus" (*The Book of Exodus*, 839).

Conclusion

the first two tablets after being confronted with Israel's disobedience. But while in Exodus the second set of tablets contain a modified set of rules and exhortations with more emphasis on cultic rules like keeping festivals, tithing, and rules for offering sacrifices (Exod 34), in Deuteronomy the second set of tablets contains the same "ten words" as the first, and these words are seen as the summary of the law.[4] The moral vision of the decalogue clearly dominates the cultic and priestly principles. This trajectory of emphasis on justice rather than observing the cult is continued by Israel's prophets and Jesus of Nazareth.

Jesus accepted the authority of the "ten words," but at the same time he radicalized them (by relating killing to anger and sexuality to lust, for instance) and he exercised the freedom to measure and criticize them according to his understanding of God as the ultimate reality in his life (see our discussion of the sabbath).

For Christians the liberating activity of God includes the life, death, and resurrection of Jesus Christ. The liberating word, the good news, the gospel (in Greek, *euangelion*), which God speaks into our conscience, is grounded in the divine act of cross and resurrection, which demonstrates that God's love is stronger than the forces of death. Political, economic, and religious self-interest led to Jesus' arrest, torture, trial, and crucifixion. By raising Jesus from the dead, God confirmed God's faithfulness and at the same time verified and validated Jesus' vision of life. The exodus in the Hebrew Bible and the resurrection of the crucified Jesus in the Christian Bible therefore feed on the same reality that God is the God who liberates people from the estranging powers of death and oppression. Both, thereby, want to restore the beauty of creation.

In that context of God's liberating activity the "ten words" are not "laws" or "commandments." They are the structures of a God-given freedom. They are invitations to a culture of freedom. They incite not merely obedience but also responsibility. One must not lose sight of this. I have sought to maintain an evangelical emphasis in that what God has done precedes what we can do. God does for us what we cannot do for ourselves. God frees us from our selfishness and opens up our lives to God and to the "other." But this freedom is structured into a life for God and for others. Our worship to God and our compassion for God's creation are not merely the results of faith, they are the content and structures of faith.

---

4. For more details see Appendix 1.

Toward a Culture of Freedom

Given this grounding in God's nature as being "for and with us," each of the words does not only mean "you *shall* . . ." or "you *shall not* . . . ," but as people who have been set free and have been reconciled with God, "you *will* worship God and as part of that worship you *will not* exploit others." The following points gather up what we have discovered as distinctive and relevant in our reading of the "ten words":

- The "ten words" are grounded in God's liberating action, which for Christians includes the life, death and resurrection of Jesus Christ. The exodus of Israel from slavery in the Hebrew Bible and the resurrection of the crucified Jesus in the Christian Bible are the two integrating foci of the biblical narratives.

- Faith in the God of Moses and Jesus includes appropriating God's liberating activity for our own life and echoing it through our thoughts, words and deeds in the world. "You shall not oppress a resident alien; you know the heart of an alien, for you were aliens in the land of Egypt" (Exod 23:9; cf., Exod 22:21; Lev 19:34). This integration of faith into our life is well formulated in the recent *Micah Declaration*:

    > "If we ignore the world we betray the word of God which sends us out to serve the world. If we ignore the word of God we have nothing to bring to the world. Justice and justification by faith, worship and political action, the spiritual and the material, personal change and structural change belong together. As in the life of Jesus, being, doing and saying are at the heart of our integral task."[5]

- The "ten words" are structures of freedom. Taking them seriously and implementing them will help create a culture of freedom which is an important context for a civil society and for a meaningful and successful life.

- The appropriate response to the "ten words" is not blind obedience but creative responsibility. The "words" are not casuistic laws that set out what exactly needs to be done or not done in each particular situation. They are guidelines that steer us in the right direction. They are principles that aid our response to the moral and spiritual challenges that we face.

- In our response to moral and spiritual challenges we need to distinguish between ultimate and penultimate commitments. Honoring God's

---

5. Micah Network, "Micah Declaration on Integral Mission."

Conclusion

name by refusing to have other gods and centering our whole trust in the God of Moses and Jesus is an ultimate commitment. It is the ground for everything else. From this follows that honoring our parents, keeping the sabbath, being faithful in our marriage, working for peace and justice are all worthy and important commitments. They are related to our faith in God. But they are not the same as our faith in God. Faith in God for God's own sake is the necessary ground from which all other commitments derive and by which all other commitments are sustained, validated and measured.

- Jesus' interpretation of the decalogue has summarized tendencies in the Hebrew tradition that emphasize the interlocking of motivation and action. For an activity to be moral, both the motivation and the consequences must be considered. With such an understanding one cannot use war and violence in the pursuit of peace. Peaceful ends and peaceful means belong together. Killing may therefore be related to anger; and sexual exploitation to lust. One should not argue for or against euthanasia as being the best option for a particular person without considering the social consequences of such an action.

- I have emphasized the distinction between individual, personal, and social ethics. Individual ethics has to do with activities that only concern the individual, for instance, whether I go for a walk each day to keep fit. Personal ethics is concerned with those thoughts and deeds that affect others, like smoking in a restaurant or driving under the influence of alcohol or drugs. Social ethics has to do with structures. On a personal level I may give $100 a week to a good cause. That is important, but not enough. To help the poor or to address climate change, structural changes on the political and economic level, like the UN Millennium Goals and the Kyoto Protocol, need to take place. This responsibility to apply faith to structures is often overlooked or downplayed by churches.

- Where consequences or sanctions are mentioned—as in the words about idol worship, honoring God's name, and keeping the sabbath—they are reminders that our activity or inactivity, our speaking or keeping silent has consequences. Implementing the "ten words" contains the promise of creating a culture of freedom. Disregarding the "ten words" will intensify a culture of individualism, selfishness and greed. We are relational beings. We need to affirm our relational responsibility—to God, to each other, to the environment—if we are to live a meaningful and successful life. The consequences of not accepting that responsibility and turning the focus on the self is in the Bible called "judgment."

- The "ten words" were spoken into a defined community with which God had made a covenant. However, the affirmation that Yahweh is not only the God of Israel but the "creator of heaven and earth"—the Psalmist summarizes the message of the creation narratives in Genesis 1 and 2: "The earth is the Lord's and all that is in it, the world, and those who live in it" (Ps 24:1)—authorizes us to apply the "ten words" to ourselves. We live in a global community in which all major challenges to human life on earth transcend national borders and interests. Therefore, without intending to be imperialistic, we suggest that the "ten words" contain promise for all people everywhere.

- The ethos of the "ten words" contains a certain leaning—a partiality. God liberates slaves, rather than validating those in power. "Coveting" is mostly exercised by the rich to the disadvantage of the poor. In relation to the sabbath, concern was not only focused on the patriarch and his immediate family, but also on the rest of the clan, including slaves and servants. Indeed the ecological relevance is underlined by the fact that the earth also needs and deserves rest.

- The "ten words" suggest a way beyond legalism on the one hand and anarchy or situationalism on the other. They are not "laws" or rules that one can easily and immediately apply to each situation. They do not exclude human agency and human responsibility, but they invite people to enter the process of moral decision-making and moral action. At the same time, they provide clear guidance—to worship God, not to kill, not to commit adultery, etc.—and thereby resist a modern (and postmodern) tendency toward the view that truth is relative. The "ten words" provide guidelines with which one can approach, interpret, and negotiate an ethical challenge.[6]

- The fact that generally the "ten words" contain no sanctions (except for the second word) shows that they are future-oriented. They can be applied to ever new situations. For instance, to honor one's parents is a universal guideline, but how that is done will vary from culture to culture.

- As Christians, we pay special attention to how the "ten words" were received by Jesus and by the early Christian churches. The fact that the

6. For more details see Appendix 2.

Conclusion

decalogue has played a significant role in all Christian traditions encourages us to seek its relevance for today, whereby Christians recognize Jesus Christ as the ground and the norm for their spirituality and for ethical decisions and actions.

With these general comments in mind I will now summarize the central message of each chapter.

The *overture*—chapters one and two—is indispensable for understanding the "ten words." Apart from the overture the theological vision contained in the "ten words" becomes sterile morality. The overture spells out that God speaks God's "Yes" into our lives and at the same time seeks to free us from those things that hinder our relationship with God, with each other and with the environment. The "ten words" are therefore not ready-made and clearly formulated laws to keep. They are invitations to a meaningful and flourishing life. They are principles for shaping a culture of freedom. They are guidelines to keep the journey of freedom on track. In ever new situation they seek to keep the human longing for liberation alive.

If God is God in our life, then "we won't need any other gods." The *first word*—chapter three—challenges us to name those things that claim our ultimate allegiance, dethrone them and make God, the God of Moses and Jesus, the central concern in our life. Having named and accepted responsibility for that central concern, all other realities in life "fall into place." On the other hand, if the central concern remains unclear and elusive, the whole network of life's relationships becomes distorted.

If God is to become interesting by making a *difference* and adding something *new* to our life, then God's deity, God's "otherness" must be recognized and protected—chapter four. The *second word* therefore reminds us that we should not take any part of creation, like stones, wood, or metal and shape them into representations of the creator. By objectifying God in images we try to make God part of our reality—and then nothing new can be expected. Christians meet God on God's terms by accepting God's self-revelation in Jesus Christ.

The *third word* about honoring God's name—chapter five—means that with our words and deeds we have the privilege and responsibility to look after God's reputation in the world. As believers we are the letters that people read to decipher the truth of God. We honor God's name by echoing God's compassion in our thoughts, words and deeds.

The *fourth word* about the sabbath—chapter six—occupies an important place in the decalogue. For most Christians the sabbath is the first day of the week, symbolizing the fact that the other days of the week are grounded in God. The sabbath does not separate us from life. It is an important interruption in the flow of time to recall our need for worship and at the same time to remind us of our responsibility towards our fellow human beings and to the garden in which we have been placed.

The *fifth word* to honor father and mother gives us occasion to discuss problems related to the elderly in our performance-oriented culture—chapter seven. A culture of freedom creates an ethos in which the dignity of the elderly is respected. Such affirmation results in structures like an adequate health care and pension scheme, the promotion of palliative care, and the advancement of the hospice movement. We also noted that the threat of climate change makes generational responsibility imperative.

The *sixth word* about "killing"—chapter eight—reminds us how difficult it is to find a translation that is faithful to the intention of the text. The covenant context of the decalogue and the formulation "anti-social killing" allows us in our global setting to relate this word to contemporary issues of war, violence, capital punishment, abortion, and killing by omission.

We placed the *seventh word* concerning adultery—chapter nine—in the larger context of sex, love, and marriage. We affirmed the joy of sexuality but at the same time recognized that selfishness, power, and lust can deform sexuality into violence, mainly against women and children. The context of love, marriage, and family seeks to guard and guide the joy of sex as a part of a meaningful and successful life.

Since it is fairly obvious that one should not steal bikes and cars, I retrieved another, perhaps even the earliest dimension of the *eighth word*, namely not to steal (kidnap) people—chapter ten. A number of illustrations demonstrate that stealing people's freedom is a major challenge to any culture and still a major problem today. At the same time, there are many stories that encourage us to transform a culture of stealing into a culture of sharing.

With the *ninth word* we become aware that we can diminish and even destroy fellow human beings by bearing false witness against them—chapter eleven. We considered illustrations from the academic and political world of how the lives of others can be traded cheaply when one's own ideology and advantage is at stake.

Conclusion

The *tenth word* about coveting addresses the basic desire to use others and what they have for one's own advantage—chapter twelve. Coveting is deceptive. It does not deliver what it promises.

We conclude our meditations by encapsulating each of the "ten words" in language that conflates the then and the now, what it meant and what it means.

> The God in whom you believe is a lover of freedom. God provides both resources and structures for a culture of freedom.
>
> 1. Therefore, let God be the central passion in your life.
> 2. God is different from us and therefore is able and willing to surprise us with joy, freedom, and meaning.
> 3. We have the privilege of representing God in our world.
> 4. Nothing can separate us from God's love. God's grace precedes and inspires all we do. That is cause for celebration.
> 5. Respect the elderly; you will be one of them.
> 6. Revere life—with a special leaning for those who have no voice, no power and no friends.
> 7. Let love lead you to happiness—and remember that love does not violate the freedom of others.
> 8. You are only as free as you engage yourself for the freedom of others, especially the disadvantaged.
> 9. Protect the reputation of others by living truthfully and speaking words that bring life.
> 10. Do not crave what others have—but learn that in sharing you will increase your own happiness.

Appendix 1

Understanding and Interpreting the Decalogue

INTRODUCTION

ALTHOUGH THE DECALOGUE BELONGS to the "classics" of human history, like most texts, it can get into the wrong hands and be misused to justify racism, murder and violence. From white supremicists in America to the "Lord's Resistance Army" in Uganda and Sudan, people and movements have justified their immorality and injustice by appealing to the ten commandments.[1] Therefore, we must ever again reclaim the text so that it serves to fulfill its intention, which in the case of biblical texts is the cause of God's passion for freedom, justice, and peace.

The interpreter of biblical texts faces the task of merging the horizons between the "then" and the "now," between what they meant then and what they mean now. Fortunately, biblical scholarship has provided us with the tools to come close to the original meaning of the texts. Good and reliable biblical scholars seek to understand texts on their own terms. At the same time they realize that many biblical texts have more than one layer of meaning. They are not frozen into their original setting. They have a surplus of meaning. They point beyond themselves. They have the inner propulsion to speak into ever new and changing situations. It is, therefore, not enough to know the "surface meaning" of biblical texts. One must also try to discern their *intention*, which is then applied to ever changing situations. Texts, especially "classics," point beyond themselves and open up new possibilities of meaning. The interpreter will therefore try to discern the history of a text and thereby "enter" that history in order to detect the relevance of the text for our present situation. Such situations are different in New York, Sydney, Bangkok, London, Tehran, Moscow, and Johannesburg, not to speak of the

---

1. See Langston, *Exodus*, 208–18. Regarding the LRA see Batstone, *NOT for Sale*, chapter 3: "Its commander, Joseph Kony, claims that he will create a society based on the Ten Commandments" (111).

APPENDIX 1

poppy fields in Myanmar, the killing fields in Darfur, the battle fields in Iraq and Afghanistan, and the parched countrysides of Africa and Australia. To know the relevance of texts and to be faithful to their intention we—each one of us, and we as a community—must enter the process of interpretation. We must interpret not only the texts themselves, but also our own situation, and then bring the two into conversation with each other. That is what we have tried to do with respect to the decalogue. The following information may be of some help to pave the way from the past (what it meant) to the present (what it means).

LITERARY CONTEXT

The two literary sources for the decalogue are Exodus 20:2-17 and Deuteronomy 5:6-21.[2] In each book the context in which the "ten words" are narrated is quite different.

In Exodus the decalogue is part of the story about God offering a covenant to Israel and announcing the covenant stipulations (Exod 19-24 and 32-34): "'... if you obey my voice and keep my covenant, you shall be my treasured possession out of all the peoples.' ... The people all answered as one: 'Everything that the LORD has spoken we will do'" (Exod 19:5-8). As is the case with the "ten words," so also the whole covenant and its regulations are grounded in Yahweh's initiative and his appearance to Moses and the people: "I am the LORD your God . . . " (Exod 20:2). Yahweh writes "the law and the commandment" on two tablets of stone and gives them to Moses (Exod 24:12). The appearance of Yahweh is therefore interlinked with giving the "ten words" (Exod 20) and the "book of the covenant" (Exod 24:7), which interprets the principles contained in the "ten words" for the new situation in Canaan (Exod 21-23). This is followed by the covenant ceremony in Exodus 24. With Exodus 25-31 the narrative is interrupted by extensive instructions for the building of the ark of the covenant and the tabernacle and by regulations that are mainly concerned with cultic and priestly matters. These are then named, as were the laws and commandment in Exodus 24, "the two tablets of the covenant, tablets of stone, written with the finger of God" (Exod 31:18). Exodus 32 picks up where the story of the book of the covenant left off at the end of chapter 24. While Moses was on the mountain receiving the tablets with the covenant from God, the people disobeyed God by collecting their jewelry and building a representation of

---

2. For related and similar texts see the "Introduction," p. 6, n. 5.

Understanding and Interpreting the Decalogue

the LORD in the "image of a calf" (Exod 32:4–5). Both God and Moses are angry. God decides to "consume" his people (Exod 32:10) and Moses "threw the tablets from his hands and broke them at the foot of the mountain" (Exod 32:19). But, recalling the promises of God's faithfulness—"keeping steadfast love for the thousandth generation" (Exod 31:7)—Moses intercedes for his people and God changes his mind. Moses prepares two new tablets on which God writes. He does not repeat what was in the first two tablets but continues the rules for their new life in Canaan.

Deuteronomy is a different type of literature to the Exodus. While Exodus relates a *narrative* of Israel's oppression in Egypt, followed by the journey of liberation, the revelation of the law, and the establishment of the sanctuary, Deuteronomy is a long *sermon* or a collection of *sermons* which relate God's covenant to the lives of the people in order to shape a civil society. Deuteronomy 4:44—11:32 follows a similar plot to the Exodus narrative but at the same time modifies the narrative in significant ways. It interprets the Exodus version by insisting that the second set of tablets includes the same material as the first:

> ... the LORD said to me (= Moses), "Carve out two tablets of stone like the former ones, and come up to me on the mountain, and make an ark of wood. I will write on the tablets *the words that were on the former tablets*, which you smashed, and you shall put them in the ark." So I made an ark of acacia wood, cut two tablets of stone like the former ones, and went up the mountain with the two tablets in my hand. Then he wrote on the tablets *the same words as before, the ten commandments that the LORD had spoken to you on the mountain out of the fire on the day of the assembly*; and the LORD gave them to me. So I turned and came down from the mountain, and put the tablets in the ark that I had made; and there they are, as the LORD commanded me. (Deut 10:1–5)

Where the Exodus has the many laws (and, as part of them, the decalogue) as well as the cultic and priestly material on the two sets of tablets, Deuteronomy has the "ten words" only on both sets. The composers of the Deuteronomy are obviously more interested in the moral vision than in cultic and priestly material. The "ten words" are summarized in the exhortation: "Hear, O Israel: The LORD is our God, the LORD alone. You shall love the LORD your God with all your heart, and with all your soul, and with all your might" (Deut 6:4–5). The interrelation of love for God and commitment to justice is emphasized at the conclusion of this section, Deuteronomy 10:12–22:

> So now, O Israel, what does the LORD your God require of you? Only to fear the LORD your God, to walk in all his ways, to love him, to serve the LORD your God with all your heart and with all your soul, and to keep the commandments of the LORD your God and his decrees that I am commanding you today, for your own well-being.... the LORD your God ... executes justice for the orphan and the widow, and who loves the strangers, providing them food and clothing. You shall also love the stranger, for you were strangers in the land of Egypt.

This theological vision of the decalogue, being the spiritual and moral foundation of the covenant, has proven to be more influential in the history of interpretation than the much more complicated narrative in the Book of Exodus.

AUTHORSHIP AND DATE

The first five books in the Bible—Genesis, Exodus, Leviticus, Numbers, and Deuteronomy—are often referred to as the "five books of Moses." Although there may be some sayings and even narratives that go back to the time of Moses or even Moses himself (ca. thirteenth century BCE), the books as we have them today were not written by Moses. They are the end-products of a long process of development. Old Testament scholars have reconstructed a variety of oral and written sources and there are different theories as to the dates and authors of those sources and how and when they evolved into the books as we have them today.

The same is true for the decalogue. We have already seen that the "ten words" in Deuteronomy is a reworking of the Exodus version. Scholars have tried to reconstruct an early form of the decalogue which may or may not go back to Moses, but no consensus has been reached on that point.[3] Since our discussion is not an academic work about the decalogue as such but rather its significance as a "classic," we have largely ignored the question of the origins of the "ten words."

---

3. For details see Harrelson, *The Ten Commandments and Human Rights*, 19–45.

Understanding and Interpreting the Decalogue

THE COVENANT CONTEXT

The "ten words" are part of the covenant God made with Israel. In the narrative, they were given at Sinai. Sinai in turn is interrelated with the exodus. Consequently, the liberation of God's people from slavery and oppression (the exodus) and the declaration of the "ten words" are inexorably interlinked. The decalogue itself interrelates the giving of the covenant with the exodus (Exod 20:1–2; also Exod 19:4–6). Israel's God, God's nature, and the content of God's will are therefore related to what happened in the exodus and at Sinai. In that order! The God of the exodus makes a covenant to structure the journey of liberation.

Most of us are not Jews and we don't live in Israel. We are therefore not the immediate addressees of the covenant and of the "ten words." The gulf of time and culture is deep and wide. Nevertheless, when we hear the "ten words" as being addressed to us today we take notice and become interested for the following reasons:

- They are part of the Bible which all Christians and all Christian churches accept as authoritative for their faith and practice.

- Israel itself claimed a universal relevance for its God by adding Genesis 1–11—God as creator of heaven and earth and of all human beings—as a prelude to its own history under God. At the genesis of its journey with God this universal relevance is underlined. In Abraham "all the families of the earth shall be blessed" (Gen 12:3). Israel's destiny is to be "a light to the nations" so that God's "salvation may reach to the end of the earth" (Isa 49:6). In worship Israel is reminded that "the earth is the LORD's and all that is in it, the world, and those who live in it" (Ps 24:1).

- The God of Israel and Moses shared his life with Jesus of Nazareth and thereby demonstrated God's commitment to all human beings, indeed to all of creation.

- The "ten words" have an inherent truth-claim that has stood the test of time. They have been helpful and transformative in many different cultures and contexts.

We therefore conclude that the "ten words" contain a universal intention. Using covenantal language, the Sinai covenant must be seen together with the Noahic and Abrahamic covenants (Gen 8–9 and 12–17), both of which emphasize God's universal compassion and relevance. This is intensified with the New Covenant in the life, death, and resurrection of Jesus Christ. In Jesus Christ, God demonstrated God's love for God's creation by reconciling the world to himself (John 3:16; 2 Cor 5:17–21; Rom 5). God's covenant, and with it the "ten words," therefore, have an immediate appeal to all people who believe in the God of Moses and Jesus. At the same time it is an invitation to a culture of freedom for all people.

Today humanity has become a global village. All major challenges to humanity—from poverty and terrorism to the nuclear threat and climate change—are global problems. There is a growing awareness that we need a global morality. What the decalogue was to Israel 3000 years ago, the *Universal Declaration of Human Rights* is to all people in our time. Following the atrocities and the attempted genocide during World War II, the United Nations was created in 1945 with the specific objective

- to save succeeding generations from the scourge of war, which twice in our lifetime has brought untold sorrow to mankind, and
- to reaffirm faith in fundamental human rights, in the dignity and worth of the human person, in the equal rights of men and women and of nations large and small, and
- to establish conditions under which justice and respect for the obligations arising from treaties and other sources of international law can be maintained, and
- to promote social progress and better standards of life in larger freedom,

AND FOR THESE ENDS

- to practice tolerance and live together in peace with one another as good neighbors, and
- to unite our strength to maintain international peace and security, and to ensure, by the acceptance of the principles and the institution of methods, that armed force shall not be used, save in the common interest, and
- to employ international machinery for the promotion of the economic and social advancement of all peoples,

HAVE RESOLVED TO COMBINE OUR EFFORTS TO ACCOMPLISH THESE AIMS.[4]

---

4. United Nations Conference on International Organization, *Charter of the United Nations*.

Understanding and Interpreting the Decalogue

In 1948 the *Universal Declaration of Human Rights* was issued. It has been hailed as one of the important landmarks in the history of humanity. It sets a "common standard of achievement for all peoples and all nations" by which nations should measure their treatment of citizens and by which citizens could know their own rights over against the state and the human community.

This declaration was followed 20 years later, in 1966, by two covenants, the *International Covenant of Economic, Social, and Cultural Rights*, the *International Covenant on Civil and Political Rights*, and the *Optional Protocol* to the latter covenant. For governments that have ratified it, this protocol allows individual persons to file complaints concerning human rights matters with an international Human Rights Committee. Together with the *Universal Declaration* these covenants form the *International Bill of Human Rights* which sets a moral and juridical standard for the human community. Over a hundred nations have ratified these covenants and have thereby promised to use all available urgency to implement these human rights in their area of jurisdiction.

The *International Bill of Human Rights* is backed up by many more declarations and conventions that deal with the definition and effective implementation of individual human rights. Recent examples are the *Declaration on the Elimination of All Forms of Intolerance and Discrimination Based on Religion or Belief* (1981), the *Convention against Torture and Other Cruel, Inhuman or Degrading Treatment or Punishment* (1984), and the *Convention on the Rights of the Child* (1989). A convention on religious liberty, a declaration or convention on conscientious objection, and a declaration on the rights of indigenous peoples are in the process of preparation.[5]

In our global context we need to hear the "ten words" as an invitation and a contribution towards the creation of a universal ethos where the best of every culture is preserved, where all human life is welcomed, where human dignity is affirmed, where ecological responsibility is practiced and where compassion, justice and peace are the foundation stones for a promising future.

---

5 The official human rights instruments are accessible in United Nations, *Human Rights: A Compilation of International Instruments*. A list of the countries that have ratified or signed the various instruments is found in United Nations, *Human Rights—Status of Human Rights Instruments*. Both of these publications are regularly updated.

Appendix 1

NUMBERING

The numbering of the "ten words" varies in both Jewish and in Christian traditions. In Jewish traditions the introduction ("I am the LORD your God...") is numbered as the first word. Words two and three (not to follow "other gods" and not to fabricate "carved images" of God) are drawn together in the "second word" in order to keep to the number "ten." Although I do not follow this numbering, I have consistently emphasized that it is theologically important to ground the "ten words" in God's liberating activity. The decalogue cannot be adequately understood apart from its grounding in God.

Martin Luther followed the Roman Catholic church by either ignoring the "second word" (about making "carved images" of God) or by drawing the first and second word together into the first commandment. To make up the number ten the last commandment was divided into two (coveting the neighbor's "wife" and coveting his "house").

I have followed the numbering that is most clearly presented by the biblical text and as such is followed by the Reformed and Orthodox churches.

TWO SETS OF TWO TABLETS OF STONE

According to the biblical narrative God wrote the "ten words" and/or the covenant on "two stone tablets" (Deut 4:13; also Deut 10:1, 3–4; Exod 34:1, 4, 28). If, as the text in Deuteronomy suggests, the "ten words" were given on two tablets of stone, then the question arises as to how the "ten words" were originally divided. The text does not tell us and, therefore, we do not know. Suggestive is the possibility that the first tablet majored on the relation between God and humanity, perhaps with the word about the sabbath as a conclusion and transition because it contains elements of relationship to God and responsibility to others and to nature. The second tablet would then commence with the word to honor father and mother. It would echo God's nature in our relationship to each other and to the rest of the world. This order cannot be turned around. Relationship to God and relationship to the world belong together—but with a procedural priority for our relation to God.

This suggests a way beyond the old controversy between evangelicals and liberals. Evangelicals tend to understand God in terms of doctrinal correctness and personal piety, with mission understood as conversion of individuals. Liberals, on the other hand, tend to reduce God to what is

Understanding and Interpreting the Decalogue

acceptable to the human intellect with more emphasis on ethics than on faith. The "ten words" in particular, but also the biblical narrative as a whole, suggest a vision in which God's liberation from oppression (exodus) and God's reconciliation with Godself (resurrection of Jesus Christ) precedes and initiates human response. The appropriate human response includes the faith and baptism of individuals but it cannot be reduced to this personal response. To be true to the God of Moses and Jesus, our faith must echo God's activity of speaking good news into the human conscience and liberating people from oppression and slavery.

ECHOES OF THE "TEN WORDS" IN HISTORY[6]

There is a small lake in southern Bavaria near the German–Austrian border, the *Königssee*. It is surrounded by mountains and it can be toured by battery driven boats. At one point of the tour the boat stops. The captain puts a trumpet to his mouth and the resulting sound reverberates seven times, back and forth between the mountains. The decalogue is like that. It reverberates in history, especially in the history of Jewish and Christian people. It is part of their Holy Scriptures and as such has special authority for them.

Jews through the ages and around the world tell with reverence the story of when Moses went up to Mount Sinai to receive "the two tablets of the covenant, tablets of stone, written with the finger of God," (Exod 31:18; also Exod 32:15–16; 34:1; Deut 9:9–11, 15) and with it the "ten words."[7] For them it was a foundational event. It meant the structuring of their God-given freedom. The God who had liberated them from slavery now gave them the "tablets of the covenant" to structure their life together.

It is therefore to be expected that the decalogue also found its way into Israel's worship:

> Hear, O my people, while I admonish you; O Israel, if you would but listen to me! There shall be no strange god among you; you shall not bow down to a foreign god. I am the LORD your God, who brought you up out of the land of Egypt. Open your mouth wide and I will fill it. (Psalm 81:8–10)

---

6. For details see Langston, *Exodus*, 186–221; Kuntz, *The Ten Commandments in History*; and Childs, *The Book of Exodus*, 431–37.

7. In Deuteronomy there is only the decalogue on the two tablets of stone (Deut 4:13, 10:1–5).

Appendix 1

> Gather to me my faithful ones, who made a covenant with me by sacrifice! The heavens declare his righteousness, for God himself is judge. . . . "Hear, O my people, and I will speak, O Israel, I will testify against you. I am God, your God." (Psalm 50:5–7)

The prophets of the eighth century BCE also knew the decalogue or of parts of it. The prophet Hosea—active ca. 750-725 BCE—alludes to the introduction to the decalogue: "... I have been the LORD your God ever since the land of Egypt; you know no God but me, and besides me there is no savior" (13:4; also 12:9). He also seems to have known the commandment not to follow other gods: "The LORD said to me again, 'Go, love a woman who has a lover and is an adulteress, just as the LORD loves the people of Israel, though *they turn to other gods* and love raisin cakes'" (3:1). A more general reference is found in Hosea 4:1-2: "Hear the word of the LORD, O people of Israel; for the LORD has an indictment against the inhabitants of the land. There is no faithfulness or loyalty, and no knowledge of God in the land. *Swearing, lying, and murder, and stealing and adultery break out; bloodshed follows bloodshed.*"

The prophet Micah—active around 700 BCE—refers to the commandment not to covet: "Alas for those who devise wickedness and evil deeds on their beds! When the morning dawns, they perform it, because it is in their power. They *covet* fields, and *seize* them; houses, and take them away; they oppress householder and house, people and their inheritance" (2:1-2).

About the same time, the prophet Isaiah refers to the commandments not to kill and not to covet: ". . . the vineyard of the LORD of hosts is the house of Israel, and the people of Judah are his pleasant planting; he expected justice, but saw *bloodshed*; righteousness, but heard a cry! Ah, you who *join house to house*, who *add field to field*, until there is room for no one but you, and you are left to live alone in the midst of the land" (5:7-8).

A century later the prophet Jeremiah—active 627/6-600 BCE—reveals knowledge of the decalogue: "Here you are, trusting in deceptive words to no avail. *Will you steal, murder, commit adultery, swear falsely, make offerings to Baal, and go after other gods that you have not known*, and then come and stand before me in this house, which is called by my name, and say, '*We are safe!*'—only to go on doing all these abominations? Has this house, which is called by my name, become a den of robbers in your sight? You know, I too am watching, says the LORD" (7:8-11).

Understanding and Interpreting the Decalogue

Jesus and the early Christian churches recognized the authority of the decalogue. They referred to it extensively without ever citing it as a whole.[8] Jesus summarized the "ten words" into the double commandment of loving God and loving your neighbor.

> As he (Jesus) was setting out on a journey, a man ran up and knelt before him, and asked him, "Good Teacher, what must I do to inherit eternal life?" Jesus said to him, "Why do you call me good? No one is good but God alone. *You know the commandments: 'You shall not murder; You shall not commit adultery; You shall not steal; You shall not bear false witness; You shall not defraud; Honor your father and mother.'*" He said to him, "Teacher, I have kept all these since my youth." Jesus, looking at him, loved him and said, "You lack one thing; go, sell what you own, and give the money to the poor, and you will have treasure in heaven; then come, follow me." When he heard this, he was shocked and went away grieving, for he had many possessions. (Mark 10:17–22; parallel in Matt 19:16–22 and Luke 18:18–23)

In Mark 7:8–13 (Matt 15:3–6) Jesus criticizes the Scribes and the Pharisees for not taking the "ten words" seriously enough. They escape the moral claim of God upon their lives by replacing the *ten commandments* with traditions that are comfortable and convenient.

> "*You abandon the commandment of God and hold to human tradition.*" Then he said to them, "You have a fine way of rejecting the commandment of God in order to keep your tradition! For Moses said, 'Honor your father and your mother'; and, 'Whoever speaks evil of father or mother must surely die.' But you say that if anyone tells father or mother, 'Whatever support you might have had from me is Corban' (that is, an offering to God)—then you no longer permit doing anything for a father or mother, thus *making void the word of God through your tradition that you have handed on*. And you do many things like this."

Jesus unmasks the human tendency to use religious laws, language and rites ("traditions") to escape God's claim upon our life. He wants to understand the *ten commandments* as the "word of God" that liberates and disciplines our conscience at the same time.

---

8. For instance Mark 7:9–13 (parallel in Matt 15:4–6); 10:17–22 (parallel in Matt 19:16–22; Luke 18:18–23); Matt 5:21–37; Rom 13:8–10; Gal 5:13–14; Eph 6:1–3; Jas 2:10–11.

Appendix 1

A further emphasis is that Jesus and the church in which the Gospel of Matthew was written radicalized the commandments. Not only killing but also its root, anger, is unmasked (Matt 5:21–22). Committing adultery is related to the look that wants to possess (Matt 5:27–28). Bearing false witness against one's neighbor is radicalized to mean that swearing should be avoided altogether; one's word should be "'Yes, Yes' or 'No, No'" (Matt 5:33–37).

The apostle Paul also shows knowledge of the decalogue.

> Owe no one anything, except to love one another; for he who loves his neighbor has fulfilled the law. *The commandments, "You shall not commit adultery, You shall not kill, You shall not steal, You shall not covet," and any other commandment, are summed up in this sentence, "You shall love your neighbor as yourself."* Love does no wrong to a neighbor; therefore love is the fulfilling of the law. (Rom 13:8–10)

Paul picks up Jesus' intention. He wants to safeguard the nature of the gospel from falling back into law and legalism. Ultimately, for Paul, it is the "law *of Christ*" (Gal 6:2) to which Christians have bound their conscience. But the "law of Christ" is *love*. Unconditional love. Love of God and love of neighbor. The *ten commandments* are part of the long history of love as the expression of God's solidarity with and commitment to God's people.

In the post-Pauline moral instructions to Christian households we find another reference to the *ten commandments*:

> Children, obey your parents in the Lord, for this is right. "*Honor your father and mother*"—this is the first commandment with a promise: "*so that it may be well with you and you may live long on the earth.*" And, fathers, do not provoke your children to anger, but bring them up in the discipline and instruction of the Lord. (Eph 6:1–4)

Also the Epistle of James shows that the "ten words" were well known and used in the early churches:

> You do well if you really fulfill the royal law according to the scripture, "You shall love your neighbor as yourself." But if you show partiality, you commit sin and are convicted by the law as transgressors. For whoever keeps the whole law but fails in one point has become accountable for all of it. For the one who said, "*You shall not commit adultery,*" also said, "*You shall not murder.*" Now if you do not commit adultery but if you murder, you have

Understanding and Interpreting the Decalogue

become a transgressor of the law. So speak and so act as those who are to be judged by the *law of liberty*. (Jas 2:8–12)

The *Didache* (ca. 120 CE) refers to the *ten commandments* as part of the "way of life" which is contrasted with the "way of death."[9] The way of life contains the double commandment of love—love God and neighbor—and the golden rule ("do not do to another what you would not want done to you"). This is elaborated by a number of exhortations from Paul and the Gospels. After that we have the following list of instructions which include references to the decalogue:

> You shall not commit murder, you shall not commit adultery, you shall not commit pederasty, you shall not commit fornication, you shall not steal, you shall not practice magic, you shall not practice witchcraft, you shall not murder a child by abortion nor kill that which is born. You shall not covet the things of your neighbor, you shall not swear, you shall not bear false witness, you shall not speak evil, you shall bear no grudge. You shall not be double-minded nor double-tongued, for to be double-tongued is a snare of death. Your speech shall not be false, nor empty, but fulfilled by deed. You shall not be covetous, nor rapacious, nor a hypocrite, nor evil disposed, nor haughty. You shall not take evil counsel against your neighbor. You shall not hate any man; but some you shall reprove, and concerning some you shall pray, and some you shall love more than your own life. (*Did.* 2)[10]

It has become obvious that the decalogue remained alive in the Jewish and Christian traditions. That has continued throughout the history of the Christian church to the present day. Most churches include the decalogue in their catechism and Sunday School material. Major theologians in all Christian traditions, but also philosophers and lawyers, have given serious attention to the "ten words."

Since earliest times, therefore, the decalogue has been an important part of the content of faith in Christ. It contains an inherent authority that has challenged people through the ages and in different situations. It would

---

9. The *Didache* (from the Greek meaning "teaching") is an early Christian catechetical writing that did not quite make it into the Canon.

10. A similar and even longer list of virtues and vices including different appeals to the *ten commandments* is found in another early Christian writing, the *Epistle of Barnabas* (ca. 120 CE). There it is described as the "way of light" (chapter 19).

therefore not only be arrogant, but it would be foolish if we did not consider its claim upon us today.

A "CLASSIC"

The fact that we have two or more versions of the "ten words," that most commandments contain no sanctions, that the "ten words" have been positively received by Jesus and the early Christians, and that they have found the interest and attention of many theologians and philosophers through the ages demonstrates that their relevance transcends each particular situation.

Such a text that points beyond itself has been called a "classic."[11] A "classic" is a text (or a work of art or a ritual) with a surplus of meaning. It draws its readers or listeners into its orbit. It impinges upon our lives and teases questions and desires into awareness. It suggests solutions to difficult questions and problems. It merges horizons between past and present and inter-relates situations and cultures. Encountering a "classic" means "that here we recognize nothing less than the disclosure of a reality we cannot but name truth."[12]

It has often been said that only those who have come to terms with the past can honor the present and constructively anticipate the future. Although we live in the present, it is wise to shape our values in dialogue with the past and in responsible anticipation of the future. We cannot simply assume that our moral vision or sensitivity is superior to that of the past. The inherent authenticity of the ethics of Jesus, the environmental vision of Francis of Assisi, the reverence for life of Albert Schweitzer, the power of non-violence of Mahatma Gandhi and Martin Luther King Jr., the tenacity of Nelson Mandela, the moral credibility of Aung San Suu Kyi, and the commitment to what is right by Dietrich Bonhoeffer and Oscar Romero, all coming from different cultures and traditions, are important reminders that we must not overlook or even reject the past. We must listen to it, test it, digest it, and then apply it to our way of life.

In that regard it is generally recognized that the decalogue is one of the great moral visions of the past. We have already noted that its moral authority is mentioned alongside Jesus' Sermon on the Mount and the *Universal Declaration of Human Rights*. The decalogue has shaped "Western" culture

11. Tracy, *The Analogical Imagination*, 99–153.
12. Ibid., 108.

Understanding and Interpreting the Decalogue

and "Western" morality, and still enjoys great moral authority at least in the so-called "Western" world. It belongs to those treasures of our culture that no person can ignore.

PERSONAL RESPONSIBILITY

With the personal address *"you* shall . . . ," the commandments are addressed to *individuals* in a community. In Israel's history, the community was much more dominant and important than the individual. But even then it was recognized that each person is ultimately responsible for his or her own action or inaction. We are part of a community, but we must not "hide" within or behind the group. Each individual is a *moral agent* and as such responsible for what he or she says and does.

It is interesting that we find the same affirmation of the individual in the gospel stories, in which people in the presence of Jesus experience faith in God and Jesus interprets those encounters: "*Your* faith has made you whole." (Mark 5:34 [Matt 9:48; Luke 8:48]; Mark 10:52 [Luke 18:42]; Matt 9:22; Luke 7:50; 17:19)

THE ADDRESSEES

The "ten words" are addressed to adults. This is not kids' stuff. Adults are addressed as responsible moral agents, as people who can make a difference. We all know how difficult it is to make a difference. What can I do to reduce landmines in Cambodia? What can I do for structuring a new society in East Timor? What can I do to reduce the CO_2 emissions and create a sustainable biosphere? We seem to be determined by international systems that allow little room for individual freedom and responsibility. And yet, just as one little snowflake, light as a feather, can be the final weight to make the branch of a tree break, so each individual decision and action can make a difference. The "ten words" call for an intentional and committed response to become creatively and constructively involved in the business of life.

BEYOND CASUISTRY

The decalogue needs to be distinguished from casuistic laws. Casuistic laws are prescriptive and situational. They describe ethical situations and then prescribe actions and list sanctions. Consider these examples:

Appendix 1

> When individuals quarrel and one strikes the other with a stone or fist so that the injured party, though not dead, is confined to bed, but recovers and walks around outside with the help of a staff, then the assailant shall be free of liability, except to pay for the loss of time, and to arrange for full recovery. (Exod 21:18–19)
>
> When a slave owner strikes a male or female slave with a rod and the slave dies immediately, the owner shall be punished. But if the slave survives a day or two, there is no punishment; for the slave is the owner's property. (Exod 21:20–21)
>
> When people who are fighting injure a pregnant woman so that there is a miscarriage, and yet no further harm follows, the one responsible shall be fined what the woman's husband demands, paying as much as the judges determine. If any harm follows, then you shall give life for life. (Exod 21:22–23)

In each case a particular situation is described—in a fight someone is hurt; a slave owner strikes a slave; a pregnant women is injured. For each case the sanctions are mentioned. With such laws, individual responsibility is focused on knowing and obeying given laws, norms and rules that operate in a given community. That is basically the procedure in our legal systems and it is also practiced in some of the larger and more structured churches, like the Roman Catholic church. In such cases individual responsibility is reduced to knowing and keeping the prescribed laws and rules. In contrast, the "ten words" are much more general. They leave more room for individual interpretation, creativity, and application.

At the same time, the seriousness of the moral claim of the "ten words" is underlined by the fact that in other parts of Israel's law-codes, transgression against some of the commandments is punished with the death penalty. Consider these quotations from the Exodus:

> Whoever strikes a person mortally shall be put to death. (21:12)
>
> Whoever strikes father or mother shall be put to death. (21:15)
>
> Whoever kidnaps a person, whether that person has been sold or is still held in possession, shall be put to death. (21:16)
>
> Whoever curses father or mother shall be put to death. (21:17)

From our perspective we would question these sanctions, especially the death penalty. Capital punishment is the harshest judgment possible. But it underlines the seriousness of these moral challenges in those days.

IMPLEMENTATION

As is the case with all moral visions, there is the problem of implementation. The church has struggled with that issue from the beginning. Can the "words" be obeyed and implemented? There were times when some church traditions thought that it was easier to keep the decalogue than it was to keep the Sermon on the Mount. Therefore the laity was expected to keep the decalogue, while the clergy was expected to keep also the Sermon on the Mount. Such distinctions are not helpful. They fail to recognize that before God all believers are equal. At this point the discussion becomes personal, as to whether we are willing to accept responsibility for what we recognize as being right.

ETHICS STARTS "AT THE POINT OF PAIN"

Ethical reflection always has a critical thrust. It questions the status quo. It has its impact "at the point of pain." We have to be constantly aware of the danger of using our ethical reflection merely to validate what we find comfortable and what serves our interest. Racists who use biblical texts to argue for apartheid, or people who use theological arguments to justify slavery or the submission of women to men have functionalized ethics to serve their own ideological purposes.

Ethical reflection must therefore be accompanied by a healthy suspicion. Reason is never neutral. So-called "scientific objectivity" is easily used to please the hand that feeds us. For the Christian, reason must therefore submit to the authority of the word of God and then explicate and explain what the word of God means in our respective situation.

JESUS CHRIST THE NORM

For Christians the ethical challenge is shaped by their faith in Jesus Christ. This faith encompasses their human existence in all its manifold relationships. The Christian therefore asks: "What must I, *as a Christian*, do in this or that situation?" "What is the *will of God* for me in and for this situation?" The Bible uses many pictures to say that Christians are people whose personal vision of life is determined by their faith in Christ. They are called "new creatures," they "have died with Christ and risen with him to newness of life," their "mind is renewed," they are the "salt of the earth," the

Appendix 1

"light of the world," "a chosen race, a royal priesthood, a holy nation, God's own people."[13]

In a free and voluntary decision, Christians have responded to God's initiative and have interlocked their personal identity with the story of Jesus. Christians therefore want the *story of Jesus* to shape their identity and thereby influence and indeed determine their ethical decisions. Their personal identity is at stake in their ethical decision-making. The apostle Paul spells it out clearly. He interprets the *freedom* that he has experienced through faith in Christ: "I have been crucified with Christ; and it is no longer I who live, but it is Christ who lives in me. And the life I now live in the flesh I live by faith in the Son of God, who loved me and gave himself for me" (Gal 2:20).

Since the story of Jesus is found only in the Bible, ethical reflection and action from the Christian perspective is by necessity biblical. We need to be clear at this point. I am not saying that the Scriptures as a whole or the decalogue in particular have a ready-made answer for our moral challenges or that they cannot teach anything new or different from what we know of Jesus and his vision of life. I am also not saying that faith in Jesus Christ has a direct and non-controversial answer to every moral challenge. What I am saying is that for Christians, Jesus Christ is the norm by which we measure our moral vision. If, for instance, Christians in Mississippi justify racism with biblical texts, or churches in South Africa find biblical justification for Apartheid, or churches all over the world still hold on to patriarchy and the subordination of women, or most nations still use the instrument of war for solving human conflicts, then "in the name of Jesus" other Christians will protest and argue for alternative solutions.

For Christians, besides carefully listening to the story of Jesus, there is another factor that flows into making a responsible ethical decision. Although faith is experienced by each individual, it does not individualize us. It places us in a *community of believers*, the church. The church is the place where the story of Jesus is heard in its colorful variety, and where Christ is believed and obeyed. The Christian therefore asks, "Who must I become, what must I do, how must I act, as a believer in Christ and as a member of the community of faith?"

For Christians, the story of Jesus is written into our lives by the ministry of the *Holy Spirit*. It is important to mention the Holy Spirit, because

---

13. Allusions are to 2 Cor 5:17; Matt 5:13–16; Rom 6:3–4; 12:2; 1 Pet 2:9.

Understanding and Interpreting the Decalogue

ethical decisions and actions are not merely rational. They are made and implemented with our whole being. Intuition, personal commitment, taking risks, and leaning into the future are as important as rational insights. It is the Holy Spirit who feeds the story of Jesus into the innermost recesses of our lives. And the outward fruits of our lives show what happens in the innermost recesses of our hearts. Jesus appropriated some lessons from nature when he taught how to distinguish between right and wrong, and between true and false people:

> Beware of false prophets, who come to you in sheep's clothing but inwardly are ravenous wolves. You will know them by their fruits. Are grapes gathered from thorns, or figs from thistles? So, every sound tree bears good fruit, but the bad tree bears evil fruit. A sound tree cannot bear evil fruit, nor can a bad tree bear good fruit. Every tree that does not bear good fruit is cut down and thrown into the fire. Thus you will know them by their fruits. (Matt 7:15–20; also Luke 6:43–45)

Having said all that, we must also be aware that there is a difference between a Christian reading the Hebrew Scriptures and a Jewish believer doing the same. As Christians we have great respect for the Hebrew Scriptures. They were the Bible of Jesus and Paul and of the earliest churches. At the same time, for Christians a new authority was given with the resurrection of Christ. For Christians, Jesus Christ is the interpreter of the being of God (John 1:18); he is the *one* word of God that we are to hear, trust and obey. This *one* word of God is the measure, the canon for all other words. Christians therefore read and understand the Hebrew Bible in general and the "ten words" in particular in light of their understanding of the story of Jesus.

This one word which we are invited to hear, trust and obey comes to us as invitation and challenge, as indicative and imperative, as gospel with its moral claims.[14] Our questions about what we must do are related to the awareness of what God has done for us. Hearing and believing what God has done for us provides the resources that empower us to meet the challenges of life. Hearing and believing precedes doing. If we do not remain aware of the deep and rich wells from which we can feed our faith, then the living reality of the gospel easily results in a cold and sterile moralism.

---

14. For more details see: Barth, "Gospel and Law"; Barth, "Church and State"; Jüngel, "Gospel and Law. The Relation of Dogmatics to Ethics"; Tödt, *Perspektiven Theologischer Ethik*, 12–20.

We must therefore carefully guard the priority of the liberating reality of the gospel. Yet at the same time we must maintain that the gospel is not merely the religious icing on our life, but that it claims our whole life and has its own distinctive content. "For freedom Christ has set us free; stand fast therefore, and do not submit again to a yoke of slavery" (Gal 5:1).

CONCLUSION

The ten commandments can only be properly understood and appreciated if they are seen in the context of a living and intentional faith relationship to God. It is God who speaks through them, and if God is not recognized as God then the commandments lose the very ground from which they emerge.

This does not mean that they have no value apart from faith in God. God is creator of heaven and earth and therefore what God "says" has value and significance for all of creation. But apart from a living faith in God, what is intended as the structure and discipline of freedom can easily become sterile human morality.

For people of faith the "ten words" must be heard with utter seriousness and can only be suspended or modified if faith in Jesus Christ makes such modification necessary. Indeed for believers the "ten words" are not really commandments; they are indications of who believers as believers want to be and what they do and not do.

Since God and freedom belong together, the "ten words" do not want to quench life and joy and human fulfillment. They want to be guide-posts to a happy and fulfilled life, and they want to warn against ways that lead to illusion, estrangement and destruction. The challenge to Christians and their churches is, firstly, to integrate the vision of the decalogue into their lives, and then, secondly, to witness to that vision in a world that yearns for good news that fuel the journey toward a culture of freedom.

Appendix 2
Making Ethical Decisions from a Christian Perspective

INTRODUCTION

THE BIBLE—THE ONLY AUTHORITY which all Christians accept for their faith and life—is not a book of laws and rules that supply ready-made answers to our ethical problems and moral challenges. Indeed, most modern problems—one only has to think of climate change, nuclear power stations, modern warfare and genetic engineering—were unknown in biblical times. That implies, we either regard the Bible as irrelevant for our attitudes and behavior, or we seek a way to bridge the gulf from the biblical message to our life and the ethical challenges that confront us. I prefer the second option, and I want to suggest a method to relate the biblical message to our situations. If we do not have a methodology, if we face ethical challenges unprepared, the danger is that we merely follow our subjective feelings or intuition—and these feelings are often dominated by our self-interest or unwillingness to enter the fray of ethical decision and actions. I am suggesting four steps to deal with an ethical challenge: (1) looking and listening; (2) reflecting; (3) deciding; and (4) acting. But first of all, we need to agree on some ground rules.

Beyond Legalism and Morality

As I said, for Christians the biblical message is the final authority in matters of faith and practice. However, neither the Bible as a whole nor the decalogue or the New Testament in particular are blueprints for moral action. The Bible is neither a legal compendium nor a moral catechism. Essentially it is the story of God's passion for God's people and for God's world. God calls people to the journey of freedom. At the same time and with the same passion, God liberates and empowers those who respond. God frees them for prayer and worship, for caring for each other and for being good stewards of the earth. All commands, laws and exhortations need to be seen and interpreted in that context. The events that shape the biblical ethos are the exodus from oppression in the Old Testament and the resurrection of Jesus Christ in the New Testament. Both are events of liberation. Those who want to echo the biblical ethos are challenged to develop an ethic of freedom.

Faith therefore cannot be adequately captured in terms of morality. It is about "being" before it is about "doing." It is a relationship of love and trust. But as is the case with any meaningful relationship, faith includes rigor, responsibility, and discipline. It entails the call to discipleship and obedience. The Bible describes its ethical thrust in general concepts like love, peace, justice, joy, patience, empathy, solidarity, compassion, kindness, openness, beauty, courage, forgiveness, and nonviolence. These dimensions describe an ethos which invites and inspires people to accept responsibility for what they know and then act accordingly.

Responsibility

There are two dimensions to the biblical ethos. We said above that it is *general* rather than particular. The Bible is not a collection of laws and rules and dogmas. At the same time, the word of God aims at *concreteness*. It wants to be transformative in ever new and ever changing historical constellations. We need to locate Christian responsibility at the intersection between the word of God and the situation.

Christians are challenged to accept responsibility for what has become their ultimate concern. "For freedom Christ has set us free. Stand firm, *therefore*, and do not submit again to a yoke of slavery" (Gal 5:1). Just as in the faith-event, Christians have discovered their relation to God, to fellow human beings, to nature, and to history, so now they are responsible in and for that network of relationships. They are "fellow workers with God" (1 Cor 3:9) in that they seek to relate the word of God to the situation at hand and accept responsibility for that action. Thereby freedom becomes historically manifest. It may be with fear and trembling, but in accepting responsibility for what they know, Christians become who they are called to be. Otherwise Christian freedom remains abstract and individualistic. The believer and the community of faith bridge the gulf between revelation and their respective situation.

According to the Catholic Catechism, "[t]he task of interpreting the Word of God authentically has been entrusted solely to the Magisterium of the Church, that is, to the Pope and to the bishops in communion with him."[1] Individual believers and their communions of faith are expected to obey. Whether it is abortion or women's ordination or attending the weekly Eucharist, they are expected to conform to the decisions of the church hierarchy.

For many Protestant Christians it is somewhat different. In various Protestant denominations there may be a general ethos and set of expectations, but ultimately each believer and each congregation must make their own ethical decisions. Baptists are often more cautious with regard to alcohol and abortion than Episcopalians. Mennonites are more anti-war than Baptists. Homosexuality, conscientious objection, and whether women can be bishops are issues dividing many churches. Most of the serious moral challenges today were unknown in the ancient world and are therefore not directly addressed in the Holy Scriptures. Since at least in many Protestant churches, members and local congregations are encouraged to relate the word of God to their situation, the question arises as to how we can arrive at responsible ethical decisions—decisions that do justice to the issue at hand, to the situation, and to perceptions of truth—and how such decisions can be implemented effectively. To do that we need to develop a method which promises to lead to an adequate moral decision, and then we need the means and the courage to implement what we have decided.

Partiality

One of the general categories that make up the biblical ethos is a certain leaning that is inherent to the biblical story and therefore distinctive of God's being. "God is love" (1 John 4:8), and love is partial. God's passion is to make human life fully human. That includes a special passion for those who are left on the sides of the roads of life. Theologians have in recent years spoken of God's preferential option for the poor and vulnerable.[2] When God's people are oppressed, God longs for their liberation and invites people like Moses to participate in that liberating activity. With the law codes in Israel, special care is taken to ease the fate of the poor, the slave, the orphan, the widow, and the stranger. The prophets condemn those leaders of religious, economic and political institutions who are not concerned with protecting the dignity of persons. Jeremiah provides an eloquent summary

---

1. *Catechism of the Catholic Church*, Part 1, Section. 1, chapter 2, article 2, III, §100, 30.

2. For instance Gutierrez, *A Theology of Liberation*, xxv–xxvii.

when he announces that knowing God means to do justice (Jer 22:15–16). Indeed, we may safely say that the Psalmist gathers up the tendency and the intention of the whole biblical message when he hears God speaking into his conscience: "Give justice to the weak and the fatherless; maintain the right of the afflicted and the destitute" (Ps 82:3). And the writer of Proverbs relates this directly to God's action in history: "the LORD will plead their cause" (Prov 22:22). Moreover, "he who oppresses a poor man insults his Maker, but he who is kind to the needy honors him" (Prov 14:31). It is therefore the privilege and responsibility of faith to tune into God's healing and saving passion for the world. The people of God "speak out for those who cannot speak, . . . (they) defend the rights of the poor and needy" (Prov 31:8). Through our attitude and action we reveal who our God is.

Jesus, to use Luke's words, tuned into that passion by announcing liberation to the oppressed and promising grace to the poor, to the hungry and the sorrowful (Luke 4:18–19, 6:20–21). As messenger of the "kingly rule of God," he healed the sick, drove out demons, and shared his life with the marginal people of society.

The earliest Christian communities were shaped by Jesus' new understanding of reality. Faith in the risen Christ transfigured racial, social and sexual barriers and injustices into a new reality of community life in which there "is no longer Jew or Greek, there is no longer slave or free, there is no longer male and female" (Gal 3:28). Indeed, the long and dominant theological tradition that locates the presence of Christ primarily in the preaching of the word and the (proper) administration of the sacraments should be supplemented by the early Christian praxis that Christ is also found in the vulnerable child (Mark 9:36–37), in the hungry, the stranger, the naked, and the prisoner (Matt 25:31–46). If the church wants to be found where Jesus Christ is active in the world, then it must show healing, saving, and liberating solidarity with those whose human dignity is injured or threatened. At the occasion of receiving the Union Medal from Union Theological Seminary, New York, on March 16, 2006, Desmond Tutu said this:

> Biblical truth could never be an opiate to the people, for it spoke of a God who was notoriously biased, biased in favor of the poor, of the despised, of the weak, who rejected as abomination a religion no matter how elaborate and meticulous its ritual and worship if

it did not issue in a concern for those who turned out to be God's favorites, the orphan, the widow and the alien.[3]

With these observations in mind let us follow the suggested steps of relating God's word to the spiritual and moral challenges of our time and to situations in which we may find ourselves.

LOOKING AND LISTENING

The first thing we have to do when we confront an ethical challenge is to identify the issue and become aware of the facts related to it.

Naming

If we are confronted with a moral issue we need to define and analyze it as clearly as possible. When we deal, for instance, with the problem of torture, we need to distinguish torture from related issues like child and spouse abuse or degrading treatment of prisoners. Such matters are important of course, and they are legitimate concerns in themselves. But it only clouds the issue at hand, and it limits an effective implementation if the issue is not defined as precisely as possible.

Part of understanding the problem is becoming informed about the *facts*. To continue the above illustration, we would need to ask why and where torture takes place. How widespread is its practice? Is it tied to a particular political, cultural, or economic system? Are there structural configurations which encourage torture? What are the motivations for using torture—revenge, punishment, getting information? Does it deliver the desired outcomes? What are its effects on torturer, tortured and the governments and societies that allow torture to take place?

Abortion provides another example. To arrive at a responsible decision, we would need to know how many women abort, and for what reasons they do so. If the national law forbids abortion, how many women abort illegally or go to another country to abort? What effects do such practices have on the societal ethos? How many women are driven into psychological, financial, and social despair in case they give birth to a child? Into what kind of family will the new life be born? What are the moral obligations to the unborn, to the mother, to the family, to society? Is there any scientific evidence as to when a growing life can be called "human"? What are the

3. As quoted in Mack, "Desmond Tutu Receives Union Theological Seminary's Highest Honor."

long-term effects on the woman who aborts? These and many other factors add to a proper understanding of the problem.

Ethical verdicts have often been made on a misunderstanding of scientific facts. Masturbation, to give only one example, was forbidden because people thought that new life was solely in the male sperm, while the woman's womb was only the incubator. There was no appreciation that female ovulation and female eggs are necessary for the creation of new life, and that sexuality is more than a means of procreation. With that lack of understanding masturbation was seen as wasting male sperm and thereby destroying human life.

Personal Interest

We need to be honest and ask whether we have a personal stake in the matter at hand. Our attitude to divorce or abortion or homosexuality is probably different if we or one of our children have been divorced or have aborted or are homosexual. Perhaps we take a deep personal interest in the Aborigines in Australia or the Dalits in India and therefore tend to prejudge issues related to them. Perhaps the church or denomination to which we belong has not taken a clear stand on issues like racism, apartheid, equality of women, and we feel uncomfortable being a member of such a church. We may even be convinced that our faith in Jesus Christ is at stake in our attitude to such issues. Our personal relationship to the problem at hand is part of understanding the problem itself.

Listening

How often have we deliberated an issue without ever listening or giving a voice to the people whose lives are affected? We announce verdicts on homosexuality without ever listening to the stories of gay and lesbian people. We make judgments on abortion without giving a voice to the unborn child. We support war without ever considering the social costs that a society has to pay by allowing their sons and daughter to go to war. Since responsible ethics have to do with making human life human, part of the process of reaching a responsible ethical decision is to listen to the people who are personally affected, and speaking "out for those who cannot speak" (Prov 31:8).

Making Ethical Decisions from a Christian Perspective

REFLECTING

Having defined the issue and having informed ourselves about the relevant facts, including listening to those who are affected, we now bring what we have discovered into conversation with the resources of faith and ethics.

Conscience

Before we can reach a responsible ethical decision and then engage in corresponding action, we must bring our understanding of the problem into correlation with the ethical guidance which we accept as being authoritative for us. The negotiation of the various factors that influence our ethical decision takes place in the conscience. "Conscience" is a real, but at the same time an elusive concept. The conscience determines and guards our personal integrity. It is rational in that it interrelates the problem at hand with the ethical principles that we know and accept. It is volitional in that it drives towards action. But it is more. It discerns whether with an ethical challenge our own identity is at stake. In an extreme case a person is prepared to die rather than to transgress against the voice of conscience. A mature democracy will therefore make room for conscientious objection to participating in war. For the Christian the ultimate authority for their ethical decision is not the law of the land or of the church, but the content of their faith in Christ.

Since faith is not only a personal but also a social reality, ethical reflection should take place in the context of a community of people with whom we journey together. Our conscience therefore submits its ethical deliberations to the community of faith for testing. Among the factors that the conscience negotiates in its ethical reflection are the following.

Human Rights

Human rights are the only moral code that is given universal relevance and acceptance today. There are voices in Asia, Africa, and Latin America that criticize human rights as being too Western. The war against Iraq has demonstrated that even Western countries have exalted national interest over their commitment to human rights by relativizing core and absolute human rights like the abolition of torture when its suits them. Yet there is no alternative. The human rights tradition is the only universally accepted moral guide. It is therefore of interest what the global community thinks of the issue at hand. Whether it is war or abortion or capital punishment or torture, we can ask whether the *International Bill of Human Rights* and the many other human rights declarations and conventions address the problem and how they deal with it. As believers we may see the providence of God being at work in the human rights tradition.[4]

Within the human rights tradition we may be confronted with conflicts of values and interests. For instance, human rights instruments distinguish between rights which are always valid, like the right to life, to freedom of thought, conscience and religion, and the prohibition of torture and slavery, and others that may be temporarily suspended in times of public emergency, when the life of a nation is threatened. In connection with the Iraq war, the question whether torture is always wrong has been raised again, although it had been thought that the international community had found a consensus on that issue. In the case of abortion, we may ask whether the unborn's right to life weighs heavier than the mother's right to privacy and her right to determine what happens to her own body.

If there are such conflicting claims, then we have to develop a hierarchy of principles and relate these to a particular situation. In facing the situation of the millions of starving children, for instance, it is obvious that the rights to food, medical care, shelter, and a basic education precede the right to a higher education or to freely leave one's country.

Biblical Message

As Christians we then ask whether directly or indirectly the biblical message speaks to the issue at hand. This may be fairly clear, as in the case of child abuse or torture. It is more difficult with regard to other issues like religious liberty, war, homosexuality, and the building of nuclear power stations. The biblical texts were written in cultures and societies which are totally different from ours, so we cannot expect that the Bible has direct answers for the major problems which we are facing today. It is clear that the biblical texts lean in a certain direction—the direction of compassion, equality, peace, and justice—but what that concretely means varies from situation to situation.

For Christians the biblical message centers in the story of Jesus who is their ultimate authority. Although that story is more than morality, on some issues the guidance is quite clear. Jesus refused, for instance, to accept

---

4. See Lorenzen, "Towards a Theology of Human Rights," 49–66; and Lorenzen, "Freedom or Security. 'Freedom of Religion' as a Human Right Today," 193–213.

Making Ethical Decisions from a Christian Perspective

the final authority of the law. When human dignity was at stake he demonstratively suspended the sabbath and temple traditions.[5] Also with regard to violence and war Jesus' commitment to nonviolence is quite decisive.[6] However, for most modern ethical challenges there is no direct word from Jesus. Every ethical decision and action must be brought into correlation with Jesus in that it must "not disturb or disrupt" the general biblical line that points to Jesus Christ.[7] It is not enough to point to one or other biblical text, like Romans 1:18–32 with regard to homosexuality, or 1 Corinthians 14:34 with regard to the role of women in the church. We must seek to discover the claim of the gospel as it is revealed in the whole biblical message (see the section about "middle axioms" below).

Tradition

We will also want to ask how the various church traditions have dealt with the issue under discussion. Here we will see how the church has too often not followed the biblical imperative of justice but has been more concerned with political expediency, patriarchal structures, the interest to please society and the state, and the will to survive. Issues like the equality of women, slavery, conscientious objection, religious liberty, freedom of conscience, and the treatment of so-called heretics provide telling examples. On the other hand, alongside the establishment churches there has always been a subversive tradition that upheld a true witness to the gospel under difficult circumstances. One only has to think of the Anabaptists in continental Europe and the Baptists in England and North America in their struggle for religious liberty; the Mennonites and Quakers in their witness to peace; the Dominican priest Bartholomew de Las Casas (1474–1566) with his protest against the inhuman treatment of Indians; the struggle of John Wyclif (1328?–1384) in fourteenth-century England and the Anabaptist leader Balthasar Hubmaier (1480?–1528) in South Germany who believed that natural law and revelation demanded equal rights and privileges for all people and therefore sided with the serfs and peasants in their struggle for freedom; the anti-slavery movement fuelled by people like William Wilberforce (1759–1833) and William Knibb (1803–1845); the Protestant Christian Dietrich Bonhoeffer (1906–1945) in his commitment to Jewish

---

5. Details in Lorenzen, *Resurrection—Discipleship—Justice*, 69–77.
6. More details in Lorenzen, "Waging Peace Today," 255–56.
7. Barth, *Church Dogmatics* IV/3,1, 126.

refugees and the Roman Catholic Archbishop Oscar Romero (1917–1980) in his engagement for the poor.

We are part of the church's tradition. It would be foolish and misplaced pride if we did not acknowledge our place in that tradition, learn from it, and try to avoid repeating the mistakes of the past.

"Middle Axioms"

In 1937, at the ecumenical conference on "Church, Community and State" in Oxford, J. H. Oldham called for "middle axioms" which are to help Christians "to know what . . . to do" without relativizing their personal freedom and responsibility. These middle axioms are "to define the directions in which, in a particular state of society, Christian faith must express itself."[8] Since then this idea has been taken up by a number of theologians and ethicists. They have developed ethical guidelines—naming them as "middle axioms," "norms," "guidelines," "principles," "criteria," "maxims," and "presumptions"—in order to guide Christians and their communities towards responsible Christian decisions in their respective situations.[9]

The chasm of time and culture is wide and deep between the biblical message and our situations. We must therefore find ways to relate the biblical message to the problems under discussion. In doing so we must try to avoid two extremes. On the one hand we must avoid a biblical, moral or situational legalism, which minimizes human responsibility and fails to do justice to the particularities of a situation. On the other hand we must avoid an arbitrary relativism, which avoids the truth question and therefore can say nothing new to the situation. Ethical guidelines do not minimize the ethical responsibility of Christians and their communities, but they provide input and suggest a possible framework for making responsible ethical decisions. To illustrate the point let us view some widely accepted general and specific ethical guidelines.

Immanuel Kant's categorical imperative would be a good example of *general* ethical principles:

---

8. Oldham, "The Witness and Action of the Church as an organized Society," 209–10.

9. Since we have no space to develop this aspect I want to share a couple of books that I have found helpful in this regard: Wogaman, *Christian Moral Judgment*; and Rich, *Business and Economic Ethics*, 169–242, 489–618.

Making Ethical Decisions from a Christian Perspective

- "Act only on that maxim which will enable you at the same time to will that it be a *universal* law."[10]

- "Man and every rational being anywhere exists as *end in itself*, not merely as means for the arbitrary use by this or that will; but in all his actions . . . he must at all times be looked upon as an end. . . . . The practical imperative will then read as follows: Act so that in your own person as well as in the person of every other you are *treating mankind also as an end, never merely as a means*."[11]

Hans Jonas responds to modern technology with its problems and promises by developing an ethic of responsibility with the single aim to pave the way for a secure future of humanity. He restates Kant's imperative as follows:

- "'Act so that the effects of your actions are compatible with the *permanence of genuine human life*'; or expressed negatively: 'Act so that the effects of your actions are not destructive of the future possibility of such life'; or simply: 'Do not compromise the conditions for an *indefinite continuation of humanity on earth*'; or, again turned positive: 'In your present choices, include the future wholeness of Man among the objects of your will.'"[12]

Philip Wogaman suggests the following general guidelines (which he calls "positive moral presumptions"):[13]

- Since faith has often devalued the material life, Wogaman insists that *creation is good* and that therefore we must lean against diminishing life in war, abortion, suicide, sexuality and ecology.

- He affirms the "*radical worth of the individual person*" which implies a presumption against capital punishment and against destroying the life of civilians in war.

---

10. Kant, *The Fundamental Principles of the Metaphysics of Ethics*, 38 (emphasis mine). See also *Critique of Practical Reason*, 30.

11. Kant, *The Fundamental Principles of the Metaphysics of Ethics*, 46–47 (emphasis mine). See also *Critique of Practical Reason*, 136.

12. Jonas, *The Imperative of Responsibility*, 11 (emphases mine).

13. Wogaman, *Christian Moral Judgment*, 72–97.

- Humans are *social beings* and part of a *global family*, therefore the Christian would argue against racism and nationalism.
- All people are *equal* and therefore the moral presumption would be against racism, slavery, class systems and the subordination of women.

In light of the challenges that we face in our present world we could add further guidelines:

- A "preferential option for the poor and oppressed" which would fuel our resolve to help refugees and asylum seekers and encourage us to support the "Make Poverty History" campaign and lobby our governments to meet the United Nations Millennium Development Goals.
- In situations of conflict, global responsibility precedes national interest, which would mean that our governments would sign up to the Kyoto Protocol as a structured international attempt to address the climate crisis.

Such general ethical guidelines could then be complemented with more *specific* criteria that relate to a clearly defined issue. For instance, with regard to war, the so-called *"just war criteria"* were developed with the intention that in case of military action, necessary compromises did not result in moral relativism or political expediency:[14]

- A war can only be declared and fought by a *legitimate legal authority* representing the constituency that is threatened.
- A war could only be just if *all other means* of solving the conflict have been *exhausted*.
- A war must have a *just cause*. Guilt must be located only on one side and it must be established beyond doubt.
- War must be engaged in for the *right motivation*. Neither revenge nor conquest, but defence against aggressors, the restoration of peace, and the punishment of the offender can be seen as such.
- To engage in war, one must be convinced that *the situation after the war will be better* than before.
- The military machinery must be able to distinguish between soldiers and civilians so that innocent *civilians may not be endangered*.

14. See Lorenzen, "Waging Peace Today," 251–54.

Making Ethical Decisions from a Christian Perspective

One can easily see that with these guidelines it would be impossible to justify war in the nuclear age. Another illustration of issue-specific guidelines would be the building of nuclear power stations, which is being considered in Australia, Indonesia, China, and many other countries. The following guidelines may be considered relevant:

- Do they help to address the climate crisis? (The answer is "yes," because they have less of an ecological footprint than comparable energy sources.)
- Are they economically viable? (This may be the case if and when coal power stations will have to pay for their emissions.)
- Are they safe, especially in an age of terrorism? (With the passion and intelligence that drives international terrorism one wonders whether such safety can be guaranteed.)
- Can nuclear waste be safely stored? (No one seems to want such storage places near their own home, and with the long life of nuclear waste we have no idea whether stable social institutions can be guaranteed for tens of thousands of years.)
- Can military use of nuclear technology be excluded? (So far there seems to be no science to do that. Given the ideological and political tensions in the world there will probably be more and more nations who would want to follow Iran in its present attempt to explore nuclear technology. The only way to guarantee safety and prevent nuclear proliferation may be international control for *all* nuclear power stations in *all* countries. Would the governments of the world agree?)

The above discussion has been discouraging because it has shown how difficult it is to arrive at responsible ethical decisions. But there is no alternative. It is an important part of a culture of freedom that as many people as possible accept responsibility for the humane future of the human race.

Special Contribution of Christian Faith

Much of what has been said is not specifically Christian. Peace, equality, and justice are also pursued from non-Christian perspectives. Christians believe that God does not only love the world (John 3:16) but that in Christ, God has reconciled the world to himself (2 Cor 5:17–21). This means "that in the world reconciled by God in Jesus Christ there is no secular sphere abandoned by Him or withdrawn from His control."[15] There can therefore be no separation between God and God's creation. For Karl Barth, for instance, activities in the "world" can become "analogies," "parables," "correspondences," testimonies to the Kingdom of God. For such words and deeds "to be true . . . (they) must be in the closest material and substantial conformity and agreement with the one Word of God Himself and therefore with that of His one Prophet Jesus Christ."[16]

At the same time, Christians and churches need to ask themselves whether they have special contributions to make to the process of ethical reflection. Christian faith can highlight special dimensions that are not immediately obvious to human reason and experience. A couple of examples may illustrate the point.

Freedom, for instance, is often understood as "the power of doing whatever does not injure another."[17] This perception, while it has propelled the industrial and scientific revolution and has fuelled western political and economic successes, has at the same time disadvantaged the economically powerless, and it favors seeing every other person as a potential invader of one's individual freedom.

Here the Christian faith reminds us that humans are not individualistic but relational beings. "God created humankind . . . male and female" (Gen 1:27). The relational nature of human life has become distorted by humanity's unbending self-will. For Christians—at least in theory—this self-will and its subsequent individualism is transfigured into a relational understanding of freedom, where relationship to God, to other human beings, to nature and to history are essential for the celebration of freedom and the humane survival of human life.

A similar point can be made with reference to *equality*. The assertion that "all human beings are born free and equal in dignity and rights" is not evident in our world.[18] Aboriginal and Torres Strait Islander people in Australia, girl children in India and China, poor black people in South

---

15. Barth, *Church Dogmatics* IV/3, 1, 119.

16. Ibid., 111. See the whole section on Barth's teaching about the "parables of the Kingdom" in ibid., 110–35; also Barth, "The Christian Community and the Civil Community."

17. So in National Assembly of France, "Declaration of the Rights of Man and of the Citizen (1789)," §4.

18. United Nations Office of the High Commissioner for Human Rights. "Universal Declaration of Human Rights (1948)," §1.

Africa, African Americans and Native Americans in the USA, Christians in Moslem countries, women and Gypsies all over the world do not enjoy equality in their respective situations. Indeed, by looking into the world as it is, there is more evidence for affirming inequality as a "natural" fact than equality.

Against the apparent inequality in our world, Christians affirm the inherent equality of all people because God has created all human beings to be equal in dignity. Individualism and selfishness, which has led to inequality, is seen as a result of turning away from grounding life in God. In Christ, God has dealt with the estranging power of sin and created a new reality, which includes equality for all people. When God's reality is given space and as such becomes historically manifest, then a community of equals is being shaped (Gal 3:28). Recently, Desmond Tutu eloquently affirmed the equality of all human persons:

> When people have been told they don't matter, they are inferior by reason of their race or skin color, nothing could be more subversive of that dispensation than the declaration that each person is created in the image of God, is a God carrier, is God's viceroy, [and] their worth is not dependent on something as extrinsic as ethnicity or skin color, which are but biological irrelevancies, . . . I am loveable only and precisely because God loves me.[19]

Consequences

"By their fruits you shall know them" (Matt 7:15–20). In the process of ethical reflection moral alternatives with their advantages and disadvantages may emerge. In considering these alternatives, it is important to become aware of the consequences they may imply. We must aim at coherence between the end and the means of an activity. If one, for instance, decides that torture may be justified in an emergency situation, the question needs to be faced how one can decide when such an emergency has come, and who will be the one to make that decision. Is not every government that practices torture today convinced that for them it is an emergency situation? In the case of euthanasia it is not only a decision for the person who is suffering and for his or her immediate family, but it also has consequences for the ethos of a society in which euthanasia is permitted. It used to be

---

19. As quoted in Mack, "Desmond Tutu Receives Union Theological Seminary's Highest Honor."

the case that countries had ministers and ministries of war. Today we have Ministers of Defense and Defense ministries. Their declared aim is peace. But it is ethically problematic if the means (war) do not cohere with the end (peace). The reason why Mohandas Gandhi and Martin Luther King Jr. opted for strategies of nonviolence, and why the apostle Paul refused coercion in his evangelism—"we *entreat you* (*beg you*) on behalf of Christ, be reconciled to God" (2 Cor 5:20)—was that ends and means must cohere. One cannot bring about nonviolent realities with violent means.

DECIDING

Having defined and analyzed the problem, and having inter-related it with the ethical guidance that is available, an ethical decision needs to be made. This is often not easy, since the advantages and disadvantages of alternative solutions, as well as the conflict of values and guidelines, make it often impossible to arrive at a clear decision. A compromise may be necessary and ambiguity needs to be accepted. Important is that, all factors considered, the compromise must lean in the direction of justice. A decision must be made, even though it may have to be modified or revised in light of new evidence or new insights. No decision is also a decision. Neutrality is not possible. We may decide with fear and trembling. But decide we must if we want to be a moral agent. In making an ethical decision the following factors may be helpful.

Honesty

In most countries politicians have lost their credibility because they prefer putting a spin on things rather than speaking the truth. Honesty and transparency are rare virtues in public life. But such virtues are required in ethical decision-making. We must be willing, for instance, to admit to ourselves and to others what role the teachings of our church or the program of our party plays in our decision-making on such issues as abortion, capital punishment, euthanasia, and war. We must be in touch with our own experiences and feelings on such issues as homosexuality, adultery, and child abuse. We must be honest about our personal advantage or disadvantage with regard to the issue at hand, for instance, arguing for higher taxes so that more money can flow to education and health.

Ambiguity

There must also be the willingness to accept moral ambiguity. A decision may have to be made even though the issue is not clear. Inactivity may be worse. There must be a willingness to compromise, and there must be a willingness to become guilty. In a fallen world, in which our self-interest is strong, it is not possible to avoid evil. The most a responsible person can do is "choosing something relatively better over something relatively worse."[20] Philip Wogaman says correctly: "It is *conceivably* an act of moral goodness, and therefore no sin, to choose a lesser evil in a situation where choice is in fact limited to actions or inactions which can only result (one way or the other) in *some* evil."[21] I would hesitate to call such a decision "positively good" as Joseph Fletcher does,[22] but in many situations moral ambiguity is certainly unavoidable.

Forgiveness

For this reason it is important to know of the reality of repentance and forgiveness. Not to take moral responsibility lightly, but to accept a moral challenge with all its risks and responsibilities, knowing that even with our best intentions, and with our most careful analysis of the issue, we remain human and fallible, and therefore continue to be dependent on God's accepting, motivating and forgiving grace.

Testing

Having made the decision, it must then be re-examined and tested in light of the ethical guidance mentioned above and in light of the consequences that it will generate. There will be "the fruits which . . . true words have borne and seem to bear in the outside world."[23]

ACTING

Having made the ethical decision, the implementation of that decision must be vigorously pursued. We all know the popular saying: "The only thing necessary for the triumph of evil is for good people to do nothing."

---

20. Bonhoeffer, *Ethics*, 261.
21. Wogaman, *Christian Moral Judgment*, 107.
22. Fletcher, *Situation Ethics*, 65.
23. Barth, *Church Dogmatics*, IV/3.1, 127.

Appendix 2

In the Epistle of James we are exhorted to "be doers of the word, and not merely hearers" (Jas 1:22), and "anyone . . . who knows the right thing to do and fails to do it, commits sin" (Jas 4:17).

Coherence

It is important that the means of a moral action cohere with its end. It is not enough to have good content; one must also have good means to make an action good. Mohandas Gandhi and Martin Luther King Jr. were committed to nonviolence because they were convinced that peace, justice and reconciliation could not be brought about with violent means. It is therefore highly problematic when wars and the arms race are justified by the claim to establish peace. One easily gets the impression that such peace is only possible on the terms of the more powerful nation, rather than living with reconciled differences.

Strategy

A strategy of the most effective approach must be worked out. Many ways which all aim to achieve the same goal can complement each other. United Nations structures, international organizations, government agencies, national groups, churches, and concerned individuals can successfully work towards the implementation of moral decisions.

CONCLUSION

With this brief appendix I have attempted to outline a procedure for arriving at responsible ethical decisions from the Christian perspective. Christian faith is centered in the story of Jesus. But from that centre it is open to the rest of the world which is God's creation. The Christian faith seeks to make its contribution to making human life meaningful and successful. It therefore views with gratitude and anticipation "whatever is true, whatever is honorable, whatever is just, whatever is pure, whatever is pleasing, whatever is commendable" (Phil 4:8). At the same time Christians must relate ethical challenges to the vision of life that has come to expression in the story of Jesus. Since the story of Jesus is interwoven with the biblical message and since both come from a very different time and culture, we must develop a methodology to relate the gospel message to our situation. Hopefully, the above considerations have helped in that direction.

Bibliography

Amnesty International. "Abolitionist and Retentionist Countries." No pages. Accessed April 3, 2007. Online: http://web.amnesty.org/pages/deathpenalty-countries-eng.

Anglican Church of Australia, Doctrine Panel. *Faithfulness in Fellowship: Reflections on Homosexuality and the Church*. Mulgrave, Victoria: John Garratt, 2001.

Anglican World Communion, Lambeth Conference 1998. "Resolution 1.10—Human Sexuality." In *Faithfulness in Fellowship: Reflections on Homosexuality and the Church*, 208. Mulgrave, Victoria: John Garratt, 2001.

Attwood, Bain and S. G. Foster, editors. *Frontier Conflict: The Australian Experience*. Canberra: National Museum of Australia, 2003.

Barnabas, Epistle of. Roberts-Donaldson Translation. No pages. Accessed July 24, 2007. Online: http://www.earlychristianwritings.com/text/barnabas-roberts.html.

Barth, Karl. *Doctrine of Reconciliation: Jesus Christ the True Witness*. Church Dogmatics IV/3.1. Translated by Geoffrey W. Bromiley. Edinburgh: T&T Clark, 1961.

———. "The Christian Community and the Civil Community." In *Community, State, and Church: Three Essays*, 149–89. Gloucester: Peter Smith, 1968.

———. "Church and State." In *Community, State, and Church: Three Essays*, 101–48. Gloucester: Peter Smith, 1968.

———. "Gospel and Law." In *Community, State, and Church: Three Essays*, 71–100. Gloucester: Peter Smith, 1968.

Bartrop, Paul R. "Punitive Expeditions and Massacres: Gippsland, Colorado, and the Question of Genocide." In *Genocide and Settler Society: Frontier Violence and Stolen Indigenous Children in Australian History*, edited by A. Dirk Moses, 194–214. Studies on War and Genocide 6. New York: Berghahn, 2004.

Batstone, David. *NOT for Sale: The Return of the Global Slave Trade—and How We Can Fight It*. New York: HarperCollins, 2007.

Bearup, Greg. "Left for dead." *The Sydney Morning Herald. Good Weekend*, April 28, 2007, 18–24.

Bonhoeffer, Dietrich. "History and Good [2]." In *Ethics*. Dietrich Bonhoeffer Works 6, edited by Clifford J. Green, translated by Reinhard Krauss, Charles C. West and Douglas W. Stott, 246–98. Minneapolis: Fortress Press, 2005.

———. "Ultimate and Penultimate Things." In *Ethics*. Dietrich Bonhoeffer Works 6, edited by Clifford J. Green, translated by Reinhard Krauss, Charles C. West and Douglas W. Stott, 146–70. Minneapolis: Fortress Press, 2005.

———. *Letters and Papers from Prison*. Edited by Eberhard Bethge. Translated by Reginald Fuller, et al. London: SCM, 1971.

———. *No Rusty Swords*. Letters, Lectures and Notes 1928–1936. Collected Works of Dietrich Bonhoeffer 1, edited by Edwin H. Robertson, translated by Edwin H. Robertson and John Bowden. London: Collins, 1965.

Bibliography

Bonnell Andrew G., and Martyn Crotty. "An Australian 'Historikerstreik'?" *Australian Journal of Politics and History* 50 (2004), 425–33.

Brownlie, Ian, editor. *Basic Documents on Human Rights*. Oxford: Clarendon Press, 1971.

Brueggemann, Walter. *The Book of Exodus: Introduction, Commentary, and Reflections*. The New Interpreter's Bible 1, 675–981. Nashville: Abingdon, 1994.

———. *Deuteronomy*. Nashville: Abingdon Press, 2001.

Catechism of the Catholic Church. Homebush, NSW: St Pauls, 1994.

Childs, Brevard S. *The Book of Exodus: A Critical, Theological Commentary*. Old Testament Library. Philadelphia: Westminster, 1974.

Clarke, David M. "Scientific Reason and Homosexuality." In *Whose Homosexuality? Which Authority? Homosexual Practice, Marriage, Ordination and the Church*, edited by Brian Edgar and Gordon Preece, 100–16. Interface: A Forum for Theology in the World 9.1–2. Adelaide: ATF, 2006.

Confessional Synod of the German Evangelical Church. "Theological Declaration of Barmen (1934)." In *Kairos: Three Prophetic Challenges to the Church*, edited by Robert McAfee Brown, 156–58. Grand Rapids: Eerdmans, 1990.

Conrad, Joseph. *The Heart of Darkness* [1902]. Project Gutenberg, 2006. http://www.gutenberg.org/etext/526.

Critchett, Jan. "Encounters in the Western District." In *Frontier Conflict: The Australian Experience*, edited by Bain Attwood and S. G. Foster, 52–62. Canberra: National Museum of Australia, 2003.

Crossan, John Dominic. *Jesus: A Revolutionary Biography*. San Francisco: HarperCollins, 1994.

Crüsemann, Frank. *Bewahrung der Freiheit. Das Thema des Dekalogs in sozialgeschichtlicher Perspektive*. Kaiser Taschenbücher 128. Gütersloh: Kaiser, 1993.

Dalberg-Acton, John Emerich Edward [Lord Acton]. "Letter to Mandell Creighton, (April 5, 1887)." In *Essays on Freedom and Power*, 358–67. Boston: The Beacon Press, 1949.

Didache, The. Roberts-Donaldson Translation. No pages. Accessed July 24, 2007. Online: http://www.earlychristianwritings.com/didache.html.

Dunnill, John. "Homosexuality in the Old Testament." In *Faithfulness in Fellowship: Reflections on Homosexuality and the Church*, 47–61. Mulgrave, Victoria: John Garratt, 2001

Dyer, Keith. "A Consistent Biblical Approach to '(Homo)sexuality." In *Whose Homosexuality? Which Authority? Homosexual Practice, Marriage, Ordination and the Church*, edited by Brian Edgar and Gordon Preece, 1–21. Interface: A Forum for Theology in the World 9.1–2. Adelaide: ATF, 2006.

Ebeling, Gerhard. *Die Zehn Gebaote*. Tübingen: Mohr (Siebeck), 1973.

Edgar, Brian and Gordon Preece, editors. *Whose Homosexuality? Which Authority? Homosexual Practice, Marriage, Ordination and the Church*. Interface: A Forum for Theology in the World 9.1–2. Adelaide: ATF, 2006.

European Baptist Mission. "The 'Berlin Conference' 1884: Declaration of the European Baptist Mission at the Jubilee Conference Towards Its 50th Anniversary in Berlin in the Year 2004." Accessed March 4, 2007. Online: http://www.ebm-masa.org/download/BerlinConference1884.pdf.

European Union. "Protocol No. 13 to the European Convention on Human Rights, Concerning the Abolition of the Death Penalty in All Circumstances." No pages. Accessed May 8, 2007. Online: http://www.eurunion.org/legislat/deathpenalty/EurHRConvProt13Decl.htm.

Bibliography

Evans, Raymond. "'Plenty Shoot 'Em.' The Destruction of Aboriginal Societies along the Queensland Frontier." In *Genocide and Settler Society: Frontier Violence and Stolen Indigenous Children in Australian History*, edited by A. Dirk Moses, 150–73. Studies on War and Genocide 6. New York: Berghahn, 2004.

Fletcher, Joseph. *Situation Ethics: The New Morality*. Philadelphia: Westminster, 1966.

———. *Moral Responsibility: Situation Ethics at Work*. Philadelphia: Westminster, 1967.

Fretheim, Terence E. *Exodus*. Interpretation: A Bible Commentary for Teaching and Preaching. Louisville: John Knox, 1991.

Fromm, Erich. *The Anatomy of Human Destructiveness*. Harmondsworth, UK: Penguin, 1977.

———. *To Have or To Be?* London: ABACUS, 1980.

Frymer-Kensky, Tikua. "Deuteronomy." In *The Women's Bible Commentary*, edited by Carol A. Newsom and Sharon H. Ringe, 52–62. Louisville: WJKP, 1992.

Garcia Bachmann, Mercedes. "Deuteronomy." In *Global Bible Commentary*, edited by Daniel Patte, 52–63. Nashville: Abingdon, 2004.

Garrett, Graeme. "Starting with the Spirit: A Personal Reflection on Sexuality and Scriptural Gifts." In *Faithfulness in Fellowship. Reflections on Homosexuality and the Church.*, 181–93. Mulgrave, Victoria: John Garratt, 2001.

Gay, Peter. *Freud: A Life for Our Time*. New York: Norton, 1988.

Global Corruption Reports. No Pages. Accessed March 10, 2007. Online: http://www.globalcorruptionreport.org

Griffith, Tom. "The Language of Conflict." In *Frontier Conflict: The Australian Experience*, edited by Bain Attwood and S. G. Foster, 135–49. Canberra: National Museum of Australia, 2003.

Gutiérrez, Gustavo. *A Theology of Liberation: History, Politics, and Salvation*. Revised Edition with a New Introduction. Translated and edited by Caridad Inda and John Eagleson. Maryknoll, NY: Orbis, 1988.

Habel, Norman C. *Reconciliation. Searching for Australia's Soul*. Sydney: HarperCollins, 1999.

Haebich, Anna. "'Clearing the Wheat Belt,' Erasing the Indigenous Presence in the Southwest of Western Australia." In *Genocide and Settler Society: Frontier Violence and Stolen Indigenous Children in Australian History*, edited by A. Dirk Moses, 267–89. Studies on War and Genocide 6. New York: Berghahn, 2004.

Hanson, Pauline. "Pauline Hanson's Maiden Speech." Accessed December 17, 2007. Online: http://www.rockhate.com/hanson/hanson1.htm.

Hardaker, David. "Women Break Silence on Honour Killings." Australian Broadcasting Company, April 18, 2007. No Pages. Accessed May 2, 2007. Online: http://www.abc.net.au/7.30/content/2007/s1900891.htm.

Harrelson, Walter. *The Ten Commandments and Human Rights*. Philadelphia: Fortress Press, 1980.

Hays, Richard B. *The Moral Vision of the New Testament: Community, Cross, New Creation*. San Francisco: Harper, 1996.

Herzog, Frederick. *God-Walk: Liberation Shaping Dogmatics*. Maryknoll, NY: Orbis, 1988.

Hochschild, Adam. *King Leopold's Ghost: A Story of Greed, Terror, and Heroism in Colonial Africa*. New York: HoughtonMifflin, 1998.

Howard, John. "Towards Reconciliation." Speech made to Corroboree 2000, the opening ceremony for Reconciliation Week, May 27, 2000. Online: http://australianpolitics.com/news/2000/00-05-27.shtml.

Bibliography

Human Rights and Equal Opportunity Commission. *Bringing Them Home.* Report of the National Inquiry into the Separation of Aboriginal and Torres Strait Islander Children from Their Families. Commonwealth of Australia, 1997.

Human Rights Watch. "Children's Rights." Accessed December 14, 2007. Online: http://www.hrw.org/children/labor.htm.

Huntington, Samuel P. *The Clash of Civilizations and the Remaking of World Order.* New York, Simon & Schuster, 1996.

Hyatt, J. Philip. *Commentary on Exodus.* New Century Bible. London: Oliphants, 1971.

Inconvenient Truth, An. DVD. Directed by Davis Guggenheim. Paramount Classics, 2006.

International Labor Organization. *A Global Alliance against Forced Labor.* Report of the Director-General. Global Report under the Follow-up of the ILO Declaration on Fundamental Principles and Rights at Work 2005. Geneva: International Labor Office, 2005.

———. "Child Labour." Accessed December 14, 2007. Online: http://www.ilo.org/global/Themes/Child_Labour/index.htm.

Jackson, Alan. "William Knibb, 1803-1845, Jamaican Missionary and Slaves' Friend." *The Victorian Web.* Accessed December 14, 2007. Online: http://www.victorianweb.org/history/knibb/knibb.html.

Johnston, William Robert. "Historical Abortion Statistics, U.S.S.R." Johnston's Archive. Accessed October 24, 2007. Online: http://www.johnstonsarchive.net/policy/abortion/ab-ussr.html.

Jonas, Hans. *The Imperative of Responsibility: In Search of an Ethics for the Technological Age.* Translated by Hans Jonas with the collaboration of David Herr. Chicago: University of Chicago Press, 1984.

Jüngel, Eberhard. "Gospel and Law. The Relation of Dogmatics to Ethics." In *Karl Barth, a Theological Legacy,* 105-26. Translated by Garrett E. Paul. Philadelphia: Westminster, 1986.

Käsemann, Ernst. *Jesus Means Freedom. A Polemical Survey of the New Testament.* Translated by Frank Clarke. London: SCM, 1969.

Kant, Immanuel. *Critique of Practical Reason* (1788). Translated with an introduction by Lewis White Beck. New York: Macmillan, 1956.

———. *The Fundamental Principles of the Metaphysics of Ethics* (1785). Translated with an Introduction by Otto Manthey-Zorn. New York: Appleton-Century, 1938.

———. *Kant's Political Writings.* Edited by Hans Reiss. Translated by H. B. Nisbet. Cambridge: University Press, 1970.

———. *Perpetual Peace. A Philosophical Sketch* (1795). In *Kant's Political Writings,* edited by Hans Reiss, and translated by H. B. Nisbet, 93-130. Cambridge: University Press, 1970.

Kellerman, D. "רֵעַ." In *Theological Dictionary of the Old Testament,* edited by G. Johannes Botterweck and Helmer Ringgren, translated by J. T. Willis, Geoffrey W. Bromiley, and David E. Green, 13:522-32. Grand Rapids: Eerdmans, 2004.

King, Martin Luther, Jr. "The Three Dimensions of a Complete Life." In *A Knock at Midnight. Inspiration from the Great Sermons of Martin Luther King, Jr.,* edited by Clayborne Carson and Peter Holloran, 121-40. New York: Warner, 1998.

Kinsey, Alfred C., Wardell Pomeroy, and Clyde E. Martin. *Sexual Behavior in the Human Male.* Philadelphia: Saunders, 1948.

———. *Sexual Behavior in the Human Female.* Philadelphia: Saunders, 1953.

Bibliography

Kociumbas, Jan. "Genocide and Modernity in Colonial Australia, 1788–1850." In *Genocide and Settler Society: Frontier Violence and Stolen Indigenous Children in Australian History*, edited by A. Dirk Moses, 77–102. Studies on War and Genocide 6. New York: Berghahn, 2004.

Kolb, Robert and Timothy J. Wengert, editors. *The Book of Concord: The Confessions of the Evangelical Lutheran Church*. Minneapolis: Fortress, 2000.

Kühlewein, J. "רֵעַ." In *Theological Lexicon of the Old Testament*, edited by Ernst Jenni and Claus Westermann, translated by Mark E. Biddle, 3:1243–46. Peabody, MA: Hendrickson, 1997.

Kuntz, Paul Grimley. *The Ten Commandments in History: Mosaic Paradigms for a Well-Ordered Society*. Edited by Thomas D'Evelyn. Grand Rapids: Eerdmans, 2004.

Langston, Scott M. *Exodus Through the Centuries*. Malden, MA: Blackwell, 2006.

Lehmann, Paul L. *The Decalogue and a Human Future: The Meaning of the Commandments for Making and Keeping Human Life Human*. Grand Rapids: Eerdmans, 1995.

———. *Ethics in a Christian Context*. New York: Harper & Row, 1963.

Lorenzen, Thorwald. "The Centrality of Preaching in Christian Worship," in *Do Not Quench the Burning Bush* (Adelaide: ATF Press, 2008, forthcoming).

———. "Freedom from Fear. Christian Faith and Human Rights Today," *Pacifica* 19 (June 2006) 193–213.

———. "Freedom or Security. 'Freedom of Religion' as a Human Right Today." In *Religions-Freiheit. Festschrift zum 200. Geburtstag von Julius Köbner*, edited by Erich Geldbach, Markus Wehrstedt, and Dietmar Lütz, 339–67. Berlin: WDL, 2006.

———. *Resurrection and Discipleship: Interpretive Models, Biblical Reflections, Theological Consequences*. Maryknoll, New York: Orbis, 1995. Reprinted. Eugene, OR: Wipf and Stock Publishers, 2004.

———. *Resurrection—Discipleship—Justice: Affirming the Resurrection of Jesus Christ Today*. Macon, GA: Smyth & Helwys, 2003.

———. *The Rights of the Child*. Baptists and Human Rights 2. McLean, VA: Baptist World Alliance, 1998.

———. "Towards a Theology of Human Rights," *Review and Expositor* 97 (Winter 2000) 49–66.

———. "Waging Peace Today." In *Gemeinschaft der Kirchen und gesellschaftliche Verantwortung. Die Würde des Anderen und das Recht anders zu denken. Festschrift für Professor Dr. Erich Geldbach*, 251–60. Ecumenical Studies 30. Münster: LIT, 2004.

Lütz, Dietmar. *Zehn Worte—Zehn Werte. Gedanken über das Grundgesetz des Glaubens*. Berlin: WDL, 2004.

Luther, Martin. "The Ten Commandments." In *The Large (German) Catechism of Dr. Martin Luther* (1529). The Book of Concord: The Confessions of the Evangelical Lutheran Church, 386–431. Minneapolis: Fortress, 2000.

———. "The Ten Commandments." In *Handbook, The Small Catechism (of Dr. Martin Luther) for Ordinary Pastors and Preachers*. The Book of Concord: The Confessions of the Evangelical Lutheran Church, 351–54. Minneapolis: Fortress, 2000.

MacIntyre, Stuart and Anna Clark. *The History Wars*. Melbourne: Melbourne University Press, 2003.

Mack, Daphne. "Desmond Tutu Receives Union Theological Seminary's Highest Honor." Cpsa.news. May 22, 2006. No Pages. Accessed June 28, 2007. Online: http://lists.sn.apc.org/pipermail/cpsa.news/2006-May/001349.html.

Bibliography

Manne, Robert. "Aboriginal Child Removal and the Question of Genocide, 1900–1940." In *Genocide and Settler Society: Frontier Violence and Stolen Indigenous Children in Australian History*, edited by A. Dirk Moses, 217–43. Studies on War and Genocide 6. New York: Berghahn, 2004.

Marr, David and Marian Wilkinson. *Dark Victory. How a Government Lied Its Way to Political Triumph*. Crows Nest, NSW: Allen & Unwin, 2003.

Marti, Kurt. "Leichenreden." In *Rosa Loui, Republikanische Gedichte, Leichenreden*, 95–155. Zürich: Buchclub ex Libris, 1975.

Marx, Karl. "Theses on Feuerbach (1845)." In Karl Marx and Friedrich Engels, *On Religion*. Classics in Religious Studies and the American Academy of Religion, 3:69–72. Chico, CA: Scholars Press, 1982.

Mayer, Günter. "אוֹר." In *Theological Dictionary of the Old Testament*, edited by G. Johannes Botterweck and Helmer Ringgren, translated by J. T. Willis, Geoffrey W. Bromiley, and David E. Green, 1:134–37. Grand Rapids: Eerdmans, 2004.

McGregor, Russell. "Governance, Not Genocide. Aboriginal Assimilation in the Postwar Era." In *Genocide and Settler Society: Frontier Violence and Stolen Indigenous Children in Australian History*, edited by A. Dirk Moses, 290–311. Studies on War and Genocide 6. New York: Berghahn, 2004.

Mellor, Doreen and Anna Haebich, editors. *Many Voices: Reflections on Experiences of Indigenous Child Separation*. Canberra: National Library of Australia, 2002.

Micah Network. "Micah Declaration on Integral Mission." September 27, 2001. No pages. Accessed July 25, 2007. Online: http://www.micahchallenge.org/english/think/aim1/declaration.

Miller, Patrick D. *Deuteronomy*. Interpretation: A Bible Commentary for Teaching and Preaching. Louisville: John Knox, 1990.

Moltmann, Jürgen. *Theology of Hope: On the Ground and the Implications of a Christian Eschatology*. Translated by James Leitch. London: SCM, 1967.

Monahan, Michael. "U. S. Statistics." Heritage House '76. Accessed October 24, 2007. Online: http://www.abortionfacts.com/statistics/us_stats_abortion.asp.

"Mt. Everest, 1996: Zwei Mal an Sterbenden vorbeigegangen?" Accessed April 4, 2007. Online: http://www.mountainfuture.at/deutsch/tod/0090_Story.htm.

Moses, A. Dirk, editor. *Genocide and Settler Society: Frontier Violence and Stolen Indigenous Children in Australian History*. Studies on War and Genocide 6. New York: Berghahn Books, 2004.

———. "Genocide and Settler Society in Australian History." In *Genocide and Settler Society: Frontier Violence and Stolen Indigenous Children in Australian History*, edited by A. Dirk Moses, 3–48. Studies on War and Genocide 6. New York: Berghahn, 2004.

Mullen, Sean. "Science and the Meaning of Homosexuality." In *Faithfulness in Fellowship: Reflections on Homosexuality and the Church*, 105–23. Mulgrave, Victoria: John Garratt, 2001.

Mulvaney, D. J. "Barrow Creek northern Australia, 1874." In *Frontier Conflict. The Australian Experience*, edited by Bain Attwood and S. G. Foster, 44–51. Canberra: National Museum of Australia, 2003.

National Assembly of France. "Declaration of the Rights of Man and of the Citizen (1789)." In *Basic Documents on Human Rights*, edited by Ian Brownlie, 8–10. Oxford: Clarendon, 1971.

Bibliography

Neustatter, Angela. "It Cuts So Deep." In *The Independent (London)* March 22, 1998. Accessed July 31, 2007. Online: http://findarticles.com/p/articles/mi_qn4158/is_19980322/ai _n14144710.

News Limited. "AWB Kickback Scandal." Accessed December 18, 2007. Online: http://www .news.com.au/feature/0,,37435,00.html/.

Newsom, Carol A. and Sharon H. Ringe, editors. *The Women's Bible Commentary*. Louisville: WJKP, 1992.

Nielsen, Eduard. *The Ten Commandments in New Perspective: A Traditio-Historical Approach*. Studies in Biblical Theology, second series 7. London: SCM, 1968.

Nietzsche, Friedrich. "Thus Spoke Zarathustra (1881)." Translated by Walter Kaufmann. In *The Portable Nietzsche*, 103–439. New York: Penguin, 1954.

Noth, Martin. *Exodus: A Commentary*. Translated by J. S. Bowden. London: SCM, 1962.

O'Donnell Setel, Deborah. "Exodus." In *The Women's Bible Commentary*, edited by Carol A. Newsom and Sharon H. Ringe, 26–35. Louisville: WJKP, 1992.

Oldham, Joseph Houldsworth. "The Witness and Action of the Church as an Organized Society." In Willem Adolph Visser 't Hooft and Joseph Houldsworth Oldham, *The Church and its Function in Society*, 207–33. Church, Community, and State 1. London: George Allen & Unwin, 1937.

Parliament of Australia, Senate. Select Committee for an Inquiry into a Certain Maritime Incident. No pages. Accessed March 10, 2007. Online: http://www.aph.gov.au/senate/ committee/maritime_incident_ctte/index.htm.

Patte, Daniel, editor. *Global Bible Commentary*. Nashville: Abingdon, 2004.

Pixley, Jorge V. *On Exodus. A Liberation Perspective*. Translated by Robert R. Barr. Maryknoll, NY: Orbis, 1987.

———. "Exodus." In *Global Bible Commentary*, edited by Daniel Patte. Nashville: Abingdon Press, 2004.

Postel, Sandra. "Denial in the Decisive Decade." In *State of the World 1992: A Worldwatch Institute Report on Progress Toward a Sustainable Society*, edited by Lester R. Brown, 3–8. New York: Norton 1992.

Pratt, Angela, Amanda Biggs, and Luke Buckmaster. *Parliamentary Library Research Brief*, 9 (February 14, 2005). Also available online at http://www.aph.gov.au/library/pubs/ RB/2004-05/05rb09.pdf.

Presbyterian Church (U.S.A). *Book of Confessions: Study Edition*. Louisville: Geneva, 1996.

———. "The Shorter Catechism." In *Book of Confessions: Study Edition*, 227–45. Louisville: Geneva, 1996.

———. "The Larger Catechism." In *Book of Confessions: Study Edition*, 247–300. Louisville: Geneva, 1996.

Rad, Gerhard von. *Deuteronomy: A Commentary*. London: SCM, 1966.

Rasmussen, Larry. "Human Environmental Rights and/or Biotic Rights." In *Religion and Human Rights—Competing Claims?*, edited by Carrie Gustafson and Peter Juviler, 36–52. Armonk, NY: Sharpe, 1999.

Reynolds, Henry. "Genocide in Tasmania?" In *Genocide and Settler Society: Frontier Violence and Stolen Indigenous Children in Australian History*, edited by A. Dirk Moses, 127–49. Studies on War and Genocide 6. New York: Berghahn, 2004.

Rich, Arthur. *Business and Economic Ethics: The Ethics of Economic Systems*. Leuven: Peeters, 2006.

Bibliography

Roberts, Doris. "Statement to US Senate Special Aging Committee: Image of Aging in Media and Marketing." September 4, 2002. No pages. Accessed March 20, 2007. Online: http://members.aol.com/jennydee/dheadlines.html#senate.

Roman Catholic Church. *Catechism of the Catholic Church*. Homebush, NSW: St Pauls, 1994.

———. *Persona Humana: Declaration on Certain Questions Concerning Sexual Ethics*. By Franjo Cardinal Seper, Prefect of the Sacred Congregation for the Doctrine of the Faith, November 7, 1975. No pages. Accessed online May 17, 2007: http://www.vatican.va/roman_curia/congregations/cfaith/documents/rc_con_cfaith_doc_19751229_persona-humana_en.html.

Rosenberg, Matt. "Berlin Conference of 1884–1885 to Divide Africa." No Pages. Accessed July 24, 2007. Online: http://geography.about.com/cs/politicalgeog/a/berlinconferenc.htm.

Ryan, Lyndall. "Waterloo Creek Northern New South Wales, 1838." In *Frontier Conflict: The Australian Experience*, edited by Bain Attwood and S. G. Foster, 33–43. Canberra: National Museum of Australia, 2003.

Schirrmacher, Frank. *Das Methusalem-Komplott*. München: Karl Blessing, 2004.

Schmidt, Werner H. *Die Zehn Gebote im Rahmen Alttestamentlicher Ethik*. Erträge der Forschung 281. Darmstadt: Wissenschaftliche Buchgesellschaft, 1993.

Schmitz, Cathryne L., KimJin Traver, and Desi Larson, editors. *Child Labor: A Global View*. A World View of Social Issues. Westport, CT: Greenwood, 2004.

Solzhenitsyn, Aleksandr I. *Gulag Archipelago 1918–1956*. Translated by Thomas P. Whitney and Harry Willets. New York: Harper & Row, 1985.

Stamm, J. J. with M. E. Andrew. *The Ten Commandments in Recent Research*. Studies in Biblical Theology, second series 2. London: SCM, 1967.

Stuart, Douglas K. *Exodus*. The American Commentary 2. Nashville: Broadman & Holman, 2006.

Tödt, Heinz Eduard. *Perspektiven Theologischer Ethik*. München: Kaiser, 1988.

Tracy, David. *The Analogical Imagination: Christian Theology and the Culture of Pluralism*. London: SCM, 1981.

United Nations. *The UN Millennium Goals*. Accessed April 6, 2007. Online: http://www.un.org/millenniumgoals/.

———. *The Millennium Development Goals Report 2005*. New York: United Nations, 2005. Accessed July 26, 2007. Online: http://unstats.un.org/unsd/mi/pdf/MDG%20Book.pdf.

———. Office of the High Commissioner for Human Rights. "Universal Declaration of Human Rights (1948)." In *Human Rights: A Compilation of International Instruments*, vol. I.1, 1–7. New York: United Nations, 1994.

———. Office of Public Information. *The International Bill of Human Rights: Universal Declaration of Human Rights; International Covenant on Economic, Social and Cultural Rights; International Covenant on Civil and Political Rights; and Some Optional Protocols*. New York: United Nations, 1978.

United Nations Children's Fund. *Child Protection from Violence, Exploitation and Abuse*. Accessed July 26, 2007. Online: http://www.unicef.org/protection/index_exploitation.html.

———. *Convention on the Rights of the Child*. UNICEF, 1989. Online: http://www.unicef.org/crc.

———. *The State of the World's Children 1997*. New York: Oxford University Press for UNICEF, 1997.

Bibliography

United Nations Conference on International Organization. *Charter of the United Nations*. San Francisco: UNCIO, 1945. Accessed May 8, 2007. Online: http://www.un.org/aboutun/charter/.

United Nations Economic and Social Council. "Human Rights. Major International Instruments. Status as at 12 March 2007." 25 April 2007. Accessed May 2, 2007. Online: http://portal.unesco.org/shs/en/file_download.php/c6e93253ecbb891e48f8c2ca0983ae 43hr_international_instruments_march07.pdf.

United Nations General Assembly, 34th Session. "Resolution 146 (1979) International Convention Against the Taking of Hostages" (A/RES/34/146). 18 December 1979. Accessed May 2, 2007. Online: http://www.unodc.org/unodc/terrorism_convention_hostages.html.

United Nations General Assembly, 44th Session. "Resolution 25 (1989) Convention on the Rights of the Child" (A/RES/44/25). 20 November 1989. Accessed July 26, 2007. Online: http://www.ohchr.org/english/law/crc.htm.

"The Unthrown Kids." No pages. Accessed December 4, 2007. Online: http://www.safecom.org.au/kids-overboard.htm.

Watson, Pamela Lukin. "Passed Away? The Fate of the Karuwali." In *Genocide and Settler Society: Frontier Violence and Stolen Indigenous Children in Australian History*, edited by A. Dirk Moses, 174–93. Studies on War and Genocide 6. New York: Berghahn, 2004.

Weinfeld, Moshe. *Deuteronomy 1–11. A New Translation with Introduction and Commentary*. The Anchor Bible, volume 5. New York: Doubleday 1991.

Westermann, Claus. *Genesis 1–11. A Commentary*. Translated by John J. Scullion, S.J. London: SPCK, 1984.

Wink, Walter. "Homosexuality and the Bible." In *Homosexuality and Christian Faith: Questions of Conscience for the Churches*, edited by Walter Wink, 33–49. Minneapolis: Fortress, 1999.

Wittgenstein, Ludwig. *Tractatus Logico-Philosophicus*. Translated by D. F. Pears and B. F. McGuinness. London: Routledge & Kegan Paul, 1961.

Wogaman, J. Philip. *Christian Moral Judgment*. Louisville, Kentucky: Westminster/John Knox Press, 1989.

Yancey, Philip. *What's So Amazing About Grace*. Grand Rapids: Zondervan, 1997.

Zahn, Gordon. *In Solitary Witness: The Life and Death of Franz Jägerstätter*. Springfield, IL: Templegate, 1964.

Ziegler, Jean. *Die neuen Herrscher der Welt und ihre globalen Widersacher*. München: Bertelsmann, 2002.

Author and Subject Index

Abortion, 105–6, 213–14
Abu Ghanem, Hamda, 156
Abu Ghanem, Reem, 156
Achille Lauro, 136
Acting. 225–26
Activism, 37
"Adelaide," 161–62
Adenauer, Konrad, 87
Adonai, 9
Adultery, 18, 111–30, 186
Aged Care, 81–94
Ageism, 82, 86–88
AIDS, 135
American *Declaration of Independence*, 17
Anabaptists, 217
Anger, 97–98, 101–2, 107
Anglican World Communion, 126, 127n9
Annan, Kofi A., 136n5
Anxiety, 157, 175
Apartheid, 104
Arms race, 39
Atonement, 143–45
Attwood Bain, 158n5, 159ns6 and 7
Aug San Suu Kyi, 29, 202
Australian government: Senate, 161
Australian Wheat Board, 140
Authority, 83
Ayatolla Khomeni, 60

Baal, 34, 44–45
Baalzebub, 34
Baptists, 126, 217
Barmen Theological Declaration, 41–42

Barth, Karl, 73, 207n14, 222, 225n23
Bartrop, Paul R., 159n6
Batstone, David, 38n10, 137, 140n16, 142, 151, 189n1
Bearup, Greg, 141n19
Bell, George, 66n10
Berlin Conference, 141, 148
Bethge, Eberhard, 66
Bible, 52–53, 206, 209–10, 216–17, 226
Birth control, 122
Bismarck, Otto von, 141
Black Madonna, 47
Black September, 136
Blainey Geoffrey, 159n7
Blair, Tony, 162
Blood revenge, 96, 101
Bomb, 38
Bonhoeffer, Dietrich, 29, 40, 62, 65–66, 73, 118, 174–75, 202, 217, 225n20
Bonnell, Andrew G., 158n5
Brueggemann, Walter, 34n1, 40n13, 44n2, 180n3

Canberra Baptist Church, 147–48
Capital punishment, 104–5, 131
Capitalism, 53
Carey, William, 149
Cargo cult, 41
Casuistry, 203–4
Categorical imperative, 218–19
Charismatic(s), 53, 126
Charter of the United Nations, 194
Child labor, 138–39
Child mortality, 135
Child prostitution, 38n10

Author and Subject Index

Child soldiers, 140
Children, 106–7
Children overboard, 161–62
Childs, Brevard S., 8n7, 166n2, 197n6
Christmas Island, 160–61
Church, 206
Churchill, Winston, 60
Clark, Anna, 158n5
Clarke, David M., 127n10
"Classic," 189, 202–3
Climate crisis, 3
Colonialism, 141–42, 148–51
Commandments: as "words," 13
  meaning of, 23
Community, 25, 79–80
Congo River, 150
Conrad, Joseph, 150
Conscience, 20–22, 165–78, 215
  freedom of, 93–94, 167
Conscientious objection, 29
Constantine, 38
Consumerism, 37, 45
Convention against Torture and Other Cruel, Inhuman or Degrading Treatment or Punishment, 195
Convention on the Prevention and Punishment of the Crime of Genocide, 147
Convention on the Rights of the Child, 113n2, 129n13, 195
Conversion, 175–76
Corpus Christianum, 103
Corruption, 140–41
Covenant, 193–95
Coveting, 18, 165–78, 187
Creation, 75–77
Creighton, Mandell, 38n11
Crotty, Martyn, 158n5
Culture, 2
Culture of death, 106–8
Culture of freedom, 79–80, 87–88, 90–91, 106, 154
Czestochow, 47

Dagon, 34
Dalia Lama, 163–64
De las Casas, Bartholomew, 217
Decalogue, 6–7, 189–208
  literary context, 190–92
  authorship, 192
  date, 192
  numbering, 196
  two tablets, 196–97
  addressees, 203
Declaration on the Elimination of All Forms of Intolerance and Discrimination Based on Religion or Belief, 195
Determinism, 1
Development, 135
Discipline, 2, 42
Divorce, 113, 120–21
Dunnill, John, 128n11
Dyer, Keith, 128n12

Ecology, 79, 142–43
Education, 134
Einsiedeln, 47
Elderly, 81–94, 186
Ellsberg, Daniel, 29
Elohim, 9
Enlightenment, 167
Environmental sustainability, 135
Equality, 115–16, 222–23
  of women, 165–66, 170
Ethics, 205
  decision making, 209–26
Eucharist, 73
European Baptist Mission, 148–49
European Union, 104
Euthanasia, 83, 88–89
Evangelical(s), 52, 196
Evans, Raymond, 159n6
Eve, 170–72
Exodus, 180–81, 197

Faith, 177–78, 207–8, 210
Family, 83, 89–90, 113, 116

Author and Subject Index

Father, 81–94, 186
Female genital mutilation, 5
Feuerbach, Ludwig, 25, 41
Fletcher, Joseph, 122n5, 225
Forced Labor, 142
Forgiveness, 163–64, 225
Fornication, 128
Foster, S. G., 158n5, 159ns6 and 7
Francis of Assisi, 60, 98, 109–10, 202
Frankenstein, 60
Freedom, 1–2, 5–7, 22–33, 42, 131–51, 186, 208, 222
   aberrations of, 26–28
   and the sabbath, 72–80
   culture of, 2–4
   of the press, 156
French Declaration of the Rights of Man and of the Citizen, 16–17, 26, 222n17
French revolution, 75
Freud, Anna, 88
Freud, Sigmund, 25, 41, 88–89
Fromm, Erich, 37n9, 107
Frontier massacres, 158–59
Frymer-Kensky, Tikua, 166n3

Gallipoli, 60–61
Gandhi, Mahatma, 29, 98, 202, 224, 226
Gay, Peter, 88–89
Gender equality, 135
Generations
   selfishness, 84, 90–91
   conflict between, 84–85, 91–94
Genocide, 158–59
Global Corruption Report, 140n17
Global Ethos, 179n1
God
   and conscience, 20–22
   and freedom, 23, 72
   and the gods, 34–42
   and history, 31–32
   as gracious, 31
   faithfulness, 46

God (*continued*)
   image of, 43–45
   jealous, 35, 55–56
   liberator, 24–33, 182, 185
   misusing God's name, 58–67
   mystery, 15–16
   name of, 44, 58–67
   nature of, 11–23, 24–33, 41–42, 49, 51–53
   objectifying, 44–45, 50–51
   otherness, 45–46, 50–51, 57
   "speaking," 11, 14–15, 22–23
   saying "yes," 15, 21–23
   universal, 40–41
   wrath of, 55–56
Golden calf, 44, 47–48
Gore, Al, 84
Grace, 56
Graham, Martha, 2
Gulag, 179
Guns, 26
Gusmao, Xanana, 29
Gutierrez, Gustavo, 211n2

Haebich, Anna, 159n6
Hall, Lincoln, 141n19
Hamed al-Bandar, Awad, 72
Hanada, Hiroshi, 141
Hanson, Pauline, 162
Happiness, 208
Harrelson, Walter, 192n3
Hays, Richard B., 28n1
Helwys, Thomas, 60
Hermeneutics, 12–13
Herzog, Frederick, 36n6
Hiroshima, 91
"History wars," 158–59
Hitler, Adolf, 41, 53, 60
Hochschild, Adam, 151n31
Holy Spirit, 206–7
Homosexuality, 125–29, 214
Honor, 155–56
Honor killings, 155–56
Honoring parents, 18, 81–94

Author and Subject Index

Hostages, 136–37
Howard, John, 159, 160–62
Hubmaier, Balthasar, 217
Human being: nature of, 115–16, 167–68
Human dignity, 5, 95–96
Human rights, 4, 83, 215–16
Human trafficking, 142
Hunger, 134
Huntington, Samuel P., 84n5
Hussein, Saddam, 27, 72, 101, 162

Ibrahim, Barzan, 72
Icon, 43–57
Identity, 46–48
Ideology, 3
Idol, 43–57
Idolatry, 49, 51–53
Images, 47–51
Immigration, 162
Immorality, 128
Individual ethics, 183
Individualism, 4, 25, 83
International Bill of Human Rights, 89, 97, 101, 179n1, 216, 195
International Covenant of Economic, Social, and Cultural Rights, 89n8, 90n9, 195
International Covenant on Civil and Political Rights, 89n8, 104, 195
International Convention Against the Taking of Hostages, 136–37
International Labor Organization, 142
Interpretation, 189–208
Iraq war, 27, 53, 101, 162

Jägerstätter, Franz, 29
Jamaica, 149
Jesus Christ, 6–7, 13, 51–53, 61, 65–67, 154, 164, 168, 205–8, 226
  and adultery, 114
  and decalogue, 183, 184–85, 199–200
  and the sabbath, 70–73

Jesus Christ (*continued*)
  and violence, 27–28
  and women, 177
  death, 28
  disobedient son, 91–92
  resurrection, 28, 33, 108–9
Jonas, Hans, 91, 219
Judgment, 55–56
Judson, Adoniram, 149
Jüngel, Eberhard, 207n14
Just war theory, 103, 220
Justice, 95–96

Kant, Immanuel, 5–6n4, 57n7, 91, 162n14, 218–19
Karlstadt, Andreas, 47
Käsemann, Ernst, 74
KGB, 179
Kidnapping, 131–32
Killing, 18, 95–110, 186
King Jr., Martin Luther, 29, 54, 98, 202, 224, 226
Kinsey, Alfred C., 123n6
Knibb, William, 149, 217
Knox, John, 47
Kociumbas, Jan, 159n6
Kony, Joseph, 189n1
Kuntz, Paul Grimley, 8n7, 197n6
Kyoto Protocol, 220

Langston, Scott M., 8n7, 189n1, 197n6
Larson, Desi, 139n15
Law, 6–7: and truth, 72–74
Laziness, 74
Least Developed Countries, 135–36
Legalism, 74–75
Lehmann, Paul, 9n8, 124
Leopold, King of Belgium, 141, 150
Liberals, 196–97
Liberation, 24–33, 77–79, 143–45
Life: meaningful and successful, 2
Lord 9
Lord Acton, 38
Lord's Prayer, 64–65

Author and Subject Index

Lord's Resistance Army, 189
Lorenzen, Thorwald, 39n12, 129n13, 216n4, 217n5, 220n14
Love, 6–7, 114–30, 186
Luther, Martin, 8–9, 36, 46, 60, 132–33, 196
Lutheran Church, 166
Lutheran World Communion, 126
Lying, 157–64

MacIntyre, Stuart, 158n5
Mack, Daphne, 213n3, 223n19
Magna Carta Libertatum, 16
"Make Poverty History," 220
Malaria, 135
Male prostitutes, 128
Mandela, Nelson, 29, 60, 164, 202
Manne, Robert, 137n9, 159n6
"Manoora," 161
Marr, David, 160n8
Marriage, 113, 118–22, 186
Marti, Kurt, 109
Martyr, 163
Marx, Karl, 25, 36
Mary, 99
Masturbation, 125, 214
Maternal health, 135
Mayer, Günter, 165n1
Meister Eckhart, 37
Mennonites, 217
Method, 209–26
Micah Challenge, 136
Micah Declaration, 149–50, 182
Micah Network, 136, 150n30
Middle axioms, 218–21
Militarism, 45
Millennium Development Goals, 73, 134–36
Minstrels, 99
Mission, 148–51
Mohammed, 49
Molech, 34
Moltmann, Jürgen, 36n7
Money, 36–37, 131

Monogamy, 121
Monotheism, 35, 40–41, 184
Monroe, Marilyn, 60
Morel, Edmund Dene, 150–51
Moses, 11–12, 16, 30, 192
Moses, A. Dirk, 159n6
Mother, 81–94, 186
Mother Theresa, 60, 109
Mullen, Sean, 127n10
Multiculturalism, 162
Murder, 96, 99–101
Muslims, 49

Nabucco, 53
Nagasaki, 91
Name, 58–67
    honoring God's name, 58–67
    of Jesus, 61
    revealing God's name, 59–60
Nationalism, 45
Neighbor, 153–55, 176–77
Neo-conservatives, 53
Neustatter, Angela, 5n3
New heart, 175–76
Nietzsche, Friedrich, 25, 120
Nonviolence 98–99, 104
NOT for sale campaign, 38n10
Nuclear power stations, 221

Old people, 82–94
Oldham, J. H., 218
Oncken, Johann Gerhard, 60
"Option for the poor," 220
Orlamünde, 47
Orthodox Churches, 196

Paisley, Ian, 87
"Palappa I," 160
Palliative care, 89
Parents, 81–94, 186
Parliament of World Religions, 179n1
Partiality, 184, 211–13
Patriarchy, 93–94, 104
Paul: and decalogue, 200

Peace, 97
Pentagon papers, 29
Penultimate concerns, 40–41, 182–83
Personal ethics, 83, 85–86, 133, 183
Pinochet, Augusto, 53
Politics of fear, 3
Pomeroy, Wardell, 123n6
Pope John Paul II, 60
Pope John XXIII, 60
Postel, Sandra, 56, 143
Poverty, 73, 79, 133–34
Powell, Colin, 162
Power, 38, 51
Preaching: Prophetic, 163
Presbyterian church, 75
Procreation, 121
Property, 131
Protestant churches, 211
Public Theology, 145, 152–64

Quakers, 217

Racism, 45, 79
Rambo, 60
Rape, 96
Rasmussen, Larry, 142n23
Rationalism, 4
Reason, 50–55
Reconciliation, 45, 56: practical, 160
Redemption, 77–79, 143–45
Reformation, 46–47, 52, 167
Reformed Churches, 196
Refugees, 106, 161–62
Religious Liberty, 217
Reputation, 155–56, 185
Responsibility, 1–2, 42, 182–83, 203, 210–11
  corporate, 134
Rest, 71
Resurrection, 181, 197
Revelation, 50–55
Reynolds, Henry, 159n6
Rich, Arthur, 218n9
Rinnan, Arne, 160–61

Robbing, 131
Roberts, Doris, 86–87
Robinson, Mary, 160
Roman Catholic Church, 46–47, 52, 125, 127, 166, 196, 204, 210–11
Romero, Oscar, 202, 218
Roosevelt, Eleanor, 101
Ruddock, Philip, 161
Russian revolution, 75
Ryan, Lyndall, 158n5

Sabbath, 68–80, 186
  and freedom, 72–80
  and time, 75–80
  and creation, 75–77
Schirrmacher, Frank, 84n5
Schmidt, Werner H., 35n5, 81n2
Schmitz, Cathryne L., 139n15
Schur, Max, 88–89
Schweitzer, Albert, 98, 109, 202
Security, 39, 160–63
Selfishness, 83: generational, 84, 90–91
September 11, 2001, 39, 101, 160
Serfdom, 132
Sermon on the Mount, 16, 202
Seventh Day Adventists, 71n3
Seventh Day Baptists, 71n3
Sexual exploitation, 137
Sexuality, 38, 45, 114–30, 186
Sharing, 175
Sharpe, Granville, 149
Sherpas, 140
Shigekawa, Eisuke, 141
Simons, Menno, 60
Sin, 33, 45
Singles, 125
Slavery, 103–4, 132, 142, 149
Smythe, John, 60
Social ethics, 83, 85–86, 133, 183
Social justice, 77–79
Sodomites, 128
Solzhenitsyn Aleksandr, 179
"Sorry," 147–48, 159
Stalin, Josef, 60

Author and Subject Index

Stealing, 18, 131–51, 186
Stolen children, 137–38
Stolen generations, 158–59
Stolyarov, Nikolai, 179
Sunday, 71–74, 186

"Tampa," 160–61
Taylor, Hudson, 149
Temptation, 170–72
Terrorism, 39
Testimony, false, 152–64
Theophany, 14
Third day, 16
Tödt, Heinz Eduard, 207n14
Torture, 213
Tracy, David, 202ns11 and 12
Tradition, 217–18
Trafficking, 38n10
Trafficking children, 137
Traver, KimJin, 139n15
Trust, 155–56
Truth, 3, 19, 21–22, 152–64, 193
Truth telling, 157–58
Turner, William, 15
Tutu, Desmond, 212–13, 223

Ultimacy, 182–83
Ultimate Concerns, 40–41
Unemployment, 76–77
United Nations, 101, 102–5, 226, 134, 179n1, 194–95
 Charter of the United Nations, 194
 Children's Fund, 137, 137n6, 138n13
 Convention against Torture and Other Cruel, Inhuman, or Degrading Treatment or Punishment, 195
 Convention on the Rights of the Child, 113n2, 129n13, 195
 Convention on the Prevention and Punishment of the Crime of Genocide, 147

United Nations (continued)
 Declaration on the Elimination of All Forms of Intolerance and Discrimination Based on Religion or Belief, 195
 International Bill of Human Rights, 89, 97, 101, 179n1, 216, 195;
 International Convention Against the Taking of Hostages, 136–37
 International Covenant of Economic, Social, and Cultural Rights, 89n8, 90n9, 195
 International Covenant on Civil and Political Rights, 89n8, 104, 195
 Millennium Development Goals, 73, 134–36, 220
 Security Council, 162
 Universal Declaration of Human Right, 4, 17, 18, 20, 89n8, 101, 104, 112n1, 129n13, 142, 194–95, 202, 222n18
Uniting Church, 126

Verdi, 53
Vietnam, 91
Vietnam war, 29
Violence, 27, 49, 53, 95–110
Von Rad, Gerhard, 97n2

War, 102–4, 214
War on terror, 101
Water, 135
Watson, Pamela Lukin, 159n6
Wedgwood, Josiah, 149
Weinfeld, Moshe, 81n3
Wesley, Charles, 60
Wesley, John, 60, 149
Westermann, Claus, 72n4
Wilberforce, William, 149, 217
Wilkinson, Marian, 160n8
Williams, Roger, 60
Wilson, Sir Ronald, 138n11
Wink, Walter, 128n12

Witness, 163
   false, 152–55
Wittgenstein, Ludwig, 67
Wogaman, J. Philip, 218n9, 219–20, 225
Women, 177
Word, 13–15
Work, 76–77
World War II, 90, 102
Worship, 60, 71, 79–80
Worshipping, 44, 48
Wyclif, John, 217

Yahweh, 9, 34–35
Yancey, Philip, 179n2
Year of Jubilee, 70

Zahn, Gordon, 29n3
Ziegler, Jean, 140n17
Zwingli, Huldrych, 47

Scripture Index

Genesis		Exodus (continued)	
1	14	6:2–8	58, 59–60
1–2	184	6:2–9	24
1–11	193	6:6–7	30
1:1	35	15:3	48
1:1—2:4a	75	16:22–27	71n2
1:27	25, 95, 116, 120, 222	19–24	190
		19:4–6	193
1:28	14, 116	19:5–8	190
1:31	69, 72n4, 180	19:11	16
1:31—2:3	68	19:15–16	16
2:2	69, 75–76	19:16–18	11
2:15–25	111	19:17	16
2:18	120	20	9, 190
2:23	115	20:1	11
2:24	121	20:1–2	193
3	165, 170–72	20:2	24, 143, 190
3:1–7	118	20:2–17	6, 12, 190
3:7	118	20:3	34,
4	95, 99	20:4–6	43
8–9	193	20:5	35n4, 65
8:21	107, 108	20:7	58
9:6b	95	20:8–11	68
12–17	193	20:10	79
12:3	193	20:11	75
19	128	20:12	81
39:1–12	111, 130	20:13	95
39:9	113	20:14	111
40:15	132	20:15	131
44:8	132	20:16	152, 153
		20:17	165
Exodus		20:22–23	46n3
1:15–19	152, 158	21–23	190
3:1–10	30	21:2–11	166
3:12	30	21:12	96, 204
3:14	32	21:15	82, 204

Scripture Index

Exodus (continued)

21:16	131, 204
21:17	82, 204
21:18–19	204
21:20–21	204
21:22–23	204
21:37	132
22:2	132
22:11–12	132
22:16–17	166
22:20	35n4
22:21	182
22:21–27	131, 144
23:1	58
23:9	182
23:10–11	70, 79
23:12	71n2
23:13	35n4
24	190
24:7	190
24:12	190
25–31	190
25:18–20	48
31:7	191
31:12–17	71
31:16–17	71n2
31:17	76
31:18	190, 197
32	43, 44, 190
32–34	190
32:1–14	46n3
32:4–5	44, 191
32:9–10	48
32:10	191
32:15–16	197
32:19	191
34	6n5, 181
34:1	196, 197
34:4	196
34:10–16	27
34:14	35
34:17	46n3
34:21	71n2
34:24	166

Exodus (continued)

34:28	6, 95, 196
35:2–3	71n2

Leviticus

5:1	152
11	128
12	128
17:12	128
18–20	6n5
18:23	128
19	107
19:3	71n2, 85
19:4	46n3, 50
19:12	58
19:17–18	97, 101
19:18	7
19:19	128
19:30	71n2
19:34	182
20	34
20:2–5	128
20:6	128
20:9	82n4, 128
20:10	112
20:13	128
22:32–33	60
23:3	71n2
24:17	96
25:1–7	79
25:3–7	70
25:8–17	70
25:39–46	132
26:2	71n2
26:1	46n3, 50

Numbers

15:32–36	71
21	48
25:1–3	34
35:9–34	95
35:11	96, 100
35:12	96
35:15	96, 100

Scripture Index

Numbers (*continued*)

35:16–18	96
35:19	96
35:27	96
35:30	96

Deuteronomy

4:9–40	43, 45
4:13	6, 95, 196, 197n7
4:20	45
4:39	35n4
4:41–42	96, 100
4:44—11:32	191
5	9
5:1	8
5:1–6	11
5:3	12
5:5	12
5:6	24
5:6–21	6, 12, 190
5:7	34
5:8–10	43
5:9	35n4
5:11	58
5:12–15	68
5:14	79
5:15	77
5:16	81
5:17	95
5:18	111
5:19	131
5:20	152, 153
5:21	165
6:4	35n4
6:4–5	7, 35, 191
6:4–9	93
6:13	58
7:1–6	27
9:9–11	197
9:15	197
10:1	196
10:1–5	95, 191, 197n7
10:3–4	196
10:4	6
10:12–22	192

Deuteronomy (*continued*)

10:20	58
12–26	12
13:5	35n4
15:12	166
15:12–17	132
19:1–13	96
19:15–21	152, 153
19:18	153
21:18–21	82n4
22:13–19	113
22:22–27	112
22:25–26	96
22:26	100
22:28–29	113, 166
23:15–16	132
24:1	113–114
24:7	131
27:15	46n3
27:15–26	6n5
27:24	96
27:16	82n4
30:11–14	7

Joshua

7:21	132
20:3	96, 100
23:7	35n4
24	42
24:14–15	42

Judges

8:30–31	121
17–18	48
17:4	44
18:17–18	44
19–21	95, 96, 99
20:4	96, 99

1 Samuel

5:1–7	34
20:42	58
21:1–6	73
25:25	61

Scripture Index

2 Samuel
5:13	121
7:22	35n4
11–12	165, 172–73
12:13	113

1 Kings
8:60	35n4
11:3	121
16:29	173
18:17–40	34
21	95, 96, 99, 152, 163, 165, 173
21:19	100

2 Kings
1	34
5:15	35n4
19:19	35n4

Nehemiah
5	82
9:13–14	71n2
10:31	71n2
13:15–22	71n2, 78

Job
7:11–21	32
24:14	96, 100

Psalms
15	6n5
18:19	26
18:35–36	26
24	58
24:1	184, 193
24:3–5	156
27:12	153
31:7–8	26
35:11	153
42–83	59
42:1–2	168
50:5–7	198
51	113

Psalms (continued)
72:17–19	67
81:8–10	197
81:9	35n4
82:3	95, 212
84:1–2	168
86:9	82
94:6	96, 100
115:5–7	50
119:174–75	168
136	43, 46

Proverbs
1:8	82n4
6:19	153
14:25	153
14:31	96, 212
15:5	82n4
18:22	113
19:26	82n4
20:20	82n4
22:13	96
22:22	96, 212
23:22	82n4
25:18	153
28:24	82n4
30:11	82n4
30:17	82n4
31:8	66, 212, 214

Ecclesiastes
4:9–12	115, 117, 120n4
7:1	153

Song of Solomon
8:6	117

Isaiah
1:21	96
1:23	153
2:2–4	97, 103
5:7–8	198
5:22–23	153
6:1–8	48

Scripture Index

Isaiah (*continued*)

11:6–8	97
25:6	97
26:13	35n4
30:27	48
40:19	44
43:1–3	21, 64
43:10	35n3
44:1–2	34
44:6	35n3
44:6–8	34
44:9–20	43
44:10	44
44:21–23	34
44:24	35n2
49:6	193
52:4–10	64
54:4–8	121
55:10–12	14
56:2–6	71n2
58:6	78
58:13–14	71n2
61:1–2	78
65:17–25	97
66:23	71n2

Jeremiah

2:1–2	121
6:13–15	58, 63
7:1–15	58
7:3–10	63
7:8–11	198
10:1–16	43
10:10	35n3
17:21–27	71n2
22:15–16	212
23:29	67
31:31–34	6
31:33	175
31:34	6
34:16–17	60

Ezekiel

18:5–18	6n5

Ezekiel (*continued*)

20:12–24	71n2
22:7	82n4
22:8	71n2
22:26	71n2
23:38	71n2
36:20–32	60
36:25–28	6
36:26–28	175
44:24	71n2

Hosea

1–3	121
3:1	198
4:1–2	198
6:9	96
8:4–6	46n3
10:5–6	46n3
11:2	46n3
12:9	198
13:1–2	46n3
13:4	35n4, 198

Amos

2:6–8	60
8:4–6	71n2, 78

Micah

2:1–2	198, 166
3	152
3:1–3	153–54
4:1–3	97, 103
7:6	82n4

Malachi

1:6	82n4
2:16	114
4:6	94

Sirach

3:1–16	82n4

Jubilees

2:25	71
50:8	71

Scripture Index

Matthew

5	107
5:1–11	24
5:5	28
5:9	28
5:13–16	206n13
5:21–37	199n8
5:21–22	95, 98, 102, 165, 169, 200
5:27	111
5:27–28	114, 118, 200
5:31–32	111
5:33–37	152, 154, 200
5:43–48	28, 154
6:1–15	58
6:9–13	64
6:21	36
6:24	36–37
7:13–23	58
7:15–20	207, 223
7:15–19	63
7:21	63
7:21–23	58n1
8:18–22	81
8:21–22	93
9:22	203
9:48	203
10:34	27–28n1
10:34–36	27–28n1
10:37–39	27–28n1
11:28–30	23
15:3–6	199
15:4–6	199n8
19:3–12	111
19:5	121
19:16–30	176
19:16–22	199
19:18	132
21:12–13	27–28n1
22:23–33	111
22:37–39	7
25:31–46	40, 212
28:18–20	33

Mark

1:16–20	30
2:23	70
2:23–28	70, 73
2:23—3:6	68
2:27	73
2:28	73
3:1–6	71, 73
3:4	70
3:6	70
3:31–35	81, 91
5:34	203
7:8–13	199
7:15	128, 169
9:36–37	212
10:2–12	111
10:7–8	121
10:9	120
10:17–22	37, 199
10:17–31	176
10:19	132
10:52	203
11:15–17	27–28n1
12:18–27	111, 120
12:28–31	7, 95
12:29–31	154
14:36	32
15:34	33

Luke

2:41–51	92
2:46	92
2:48	92
2:51	92
4:18–19	78, 212
4:16–21	131, 144
6:20–21	212
6:43–45	207
7:50	203
8:48	203
8:1–3	177
9:57–62	81
9:59–60	91, 93
10:27	7

Scripture Index

Luke (continued)

10:29–37	154
11:2–4	64
12:51	27–28n1
12:51–53	27–28n1
13:10–17	68, 71
14:1–6	68, 71
14:26	91, 93
15:4–7	33
16:18	111
17:19	203
18:18–23	199
18:18–30	176
18:20	132
18:42	203
19:1–10	131, 146
19:5	146
19:8	146
19:45–46	27–28n1
20:27–40	111
22:35–38	27–28n1
22:49–51	27

John

1:1	15
1:1–14	22
1:1–18	11, 43
1:12	14
1:13	15
1:14	13, 14, 45
1:18	13, 45, 52, 207
2:14–17	27–28n1
3	176
3:3	15
3:16	194, 221
3:30	52
5:24	15
6	22
6:35	168
6:51	168
8:1–11	111, 130
8:12	22, 168
8:38	7
9:5	22

John (continued)

10	22
10:1	41
10:9	41
10:10	22, 116
10:11	168
10:11–16	34
10:14	168
11:25	22, 168
11:25–26	108
12:44–45	52
14:6	22, 41, 168
15	22
15:1	168
15:5	168

Acts

3:15	28n2
4:10	28n2
4:12	61
5:30	28n2
10:40	28n2
12:12	177
13:30	28n2
13:37	28n2
16:14–15	177
16:40	177
17:28	31
18:18	177
18:26	177

Romans

1:18–32	217
1:18—2:1	43, 55–56
1:23	45
1:24–28	128
1:26	126
2:24	60
4:24	28n2
5	194
5:20	56, 65
6:3–4	206n13
6:9	108
6:23	107, 108

Scripture Index

Romans (*continued*)

8:11	28n2
8:31–39	33
10:4	17
10:9	28n2, 60n2
10:17	7, 14
12:1–2	8on8
12:2	206n13
13:8–10	199n8, 200
13:9	132
16:1	177
16:3	177
16:5a	177
16:7	177

1 Corinthians

3:9	145, 210
6:9–10	128
6:14	28n2
7	111
7:1–9	123
7:6	123
8:4–6	55
8:6	57
9:16	67
11–14	8on8
11:14	127
12:3	60n2
13:4–7	119
13:4–8	117–118
14:34	217
15:15	28n2
15:54–57	108
16:22	60n3

2 Corinthians

1:18–20	11, 23, 45, 72
4:4	45
4:14	28n2
5:17	206n13
5:17–21	72, 78, 194, 221
5:20	224

Galatians

1:1	28n2
2:20	65, 206
3:23–28	29, 79, 131
3:28	132, 142, 177, 212, 223
4:4–5	13, 32
5:1	7, 23, 30, 208, 210
5:13–14	199n8, 23, 30
5:13–25	24
5:19	121
5:19–21	128
6:2	200

Ephesians

1:20	28n2
4:25—5:2	131
4:28	132
5:22–33	111, 121
5:31	121
6:1–3	85, 86, 199n8
6:1–4	82n4, 200

Philippians

4:8	226

Colossians

1:13–20	51
1:15–20	43
1:15	45, 51
2:9	51
2:12	28n2
3:20–21	82n4
4:15	177

1 Thessalonians

1:9–10	28n2, 57

1 Timothy

1:9–11	128
4:3–4	120

2 Timothy

2:13	13
4:19	177

Scripture Index

Titus
3:5–7   176n5

Hebrews
1:1–2   14
1:1–3   51, 71
1:1–4   43
1:3   45
4:15–16   177
10:23–25   80

James
1:22   226
2:8–12   200–201
2:10–11   199n8
3:1–12   152, 157
4:17   226

1 Peter
1:3   176n5
1:21   28n2
2:9   206n13
4:15   132

1 John
4:8   6, 211
4:17–18   118
4:18   164
4:19   15, 118

Revelation
13:11–18   46
22:20   60n3

Didache
2   201
10:6   60n3

Barnabas
19   201n10

www.ingramcontent.com/pod-product-compliance
Lightning Source LLC
Chambersburg PA
CBHW031726230426
43669CB00007B/265